# THE CHILD
# BIBLE

# THE CHILDREN'S
# BIBLE

retold by Marjorie Newman
illustrated by Michael Codd

WORLD INTERNATIONAL PUBLISHING LIMITED
MANCHESTER

House editors: Brenda Apsley, Nina Filipek, Clive Hopwood
Design and layout: Bob Swan, Melissa Orrom, Jane Herridge

*A catalogue record for this book is available from the British Library*

ISBN 0 7498 0853 5

Phototypeset in Century Old Style
Printed and bound in Hong Kong

# INTRODUCTION
## by Marjorie Newman

When I was first asked to write a children's Bible the thought almost overwhelmed me; but as I started my research the Bible itself, with all its power and fascination, began to take hold. Once more I discovered that it *is* a very special book; and in the retelling here I have tried to make it come vividly alive for the children, while keeping as closely as possible to the original text.

Inevitably some stories had to be left out. I tried to include as many as I could – stories of adventure, loyalty, faith, love.

On one level I wanted the children to see that these are great stories about real human beings. On a deeper level I wanted them to begin to understand the relationship of God with His creation.

This was certainly one of the most difficult tasks I have ever undertaken; but my own faith gained in the doing of it, and I hope in some measure the readers will gain from it also.

Marjorie has written widely for children of all ages. She is a full-time writer, and lives in Hampshire.

MICHAEL CODD is an experienced illustrator, whose work has covered a wide variety of subjects. He has specialized particularly in children's titles, information books, encyclopedias and work with an historical background.

# Contents

# THE
# OLD
# TESTAMENT

# Creation

In the beginning there was no earth; no sky; no universe. But there was always God.

And God decided to create heaven and earth. At first He made only darkness, and water, and swirling mists. Then God said, "Let there be light," and there was light. And God saw that it was good.

God divided the light from the darkness to create day and night, morning and evening. And that was the first day.

Next, God divided the waters – some above, and some underneath. The space between them he called 'sky'; and that was the second day.

Then God gathered together the waters under the sky so that dry land appeared. Some of the water formed into great, wide seas, with sandy beaches or rocky shores. Some of the water formed into streams, pools and waterfalls. And there were deep rivers, flowing down to the sea.

On the land God made trees and plants grow. He made tall forests; brightly coloured flowers; trees for fruit, trees for shade; plants that were good to eat, plants that were beautiful to see. And in each one God put seeds so that as the first trees and plants died, others of the same kind would grow in their places. That was the third day. God was pleased with the world He was making.

To mark the days, the months, the

seasons, God made the sun, moon and stars. That was the fourth day; and God saw that it was good.

But the world was silent and still, except for the sighing of the wind in the trees, and the waves splashing on the empty shores. So God made creatures to go in the sea – great whales, tiny fish, and all sorts and sizes in between. The seas teemed with life!

Then God made birds to fly in the sky – birds that swooped and soared, perched on the rocks, and nested in the trees. And God blessed them, and said, "Have young, each of your own kind; and fill the seas and the sky." And that was the fifth day.

Then God made creatures to go on the land – wild animals, every kind of insect, snakes, lizards, turtles. And

God blessed them also, so that they would multiply, and fill the earth. And God saw that all that He had made was good.

But there was still no one to help care for the earth and its creatures. No one to love God, and talk to Him. So God made people – people in His own likeness. And God blessed them, and said, "Have many children to live on the earth, and rule wisely over it." That was the sixth day. And God saw everything He had made, and it was very good.

The work of creation was finished, so on the seventh day God rested. And He blessed the seventh day, so that it was holy.

# In the Garden of Eden

God had planted a garden in the east, and there He put Adam, the first man He had formed.

The garden was very beautiful, full of flowers and trees. In the middle of the garden God planted two special trees – the Tree of Life, and the Tree of the Knowledge of Good and Evil. And God said to Adam, "You may eat the fruit of any tree in the garden, except the fruit of the Tree of the Knowledge of Good and Evil. If you eat from that tree, you will die."

So Adam lived in the garden, which was called Eden, and cared for it. But God could see that Adam was lonely. "I'll make someone to help him," thought God.

God brought every living creature to Adam in turn, and Adam gave them names; but none of them was just right to share Adam's life. So God made Adam fall deeply asleep, and while he slept, God took out one of Adam's ribs, and closed the wound. He had formed Adam from dust; but now He formed a woman from Adam's rib, and brought her to him.

Adam named her Eve, and they were very happy together.

But in the garden lived a serpent. A wily, crafty serpent...

One day, the serpent slithered up to Eve and whispered, "If you eat from the Tree of the Knowledge of Good and Evil, you won't really die.

13

You will understand everything, and be as wise as God."

Eve looked at the serpent. Then she looked at the tree. Until then, she'd never bothered much about it; but now, the more she looked at it, the more she longed to know what the fruit would taste like. And she *wanted* to be as wise as God...

She looked around her, then she stretched out her hand...picked a fruit...and ate it. It was *delicious*!

"Adam!" she called. "Try this fruit!"

Adam knew quite well where the fruit had come from. But Eve was holding it out to him... "Taste it!" she said. And he did.

Immediately, the happy, contented peacefulness they had always felt was destroyed. First, they began to be anxious because they were naked. They hurried to make some sort of clothing for themselves from fig leaves.

By then it was evening. God always walked in the garden in the cool of the day. Now they heard Him coming!

Afraid, guilty, they hid amongst the trees. God called to Adam, "Where are you?"

It was no use trying to hide. Trembling, Adam and Eve came out. "I was afraid because I was naked, so I hid," Adam admitted.

"Who told you you were naked?" cried God. And then He said, "Have you eaten from the forbidden tree?"

Adam trembled still more, and tried to escape blame. "*You* put a woman here with me. *She* made me do it," he said.

God looked at Eve. "Why did you do it?" He asked.

"The serpent made me!" cried Eve.

Then God was very angry. He put a curse on the serpent, so that it would

for ever have to crawl on the ground; and people would always be its enemy. To Eve, God said, "From now on, when women have children they will suffer pain." And to Adam, He said, "For as long as they live, men will always have to work hard to get a harvest from the earth."

Then God looked at the clothes which Adam and Eve had tried to make from fig leaves, and He made clothes for them Himself, from the skins of animals. But Adam and Eve could no longer be trusted to live in the Garden of Eden, in case they ate from the other special tree – The Tree of Life. For now they had disobeyed God, and eaten from the Tree of the Knowledge of Good and Evil, they would one day die.

So God sent them out from the garden where He had meant them to live so happily, and an angel and a fiery sword guarded the way to the Tree of Life. Adam and Eve could never return.

# Two Brothers

Now life was different for Adam and Eve. The work of cultivating the ground was hard. But God still loved and cared for them; and presently Eve had two sons, Cain and Abel. As the boys grew up they helped with the work. Cain became a farmer, and Abel a shepherd.

Adam and Eve often made sacrifices – offerings – to God. They would build an altar of stones and light a fire on it. Then they would take one of their best lambs, kill it, and burn its body on the fire so that the smoke rose up to heaven. Or they might offer some of their best fruit or grain. They made the sacrifices gladly, to show their love for God, and to thank Him for His love for them.

One day, Cain and Abel made *their* first offering. Cain brought some of the corn from his harvest. He didn't bother to pick out the best, and he sulked as he put it on the altar. He didn't want to make the offering at all.

But Abel brought the best pieces from some of his freshly-killed sheep, and gladly offered them to God.

God accepted Abel's gift, but He refused Cain's.

Cain was furious. God said to him, "Why are you so angry? Why are you making that face? If your thoughts and actions are right, then your gifts will be acceptable. But if your thoughts are wrong, and you do not overcome them, sin will rule in your life, and things will get worse for you."

Cain was too angry to take any notice of God's warning. And he was furiously jealous of his brother. Pretending to be friendly, he said to Abel, "Let's go out to the fields." Abel went with Cain, unsuspecting. But once they were alone, Cain suddenly and violently hit Abel, and killed him.

Thinking no one would find out, Cain left his brother's body where it lay, and came home as if nothing had happened.

But God said to him, "Where is your brother Abel?"

Guiltily Cain shouted, "How should I know? I am not my brother's keeper, am I?"

Then God said, "Your brother's blood cries out to Me from the ground." And Cain realized nothing can be hidden from God.

God said, "Never again will you get a harvest from the ground. You will leave here and wander the earth for the rest of your life."

Cain cried out, "That punishment is too hard for me to bear! I'll never see *You* again! And anyone who finds me will attack me, and kill me!"

"No," said God. He put a mark on Cain. Now no one would harm Cain, but everyone would know he had killed his brother.

So Cain left the place where he had been born, and moved towards the east. And Adam and Eve had another son, Seth, and were comforted a little for the loss of their son Abel.

And in his turn Seth married and had children. And their children had children, and so on, until there were many people living on the earth.

# Noah

God looked at the world He had made, and the people He had made. He saw the people killing each other, robbing each other, cheating each other, quarrelling with each other. He saw they were thinking less and less about Him, and more and more about themselves. They had grown wicked, and God became sorry He had made them.

Only one man was different. Noah. Noah still loved God; and God loved him.

One day, God spoke to Noah. "I am going to destroy these people. My world is full of violence because of the way they are behaving. I am going to send a great flood on the earth. All life under the skies will be destroyed."

Then Noah was afraid, but God said, "Do not fear! You are a good man. I will not destroy you, or your family. We will make a covenant – an agreement. You must do as I tell you, then your lives will be saved."

And God told Noah to build an Ark. It was to be made of cypress wood, and covered with tar inside and out, so that it would be waterproof. It was to measure about one hundred and forty metres long, twenty-five metres wide, and fifteen metres high. It was to have three decks, and be divided into rooms. In one side it was to have a door, and there was to be a window.

Noah listened, puzzled. With his wife, his three sons and *their* wives, there were eight people in his family. Why need the Ark be so huge?

God went on. "You must bring into the Ark pairs of all the creatures that live – one male and one female. You must keep them alive with you. And you must take all the different kinds of food that will be needed, and store it in the Ark."

The task was enormous! But Noah trusted God, so he and his family set to work. Soon there was much hammering, sawing, bending and shaping of wood going on outside his home. The people who lived nearby jeered.

"He's building a boat! Here! Miles from the sea! And *what* a boat! It won't steer. It probably won't even float! Floods? What floods? He must be mad!"

Noah gave up trying to warn them. He simply believed God's words, and went on building.

At last the Ark was finished. Noah and his family started to gather the food. When the leaves, hay, fruit and grains were stored in the Ark, it was time to collect the animals. How was *that* to be done?

As Noah wondered, a strange thing happened. The animals came to Noah – pairs of animals, birds and insects. It was an amazing sight. God told Noah to collect seven pairs of some of them. Noah led the way into

the Ark; and two by two, the animals, birds and insects followed. Noah and his family led them all to the places specially prepared for them.

When the last one was inside, God closed the door.

The watching people were astonished, but they still jeered. It had already begun to rain. Now rain *poured* down, like water from a bucket. All the springs overflowed, and added to the flood. Higher and higher rose the water, higher than the mountain tops. Every living thing on the earth was destroyed, as God had said. But the Ark floated safely on the water, with Noah and all the creatures snug and dry inside.

For forty days and forty nights it rained. During the day, Noah cared for the animals. At night, he lay listening to the rain beating on the roof of the Ark. And then, one morning when he awoke, something was different.

The rain had stopped.

"Hurrah!" cried Noah's sons, Shem, Ham and Japheth. "Now we can get out!"

"Wait!" cried Noah. He ran to look out of the window at the top of the Ark. There was nothing to see but water. No one could leave the Ark yet.

For one hundred and fifty days the waters flooded the earth. But God hadn't forgotten Noah and all the creatures that were with him in the Ark. God sent a strong wind to blow. The wind helped to dry up the water.

And as the wind blew and the sun shone, slowly, slowly, the floods went down. Still the Ark rocked gently on the water, until one day, with a grind and a bump, it settled onto solid ground.

"Surely we can get out now!" cried Shem, Ham and Japheth. But still from the window there was nothing to be seen but water.

"We must be on a mountain top," said Noah. "We shall have to wait longer yet." And they went on with their task of keeping the animals alive.

For over two months more they waited. Now other mountain tops were showing. Noah took a raven and let it fly from the window.

"If there is dry land, the raven will find it, and not return to the Ark," he said.

Anxiously they watched the bird until they could see it no longer. They hoped it would not come back. But it did. Weary, bedraggled, it landed on the Ark; and Noah brought it inside.

"The floods still cover the earth," he said.

Seven days they waited. Then Noah let a dove fly from the window. But it returned.

Seven more long days they waited. Once more, Noah let a dove fly from the window. Once more it returned. But when Noah brought it inside, he cried, "See! The dove has an olive leaf in its beak! Olive trees grow mainly in the valleys! There must be dry land!"

Then everyone laughed and cheered. Seven more days they waited before Noah let the dove fly again. This time it did not return.

Cautiously, Noah opened the door of the Ark. He saw that the ground was dry. Then God said to him, "It is time for you to come out of the Ark; you, your family, and all the creatures."

So out came Noah. And out came the livestock, stretching and blinking in the sunshine before flying, galloping, hopping, scampering, crawling away to make their own homes, and to have young.

What a relief to see them go!

The world was clean, shining and beautiful again. Noah and his family built an altar, and Noah made a special 'thank you' sacrifice to God for saving their lives.

God was pleased. He blessed Noah and his family, and said, "You must have many children, and fill the earth with people once more. Never again will I bring a great flood on the earth, to destroy everything."

And then, across the sky, Noah and his family saw an arc of beautiful colours – red, orange, yellow, green, blue, indigo and violet – shining against the dark clouds.

"See," said God. "This is a sign of My covenant. I will put a rainbow in the sky. And whenever you see it, you can remember My promise. And My promise will last for ever."

# Tower of Babel

After the flood, Noah's sons and daughters-in-law soon had children; and *their* children had children, and so on, until Noah – who was by now a very old man – had a very large family, with many great-great-grandchildren. The families spread out a little, but they still all spoke the same language. They wandered east, looking for a good place to settle, and they came to the plain of Shinar. This was it! They would stop here.

They had discovered how to make bricks out of clay, and they decided to build a splendid city with a huge tower at its centre. A tower which would be so high, it would reach right up to heaven. A tower which would help the people to stay together, united. A tower which would show everybody what an important nation this was.

So the people started to build. Everyone helped, and the tower soon began to rise high. But God came to see what they were doing. He saw they were growing proud and arrogant. They had left Him out of their lives, and were trying to reach heaven by their own work. God knew they could never succeed. And if they went on leaving Him out, they would soon be no better than the people before the flood had been. He had to stop them.

So He did.

One morning when the people came to start work on the tower they found they couldn't understand what anyone else was saying. God had confused their language. At first the people were puzzled, angry, afraid. No matter how much they shouted, or stamped their feet, they still couldn't make themselves understood, or understand each other's instructions.

Work on the tower stopped. So many mistakes were being made, it wasn't safe to go on.

After a while, each person discovered there were a few others speaking a language which he or she could understand. These groups got together, and moved away from the rest.

So God's purpose was fulfilled. The people were scattered over the

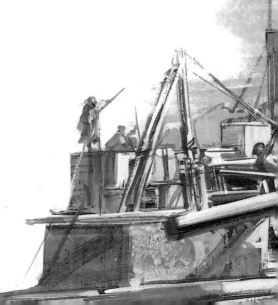

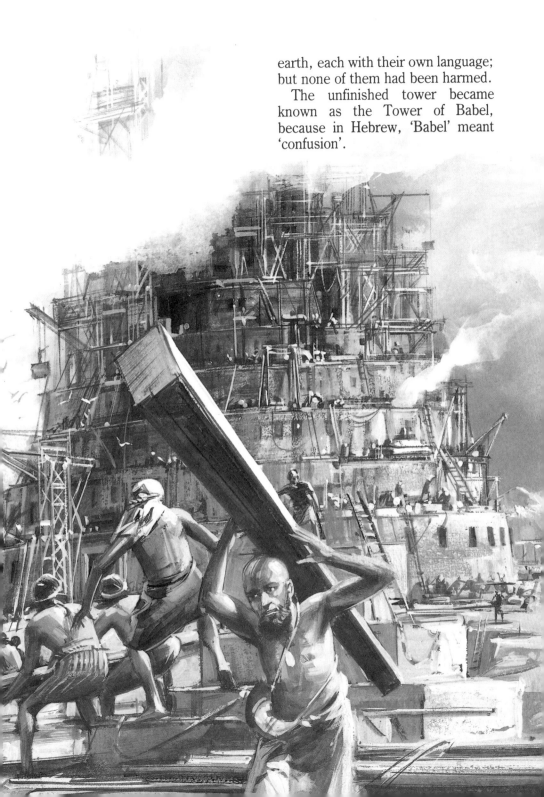

earth, each with their own language; but none of them had been harmed.

The unfinished tower became known as the Tower of Babel, because in Hebrew, 'Babel' meant 'confusion'.

# Abram

Abram was a brave man – ready to fight if the need arose; ready to do anything which God asked of him.

Abram had been living in the city of Ur, but the people there didn't worship the true God, as Abram did. In the evenings, Abram would go up and sit on the flat roof of his house, as was the custom. And there in the starlight he and God would talk together.

One evening, God said, "Abram, I want you to leave this place and go to a land which I will show you. And I will bless you, and your children, and your children's children. And you shall become a great nation."

Leave everything he knew, and set out on a journey with no idea where it would end? Abram hesitated; but only for a moment. He loved God, and believed God's promises. So preparations for the journey were made. Sarai, Abram's wife, was ready to go with him. So was Lot, his nephew.

Soon a long procession set out – family, servants, goats and sheep. Abram led the way. Nobody knew where they were going. They all followed Abram; and Abram went where God told him.

Each night they camped; each day they moved on again. Their first long stopping place was at Haran. Here Abram's father had died. Soon Abram was obeying God's command to move on.

When they had travelled as far as Shechem in Canaan, where the Canaanites lived, God said, "Abram, this is the land I will one day give to your children."

So far, Abram and Sarai *had* no children. But still Abram believed God's promises. So he stopped and built an altar. On it he offered a sacrifice of thanksgiving. But the journey wasn't over yet.

There was a famine in the land, so Abram travelled on, towards Egypt. But he was worried.

"Sarai," he said, "I've heard about these Egyptians. When they see how beautiful you are, they'll want to make you their Pharaoh's wife. He's their ruler, and they'll want to please him. They'll get rid of me by having me killed! Let's say you're my sister. Then I'll be treated well, for your sake."

Sarai agreed to the plan. It wasn't quite a lie. She *was* Abram's half-sister. Sure enough, when they reached Egypt things happened as Abram had thought. Pharaoh took Sarai to live in the palace, and sent Abram many rich gifts.

But God was not pleased with the deceit. He made Pharaoh and all his household very ill. It didn't take Pharaoh long to realize the cause of the illness, and he sent for Abram.

Guilty, ashamed, Abram trembled in front of Pharaoh.

"What have you done to me?" cried Pharaoh. "Why didn't you tell me Sarai was your wife? I might have done something very wrong! Here – take her, and go!"

Thankful to escape so lightly, Abram obeyed. Pharaoh gave orders that Abram, Sarai and Lot were to leave the country at once; but he allowed Abram to keep all the gifts he had given him.

So as the long caravan set out again, Abram was a rich man.

# Lot is Captured

Abram and his nephew Lot now owned many sheep and cattle. The herdsmen fought bitterly over who should get to the well first, for drawing enough water for all the animals took *hours*. It was also hard to find enough food for so many people and animals. The quarrelling and the fighting grew, and Abram knew something must be done.

"Lot," he said, "you and I shouldn't quarrel. There's no need. Let's separate. You choose which way you want to go, and I'll go the other way."

Lot was amazed – not by the plan, which he could see was a good one, but that Abram, the leader, should give *him* first choice! Lot looked around. He saw the rich, green grass of the plain, with the River Jordan flowing through it. There would be no problem there with grazing or water. Quickly, Lot said, "I choose the plain."

"Very well," Abram agreed quietly. So the two groups parted. Caring nothing for his uncle's welfare, Lot took his people and animals and went to live near the town of Sodom, although the people living there were known to be very wicked. Abram and his people stayed in Canaan.

God was pleased with Abram. "You may walk through this whole land," said God, "for I am giving it to you and to your offspring, who shall be too many to be counted."

So Abram built an altar of thanksgiving to God at Hebron, and settled there.

Some time after, the King of Sodom, the King of its twin town Gomorrah, and two other Kings of the plain of Jordan were attacked by five neighbouring Kings. The Kings of the plain lost the battle. Lot and his family were captured, along with many other prisoners.

Somehow, a messenger managed to reach Abram with the news. Abram didn't hesitate. No matter how selfishly Lot had behaved, he

was a member of the family, and must be rescued. Rapidly, Abram gathered his men together, and set off.

Presently they approached the place where Abram knew the attacking armies had stopped to rest. Signalling to his men to take cover, Abram peered down from the hilltop. He could see the enemy camp plainly. He could also see that his own men were heavily outnumbered. If they were to have a chance of success, he must work out a plan...

There was one thing in his favour. The enemy were off guard, celebrating their victory. They were not expecting any more resistance. Abram must make a surprise attack, under cover of darkness.

After a while, he saw how he could do it. Dividing his men into groups, he sent each group to its own place so that, unknowing, the enemy armies were surrounded.

Tensely, the men waited until night. Then, at a signal, they rushed on the camp, attacking from all sides.

In the darkness and confusion the enemy believed Abram's men were a huge army. In fear they fled, leaving behind all their possessions and all their captives.

Lot and his family were saved, and Abram was declared a hero. Returning in triumph, Abram saw the high priest himself coming out to meet them. This was a very great honour.

The King of Sodom suggested Abram let the people return, and keep for himself all the captured riches. But Abram refused. He wanted nothing from Sodom, because of the wickedness of the people who lived there.

Once more, God was pleased with Abram.

"No longer will you be called Abram, but Abraham," said God, "for I will bless you, and you will be the father of many nations. And your wife's name shall be Sarah, and I will bless her also."

# Escape from Sodom

Abraham was pleading with God, for God was planning to destroy the cities of Sodom and Gomorrah because of the wickedness of the people who lived there.

"If You find only ten good people in Sodom, will You spare it?" begged Abraham at last, looking down on the city from where he stood on the hillside.

"For only ten good people I will spare the city," God promised. And He sent two angels as messengers to inspect Sodom.

The angels looked like ordinary men. It was evening as they entered Sodom, but Lot had been sitting by the gate, and he noticed them. Knowing they were new to the town he offered them hospitality, as was the custom.

"No thank you. We'll sleep in the square," said the messengers.

This distressed Lot. "No, no! Come and stay at my house and be comfortable!" he urged.

So in the end the messengers went with him. Lot sent for water to bathe their feet. Then he got a meal ready, and they all ate together. They were still up when all the men of Sodom came banging on the door of Lot's house.

"Bring out your visitors!" shouted the men. "We want to amuse ourselves with them!"

Lot began to tremble. He knew the men meant evil. He went out to them, shutting the door behind him, and tried to calm them.

"Please, my friends! Don't harm these men!" he said. "They are my guests, under my protection! They should be left in peace!"

"Let us by!" yelled the mob. And to one another they said, "He comes here as a foreigner, then tries to tell us what's right and what's wrong!" And they shouted, "It'll be worse for you than it is for them before we've finished!"

They charged forward. But the men in the house had been listening. Quickly, they opened the door, grabbed Lot, pulled him inside, and slammed the door in the faces of the mob just in time.

Then God blinded every one of the men of Sodom, so that they couldn't see where the door was.

As the men wandered around outside, bewildered and afraid, the messengers spoke urgently to Lot. "You must escape! This town must be destroyed! Is there anyone else here who belongs to your family? You must all run for your lives!"

"My sons-in-law!" cried Lot. He rushed out to warn them. But they only laughed at him, so Lot had to leave them.

"Hurry!" cried the messengers as Lot came back alone.

Still Lot stood hesitating. Then one

messenger grabbed the hands of Lot and his wife, while the other seized the hands of Lot's two daughters, and they hurried them out of the town. Light was dawning.

"Make for the mountains! And don't stop!" the messengers ordered, preparing to leave Lot and his family.

"Not the mountains!" gasped Lot. "We'll never reach them in time! Let us take shelter in Zoar."

Zoar was a small town not far away.

"Very well," the messengers agreed. "God will spare Zoar. But make haste! And remember – don't look back!"

Shaking and exhausted, Lot and his daughters reached Zoar as the sun was fully risen. Then God rained down sulphur and fire on Sodom and Gomorrah. The towns were totally destroyed.

Lot and his daughters were safe. But in spite of the warning, Lot's wife had stopped and looked back. And as she stood there, gazing, she was turned into a pillar of salt.

Early next morning Abraham went back to the place where he had pleaded with God. He looked towards the place where Sodom and Gomorrah had been. But all he could see was thick smoke billowing up from the plain.

Then Abraham knew that God had destroyed the towns. But God had remembered Abraham, and for his sake had saved Abraham's nephew Lot.

# Abraham's Son, Isaac

Some months after Sodom was destroyed, Abraham was sitting in the doorway of his tent trying to keep out of the hot midday sun.

Suddenly, he saw three men standing close by. Amazed that anyone should be out walking in the heat of the day, he hurried forward to offer them hospitality.

"Come and rest in the shade of the trees!" he said. "Let my servants bring you cool water to bathe your feet. And let me give you a meal."

The men accepted the invitation. Then Abraham rushed around organizing everything. His servants hurried to prepare food. Sarah, Abraham's wife, baked fresh bread.

Presently, the men sat under the trees enjoying the meal. Sarah could overhear the conversation. "Where is your wife?" asked the men.

"She is in the tent," Abraham answered. By now, he was beginning to realize that these were no ordinary visitors.

One of the visitors said, "Before the year passes, and I come again, Sarah will have a son."

A son! At her age! Sarah laughed aloud. She and Abraham were old, and Sarah had given up hope of having any children.

But in due time, God kept the promise He had made to Abraham so long before, and Sarah did have a son. Abraham named him Isaac, or 'Laughter'.

Abraham and Sarah loved the boy very much. Indeed, as the lad grew, God began to fear Abraham loved Isaac too much, and would put his love for his son even above obedience to God. God decided to test Abraham.

"Abraham," said God, "take your son to the mountains, to a place which I shall show you, and there offer him up as a sacrifice."

Sacrifice his son? *Kill* his beloved only son? Abraham could hardly believe his ears. He wanted to cry out, "No! No!"

Yet Abraham had loved and obeyed God all his life...This time too, he must obey God's command...

Early next morning, Abraham rose. With a heavy heart he prepared his donkey for the journey, loading it with enough wood to make a fire for the burnt offering. Then he called to Isaac, and two of his servants. "We are going to the mountains to make a sacrifice," he said.

Excitedly, Isaac set out beside his father.

After three days, Abraham saw they were near the place which God had told him about.

"Stay here with the donkey," he ordered the servants. "My son and I will go over there, to worship God."

He forced himself to unload the wood, and gave it to Isaac to carry.

He himself carried the knife.

At first, Isaac walked happily beside his father. Then suddenly, he said, "Father – you have the knife, and I have the wood. But where is the lamb we will offer?"

Abraham's mouth went dry. Somehow he managed to answer, "God will provide the lamb."

On they went together, until they reached the exact place. Slowly, heavily, Abraham built an altar. Slowly, heavily, he arranged the wood on it. Now there were no more preparations to make. He could put the moment off no longer.

With eyes full of tears he took Isaac, bound him with rope, and laid him on the altar. He took the knife, ready to kill his only son.

But just as his hand was raised to strike, an angel of the Lord called from heaven. "Stop! Don't harm the boy! For now I know you *truly* love and trust God. You were ready to give Him your beloved son."

Isaac was safe! Trembling with relief, Abraham freed the lad. Nearby, a ram was caught by the horns in a thorn bush, so Abraham offered the ram as a thanksgiving to God.

Together, he and Isaac went back to the waiting servants, and home.

# Rebecca

Abraham was very, very old now. He wanted to see his son Isaac happily married before he died. So he sent for his most trusted servant.

"Promise me you will go to Mesopotamia, where I was born, and choose a wife for Isaac from amongst my own people," Abraham said.

This was a big responsibility. The servant was worried. "Suppose I choose a woman who won't come back with me?" he asked. "Shall I take Isaac there?"

"No!" cried Abraham. "That's the last thing you must do! God made a covenant – an agreement – with me that *this* land shall be given to my children, and to their children. I don't want Isaac to go and live in Mesopotamia! If she won't come back with you, you will be freed from your promise."

So the servant made a solemn promise. Next day he set out. He took a few more servants and ten camels with him, for he had a plan.

It was beginning to get dark as he came to the city in Mesopotamia where Abraham's brother Nahor lived. Just outside the city was a well. Here the servant stopped to wait for a while. He knew the women of the town would come to draw water every evening. This was what he needed, if his plan was to work.

He prayed to God, "Please let it be like this. I will say to one of the girls,

'Will you give me a drink of water?' If she answers, 'Yes, and I'll give your camels a drink, too,' I'll know she's the one You've chosen to be Isaac's wife."

The servant had hardly finished his prayer when a young girl called Rebecca came walking along the path to the well. She was very beautiful. She was also unmarried...

The servant's heart beat fast. Was this the right girl? He watched as she drew water. Then he spoke. "Er – will you give me a drink of water?"

"Of course!" she said, and smiled. She offered the pitcher to him. He drank. His heart still beat fast. Would she say anything more?

"I'll give your camels a drink as well," she said. She drew water from the well until all the camels were satisfied. Now the servant knew this was the girl God had chosen. But there was still a doubt. Would she leave her home and family to marry a stranger?

The servant took out some gold, to show he could pay for lodgings.

"Whose daughter are you?" he asked. "Is there room in your father's house for myself and the others to stay the night?"

"My father's name is Bethuel, son of Nahor," she replied. "We have plenty of room for you to stay with us."

Bethuel, son of Nahor! The

servant felt joy rising within him. God had brought him to the family of Abraham's brother!

Rebecca ran to tell her mother what had been happening at the well. Her brother Laban came down to speak to the servant. When Laban saw the gold the man was holding, he warmly invited the servant to lodge with them. The camels were fed and bedded down, and a good meal was prepared for the men. But before the servant could eat, he knew he must speak.

Once more his heart beat fast. He told the whole story, explaining about Isaac. "And now," he finished, "if Rebecca will not come with me, please tell me." He waited, trembling a little, for the answer.

Laban and Bethuel did not hesitate. "This is God's will," they said. "We give permission for Rebecca to marry Isaac."

What a relief! The servant praised God. Then he brought out many rich gifts which he gave to Rebecca, and to her mother and brother. They had a splendid meal, and the servant was happy.

In the morning, he and his men were ready to leave. But Rebecca's mother and brother pleaded, "Please let her stay with us for just a few more days!"

"Don't stop me," said the servant. "God has made my search successful, and I must get back to my master."

Then they called Rebecca. "Will you go with this man?" they asked.

Bravely, Rebecca replied, "Yes."

So they all set out, riding on the camels – Rebecca and her servants, Abraham's servant and his men.

All this time Isaac had been waiting, wondering what sort of wife the servant would bring back for him. One evening as he came out into the fields, he saw the camel train approaching.

Rebecca looked across the field and saw Isaac. She slipped down from her camel. "Who is that?" she cried.

"My master's son," replied the servant.

Rebecca veiled her face, as was the custom.

Isaac came running up. The servant told him all that had happened.

Isaac took Rebecca into his mother's tent. She had died, a very old lady, and Isaac had been sad. But now Isaac and Rebecca were married. They loved one another, and Isaac was comforted.

# Isaac's Twin Sons

After a while, Isaac and Rebecca had twin sons, Esau and Jacob. The two boys were completely different from each other. As they grew up, Esau was always out of doors. He became a skilful hunter. Jacob preferred to stay around the tents. He learnt to cook delicious meals. Esau soon became his father's favourite, Jacob his mother's.

One day, Jacob was cooking a good-smelling soup when Esau came in from hunting.

"I'm *starving*!" cried Esau. "Give me some of your soup!"

"Only if you'll give me your birthright in exchange!" bargained Jacob. Esau had been born first, and was counted the elder son. When their father died, Esau would inherit everything. This was his birthright.

"Never mind the birthright! I'm starving to death *now*!" said Esau.

"Promise me!" Jacob insisted.

Esau wasn't bothered about what might happen some time in the future. He was hungry, and the soup smelled good. "I promise," he said carelessly.

Jacob, well satisfied, gave his brother soup and bread.

As soon as Esau had had enough to eat, he went out again.

Jacob hurried to tell his mother what he'd done. Rebecca was pleased with Jacob. But if Esau's promise was to stand firm, Isaac must somehow be made to give to *Jacob* the elder son's blessing... They would have to wait, and watch for their chance.

Isaac grew old and blind. One day he called to Esau. "My son, go hunting, and bring back some venison. Then make me a stew, and bring it to me yourself so that I can eat, and I will give you the blessing before I die."

Rebecca overheard this. She watched Esau set out, then she hurried to Jacob. "Quickly! Go and get two of the best kids from our flock! I will make a stew using lots of herbs so that it will taste like a venison stew. You shall take it to your father, and pretend to be Esau. Then he will bless *you*."

"It won't work!" cried Jacob. "Esau's skin is rough and hairy! Mine is smooth! My father will know who I

am as soon as he touches me! He'll curse me, not bless me!"

"The curse would be on me, not you," Rebecca reassured him. "Go quickly and fetch the kids before Esau comes back!"

So Jacob obeyed his mother. She made the stew. Then she put Esau's best clothes on Jacob, and covered his hands and neck with the skins of the goats.

"Now go to your father!" she said, and put the basin of stew and some bread into his hands.

Jacob hesitated no longer. He went in to his father. "Who's there?" called Isaac.

Jacob took a deep breath. "It is your first-born son, Esau," he answered. "Sit up and eat the venison stew, then bless me."

Isaac was puzzled. "How did you manage to find the animal so quickly?" he asked.

Jacob thought fast. "God helped me," he lied.

Isaac was still puzzled. "Come close. Let me touch you!" he said.

Jacob's heart thumped. He went closer to his father, and stood still as the old man reached out and felt his hands and neck.

"The voice is Jacob's voice," said Isaac, "yet the hands are the hands of Esau. Are you *truly* my son Esau?"

"Yes, I am," lied Jacob.

So Isaac ate the meal. Then he said, "Kiss me, my son."

Jacob obeyed. Isaac could smell Esau's clothes, so he gave Jacob the blessing which should have been given to the first-born son.

"May God make you prosper. Let people serve you, and nations bow down to you. Be lord over your brothers, and let them bow down to you. Cursed be everyone that curses you; and blessed be everyone that blesses you."

Jacob left his father's tent. Hardly had he gone than Esau came back from hunting. He made a stew, and took it to his father. "My father," he said, "eat this stew, so that you may bless me."

"What?" cried Isaac. Shaking, he sat up. "Who are you?" he asked.

"I'm Esau, your son. Your first-born!" Esau answered in surprise.

Isaac could hardly speak. "Then who came to me just now? Whom have I blessed? And he *shall* be blessed, for the blessing cannot be taken away!"

Then Esau realized what had happened. "Bless me too!" he cried.

"Your brother has taken the blessing!" Isaac was distressed.

Esau was furiously angry. "He took my birthright, and now he's stolen my blessing! Haven't you even *one* blessing left for me?"

"I've just made him head of the family when I die," Isaac groaned. "I've asked God to prosper him. What is there left?"

Esau wept. "Haven't you more than one blessing to give?"

"You will serve your brother," Isaac answered. "But later you will free yourself from him."

Then Esau hated Jacob, and was determined to kill him as soon as Isaac had died.

When Rebecca heard this, she was afraid for Jacob. "Go and stay with my brother, Laban," she said. "As soon as Esau forgets what has happened between the two of you, I'll send a messenger and you can come home."

Almost petrified with fear, Jacob prepared to leave. But before he went, Isaac called him.

"My son, do not marry a woman from Canaan. Marry one of Uncle Laban's daughters. And may God bless you so that you will inherit the land, as He promised to Abraham."

Comforted a little, Jacob set out.

*Genesis 28 : 10–20*

# Jacob's Dream

All alone, Jacob started out on his journey from Beersheba to Haran, where his Uncle Laban lived. Jacob panted along, afraid in case his brother Esau should come after him to kill him.

It began to grow dark. Jacob knew he would have to rest. He found a stone which he could use as a pillow, lay down, pulled his thick cloak round him, and fell asleep, exhausted.

And he had a dream. In his dream he saw a ladder reaching from the ground nearby right up into heaven. Angels were going up and down the ladder, and the Lord God Himself stood at the top.

God spoke to Jacob. "I am the God of Abraham and of Isaac. The land on which you lie I will give to you, and to your children, and to your children's children. And they shall spread to the west and to the east; to the north and to the south. Through you and your family all the people of the earth will be blessed. And behold, I am with you and will keep you in all places wherever you go; and I will bring you again to this land. For I will not leave you until I have done everything I have promised."

Jacob awoke. He looked round. Everywhere was quiet in the starlight... But he was afraid.

"Surely this is God's house, and the gate of heaven; and I didn't know," he said.

As soon as it was light, he took the stone he had used as a pillow, and stood it up on one end to make a pillar. He poured oil over the stone and called the place 'Bethel'. And he made a promise.

"If God is with me to guard me and keep me, and bring me safely back to my father's house, then the Lord God will be my God. And of all that God gives to me, I will surely give a tenth to Him."

# Jacob Works for Laban

Jacob travelled on, and at last he neared the end of his journey. He came to a well which had a huge stone over its mouth. Sheep were lying nearby, with shepherds guarding them. Jacob spoke to the shepherds. "My friends, where are you from?"

"From Haran," they answered.

Jacob's heart beat fast. "Do you know Laban, son of Nahor?" he asked.

"Of course," they answered, staring at him.

"Is everything all right with him?" asked Jacob.

"Yes," they said. "And look – there's his daughter Rachel. She's bringing his sheep for water."

Jacob looked at Rachel as she came down the path. She was very beautiful. He hurried to move the heavy stone which covered the well. Then *he* drew the water for Laban's sheep, while Rachel watched, puzzled but grateful.

When the sheep were satisfied, Jacob greeted Rachel with a kiss. His eyes filled with tears as he explained who he was. Full of excitement, Rachel ran to tell her father. Laban came hurrying out to welcome Jacob, and bring him back home.

Jacob explained why he was running away from Esau's anger. Laban listened, and when the story was finished, Laban agreed that Jacob should stay; for whatever he'd done, he was still a member of the family, and needed help.

Next day, Jacob began to work for Laban. After a month, Laban said, "It's not right you should work for nothing, even if I am your uncle. How much would you like me to pay you?"

By now Jacob loved Rachel very much. So he said, "I will gladly work for you for seven years for no money, if at the end of that time I can marry Rachel."

Laban pretended to agree to the bargain. But he had another daughter – Leah. She was older than Rachel,

and not so beautiful. And Laban had a plan...

Jacob worked hard for seven years. Then Laban arranged a wedding, as he had promised. But under cover of darkness, and with her face veiled, Laban brought *Leah* to be the bride, not Rachel. And Jacob married her, not knowing.

When Jacob discovered he had been tricked, he was furious. But Laban said, "It's not our custom for a younger daughter to marry before the older. You shall marry Rachel but you must work another seven years for me."

There was nothing else he could do, so Jacob worked the extra seven years. But always he loved Rachel more than Leah.

Leah had lots of children, and Rachel was unhappy because she had none. She prayed to God, and at last a baby boy was born to her. They called the boy Joseph, and he was Jacob's favourite son.

Jacob had now stayed with Laban for twenty years, and had grown rich. Sometimes he used crafty tricks to

get the best cattle and sheep. Laban's sons grew jealous of him, and Jacob could see that even Laban was not as friendly as he had once been.

Then God spoke to Jacob. "Go back to your own land. I will be with you."

Jacob was afraid. Would his uncle allow him to go? He didn't want any trouble with Laban. Secretly, out in the fields where no one could overhear, Jacob told Rachel and Leah what God had said.

"You must obey God," they replied.

So Jacob waited until Laban was away shearing the sheep. Then he collected up all his family, his servants, his cattle, his sheep and his possessions and fled, making towards Mount Gilead.

When Laban discovered that Jacob had gone, he was furious. He called to his brothers to come with him, and set out in pursuit. For seven days Laban chased Jacob. Finally he caught sight of Jacob's tents camped on the mountain.

Then God spoke to Laban. "Do Jacob no harm."

Still angry, Laban pitched his tents near Jacob's camp, then rushed off to find him. Trembling, Jacob faced his uncle.

"Why did you leave like that – not even giving me a chance to say goodbye to my daughters?" Laban roared. "I haven't been able to kiss my grandchildren farewell! I could *kill* you!... But God has told me not to hurt you."

Jacob felt a little better.

But Laban was shouting again. "Why did you steal my household gods?"

For once, Jacob was quite innocent. "I haven't stolen them!" he cried. "If anyone here did steal them, that person shall die! Search the camp!"

Laban searched Jacob's tent, and the servants' tents, without finding anything. Then he came to Rachel's tent. Instead of coming to greet her father, Rachel sat on the cushions which had been on her camel. "Please don't be angry if I don't get up," she said. "I don't feel well."

Laban searched her tent, while Rachel watched him. He found nothing.

Jacob protested angrily. "When have I ever done you any wrong? I worked hard for you for twenty years! I worked in the heat, and in the bitter cold! And sometimes I didn't even stop to sleep! You kept changing my wages! You wouldn't have let me bring my own things away now, if you hadn't been afraid of my God!"

Laban was equally angry. "All that you have is really mine!" he retorted. "But I can't take anything away from you for the sake of my daughters and their children! We'd better make a covenant, an agreement."

So they set up a stone for a pillar, and agreed that Laban would not cross over to the land on Jacob's side; and Jacob would not cross over to the land on Laban's side. And Jacob made a sacrifice to God.

Then the men shared a meal together, and in the morning Laban and his brothers left for home.

And Laban never discovered that his household gods were indeed in Jacob's camp. Rachel had brought them with her, and – afraid to confess – had hidden them by sitting on them throughout the search.

# Jacob and Esau Meet

Jacob was safe from Laban. Now he began to worry about meeting his brother Esau. The last time they had been together, Esau had threatened to kill him...

Jacob decided to send messengers on ahead, to tell Esau that he was returning, and hoped for friendship between them.

The messengers set out. Soon they came hurrying back. "Esau is coming to meet you, with four hundred men!" they cried.

Four hundred men! Jacob was terrified. Esau must still be angry, and was coming to attack him!

Quickly, Jacob divided his camp into two groups. "If Esau attacks one group, at least the other will have a chance to escape!" he said. Then he cried to God, "Oh God, I beg You to save us from my brother Esau! I'm afraid he will kill everyone here, not even sparing my children! And You did promise my children should live, and have children of their own..."

All night Jacob worried. In the morning he collected up 220 sheep, 220 goats, 30 camels and their young, 50 cattle and some donkeys.

He put each group separately into the care of servants. To the first servant he said, "Take these goats to my brother as a present from me. Tell him I am coming behind you."

The servant set off.

Next Jacob sent a servant with the sheep, giving him the same message.

Next he sent the camels, and so on, until all were on their way.

"By the time Esau has received all my gifts he may stop being angry," Jacob thought anxiously.

He sent his two wives and eleven children to the other side of a brook.

Now it was almost dark, and Jacob was alone with his fear. Then, suddenly, an angel came and wrestled with him. All night they struggled, but Jacob would not give in.

As morning dawned, the angel said, "Your name shall be Jacob no longer. You shall be called Israel, for you have struggled with God and with men, and have overcome. Now let me go."

Exhausted, Jacob obeyed. "Tell me your name!" he gasped.

But the angel answered only, "Why do you ask my name?" and blessed him.

Then Jacob called the place 'Peniel', and said, "I believe I have fought with God face to face, and yet lived."

Now the sun rose high. Jacob looked up. He saw the sight he had been dreading. Esau was coming!

Hastily, Jacob went to his wives and children. He put Leah and her children in front, with Rachel and Joseph behind. Then he lead the way towards his twin brother.

When Jacob neared Esau, he stopped and bowed low seven times, quivering with fear.

But Esau ran to meet Jacob, throwing his arms round him, kissing him. They both wept a little. It was, after all, good to be together again...

Esau looked over Jacob's shoulder. "Who are all those people?" he demanded.

Jacob turned round. Proudly he replied, "Those are my wives and children. God has been good enough to give them to me."

"And what do you mean by sending me all these sheep and cattle?" Esau asked. "I have enough, my brother. Keep what is yours."

"Please accept my gifts!" said Jacob. So Esau did. And from then on, the two brothers were friends.

43

# Joseph the Dreamer

Joseph, the son of Jacob and Rachel, had ten older half brothers, and none of them liked him. The family were living in Canaan now, and Joseph was old enough to help his brothers in the work of caring for the sheep and cultivating the land. But Joseph's brothers knew he was their father's favourite, and they were jealous.

Jacob made Joseph a coat of many colours, which the boy loved, and wore all the time. His brothers wore rough tunics, and hated Joseph and his coat.

If his brothers slacked over their work, Joseph reported it to his father, and his brothers hated him all the more.

Things grew worse. Joseph dreamed a dream which he told to his brothers. "We were all in the fields, binding up the sheaves of corn. And my sheaf stood up straight, while all yours bowed down to it."

His brothers were furious. "Do you think *we* shall ever bow down to *you*?" they cried.

Then Joseph had another dream. This time he told it to his brothers *and* his father.

"In my dream the sun, the moon and eleven stars bowed down to me," he said.

Even his father was not very pleased. "Will your mother, myself and your brothers really bow down to you?" he asked. But he did not forget the dream...

One day, Jacob said to Joseph, "Your brothers have been away a very long time with the sheep. I want you to go and see if anything's wrong. They'll be near Shechem."

So Joseph set out. He reached Shechem safely, but there was no sign of his brothers, or the sheep.

As Joseph stood wondering what to do, a man spoke to him. "Are you looking for someone?"

"Yes," said Joseph. "My brothers."

"I heard them say they were going to Dothan," said the man.

"Thank you," Joseph replied, and on he went.

His brothers *were* at Dothan, tending the sheep.

But before Joseph reached them they looked up and saw him coming.

"Now's our chance! We can get rid of the dreamer for ever!" said one.

"Let's kill him, and throw him into this pit!" said another.

"We'll say a wild animal must have killed him in the desert!" cried another.

"Yes!" cried the others. "We'll kill an animal and dip Joseph's coat in its blood, then take it back and show it to our father!"

One of the brothers – Reuben – didn't want to harm Joseph, but he knew it was no use trying to dissuade his brothers while they were in this mood. He thought quickly. "If we kill him, it will mean *we* have shed his blood. Let's just throw him into the pit, and leave him," he suggested. "Joseph will never be able to climb out. He will die there."

"All right," the others agreed. Secretly, Reuben planned to rescue Joseph while the others weren't there.

Joseph came up to his brothers and greeted them. But immediately they seized him, tore off his coat of many colours and threw him into the pit. Then they sat down to enjoy a meal. The delicious smell floated down to Joseph. Bewildered and afraid, Joseph prayed to God for comfort and help.

Reuben found it hard to eat the meal or join in the laughter of his brothers. He went off to check on the sheep.

Judah, another of the brothers, looked over towards the road. He saw a camel caravan approaching. The camels were loaded with spices to sell in Egypt.

"Hey!" Judah exclaimed. "If our brother dies *here*, we gain nothing! Let's sell him as a slave to these Midianite traders! They can take him and sell him in Egypt! We shall be rid of him, *and* we'll have some money in exchange!"

Roaring with laughter, the others agreed. Roughly they hauled Joseph out of the pit. For one moment Joseph thought his brothers had tired

of their tormenting, and were freeing him; but next minute he realized what was happening. He was young, strong and good looking. The Midianites bought him gladly, paying twenty pieces of silver for him.

The traders bound Joseph with rope, and carried on with their journey. His brothers gleefully returned to their sheep.

Meanwhile, Reuben had come back. He stole over to the pit – and found it empty!

"The boy isn't here!" he cried. His brothers, laughing, told the story. Then Reuben was full of a grief he didn't try to hide; but there was nothing he could do to help Joseph now.

The brothers dipped Joseph's torn coat into the blood of one of their sheep. They took the coat back to their father, saying they had found it on the path.

Jacob cried out, "My son has been torn into pieces by wild animals." He wept, and no one could comfort him.

# Joseph, Potiphar and Prison

Now Joseph was alone, friendless in a foreign land. He was sold as a slave to Potiphar, captain of the guard, one of Pharaoh's officers. But God had not forgotten Joseph.

Potiphar lived in a large, splendid house. At first Joseph was given all the heaviest work to do. But he worked willingly and well. Potiphar soon realized that Joseph could be trusted; and after a while Joseph was allowed to move about freely, and was made chief servant of the household.

But just as Joseph's life was becoming easier, Potiphar's wife noticed him. She thought she loved him, and asked him to make love to her.

Joseph refused. "My master trusts me," he said. "It would be wicked of me to do as you ask, for you are *his* wife."

Potiphar's wife was furious. Full of revenge she went to Potiphar. "Your slave tried to make love to me!" she lied. As proof, she showed Potiphar Joseph's cloak. "When I screamed for help he fled, leaving this behind him!" she said.

When he heard this, Potiphar was furiously angry. He refused to give Joseph a chance to explain, and had him thrown into prison.

But God was still with Joseph. Even in prison Joseph's quiet strength and clear mind were soon recognized. Before long, the governor put Joseph in charge of the other prisoners. Even so, Joseph longed to be free.

When he had been in prison for a while, two of Pharaoh's servants – the chief butler and the chief baker – angered Pharaoh. They were put in the same prison as Joseph, and Joseph was in charge of them.

One morning, he found them both looking very worried. "What's wrong?" he asked.

"We both had strange dreams last night," they answered, "and there's no one here to explain what they mean."

"My God will help me to interpret them," said Joseph. "What did you dream?"

The chief butler spoke first. "In my dream I saw a vine with three branches. It grew buds which blossomed and ripened into grapes. I took some of the grapes and squeezed their juice into Pharaoh's cup. Then I took the cup and gave it to Pharaoh."

Joseph said, "The three branches stand for three days. Before three days are over, Pharaoh will send for you, and give you back your position as chief butler. You will serve him every night, just as you used to. And *please*! When you stand in front of Pharaoh, tell him about me, and get me out of here! Tell him I have done nothing wrong!"

Greatly pleased, the butler promised he would.

The chief baker heard the good news given to the butler, and hurried to tell his own dream. "There were three baskets resting on my head, one on top of the other. Each basket had bread in it, and the top basket was full of all kinds of food. I had baked the bread for Pharaoh. But birds were flying down and eating from the top basket."

Then Joseph spoke sadly. "The three baskets also stand for three days. Within three days Pharaoh will send for you. But he will have you hanged from a tree, and when you are dead the birds will peck at your flesh."

The baker was terrified. One day passed. Then another. The third day was Pharaoh's birthday, and he had a feast. He sent for the chief butler and the chief baker. He gave the butler back his old position, just as Joseph

had said. And just as Joseph had said, he had the baker hanged from a tree.

The butler, safely out of prison himself, forgot all about Joseph. Until one night Pharaoh himself had a dream…

# Pharaoh's Dreams

Pharaoh sent for all his wise men. He was worried. "I have had two dreams," he said. "In the first, I was standing by the River Nile when seven fat cows came out of the water and began to graze on the river bank. As I watched, seven *thin* cows followed them out of the water – and the thin cows *ate* the fat cows!"

Pharaoh shivered. Then he went on. "In my second dream I saw seven good ears of corn growing on one stalk. Then seven thin ears of corn sprouted on the stalk, and swallowed up the good ears. What do these dreams mean?"

The wise men talked together, trying to interpret the dreams, but none of them could do it. They grew very anxious. Pharaoh would be angry with them – he might even imprison them...

And then, at last, the chief butler remembered Joseph. He hurried to Pharaoh. "O Pharaoh, when I was in prison, I had a dream. The chief baker had a dream too. There was a young man called Joseph there, and he told us what our dreams meant."

"Bring him to me at once!" ordered Pharaoh.

A messenger ran to the prison. Joseph was brought up from the dungeons and told to shave, and put on clean clothes.

"Pharaoh has sent for you," the governor explained.

Excitedly, Joseph obeyed.

Next moment, hardly able to believe it, Joseph found himself in the palace, standing in front of Pharaoh.

Pharaoh said, "I have heard that you can interpret dreams."

"*I* cannot do it," Joseph replied steadily. "But my God will tell me what your dreams mean."

"Very well," said Pharaoh. Once more he told his dreams.

Joseph listened, then he said, "The two dreams have the same meaning. God has shown you what He means to do. The seven fat cows and the seven good ears of corn mean that

Egypt will have seven years when the harvests are good. But the seven thin cows and the seven thin ears of corn mean that the good years will be followed by seven years of famine."

Pharaoh was even more worried. Seven years of famine! Everyone would die!

Joseph could see what Pharaoh was thinking. He went on. "God has shown you this so that the people need not starve. You must find a good, trustworthy man and put him in charge of all Egypt, to see that your orders are carried out. You should command that during the seven good years, one fifth of all the grain is stored in barns. When the seven years of famine come, there will be enough food stored to keep the people alive – although even then, it must be distributed with care."

Pharaoh began to smile. "It is a good plan! Since it is through you that God has spoken – and since in all Egypt I know of no one wiser than you – *you* shall be in charge. Everyone shall obey you; and only I myself shall be greater than you."

And Pharaoh took his own ring, and put it on Joseph's finger.

Joseph's time of hardship was over. Now he wore fine clothes and a gold chain round his neck. He rode in a chariot. Men ran before it to clear the way. Everyone recognized Joseph, and bowed to him.

During the seven years of good harvests Joseph travelled throughout Egypt, making sure that a fifth of the grain was properly stored.

When the first year of famine came, the people cried to Pharaoh, "We are starving!"

But Pharaoh replied, "Do as Joseph commands, and you will all be fed."

Then Joseph ordered that the grain stores should be opened up. People from miles around came to Egypt to buy corn, for there was famine everywhere.

# Corn for Joseph's Brothers

There was famine in Canaan. Jacob said to his sons, "Why are you sitting about here, letting us starve? There is corn in Egypt. Go and buy some."

So Joseph's ten older brothers set out. Jacob wouldn't allow Benjamin, the youngest, to go, in case harm came to him.

The journey seemed long. At last, weary, travel-stained and hungry, Joseph's brothers bowed low in front of him, begging that they might buy corn.

Joseph could hardly believe it. He recognized them at once. Here were the brothers who had sold him as a slave! The brothers whom he had dreamed would one day bow down to him.

They had scarcely altered at all. But Joseph's brothers completely failed to realize that this handsome, powerful young man dressed in fine clothes was their young brother; the brother they had once hated.

Joseph didn't mean to give himself away yet. He spoke to them in Egyptian, having an interpreter translate the language to them, and having their answers interpreted to him.

"You haven't really come for food! You are spies, come to see what the situation is in Egypt!" he accused.

"No, no!" they replied in fear. "Your servants have only come to buy food. We have left behind our father and our younger brother in Canaan. If we do not get corn, they will starve."

When Joseph heard that his father and younger brother were still alive, he longed to see them. He especially wanted to see Benjamin...but how could it be managed? He decided on a plan.

"You *are* spies," he insisted. "I won't believe what you say unless you show me this younger brother. You must go and fetch him, and one of you shall be imprisoned here until you all return."

He had them all put in prison for three days.

On the third day he went to them to see what decision they had taken. He found them greatly distressed. They

spoke to one another, not knowing he understood what they were saying.

"This is our punishment for showing Joseph no mercy! Our father has lost one son – he will *never* let Benjamin come back to Egypt with us."

And Reuben said, "I *told* you not to sin against our brother! This is only what we deserve."

Joseph had to hide the tears in his eyes, but he spoke to them as harshly as before. And the brothers had to agree that Simeon should be left behind as a hostage.

With heavy hearts the others set out, their donkeys loaded with corn. Joseph had resolved to take no payment for it. Secretly, he had ordered that their money should be returned, each man's hidden in his sack of corn.

On the first night of the journey back, the nine brothers stopped at an inn to rest. One of them opened his sack – and discovered his money. He was amazed – and puzzled. The others were equally puzzled.

When they reached home, they found that their money, also, had been hidden in their sacks. It was strange. They were uneasy. And they had to tell their father that Simeon had been left behind in Egypt because the young ruler there wanted to see *Benjamin*. It was all very strange...

Jacob would not even consider letting Benjamin go. "I've lost Joseph. I've lost Simeon. And now you want to take Benjamin from me!" he cried.

Reuben vowed he would bring Benjamin back safely. But Jacob would not listen...

The corn from Egypt lasted for a while, then starvation faced them once more. There was no way out. If they didn't take Benjamin to Egypt, he would die here in Canaan. They would *all* die.

Sadly, Jacob allowed Benjamin to leave.

Joseph had been sure his brothers would return. He had been watching for them. But when at last he *saw* them, and saw that Benjamin was with them, he was so overjoyed he wept secretly.

But still he did not tell them who he was. "Bring those men to my house," he ordered his servants. "Bring Simeon also. We shall have a feast."

When the brothers found themselves being taken to Joseph's house, they were afraid. They began to explain that they hadn't *stolen* the money last time. And they'd brought double payment this time. They'd brought some gifts as well. *And* they'd brought their younger brother, just as they'd been ordered to...

Joseph answered them kindly, telling them not to worry. Then they

all sat down to a splendid meal; and Benjamin was offered far more food than anyone else.

After the meal, the sacks were loaded with corn. Joyfully the brothers set off on the journey back to Canaan.

This time, Joseph had not only ordered that their money should secretly be returned to them; he had commanded that a valuable silver cup should be hidden in Benjamin's sack.

He gave his brothers time to leave the town. Then he sent his steward after them, saying his cup had been stolen, and their sacks must be searched.

Indignantly the brothers allowed the search, sure of their innocence. To their horror, the cup was discovered; and Benjamin was ordered to return.

His brothers would not let him go back alone. In deep distress, they all returned. They bowed low before Joseph, and tried to explain.

Joseph said everything could be settled quite simply. Benjamin was to remain, as a slave. The others were free to go.

This was too much. How could they bear to go back to Jacob and tell him that Benjamin was lost to him? Judah came forward. Humbly, desperately, he pleaded with Joseph, confessing the way they had once ill-treated a younger brother, describing their father's grief at his loss...

As Joseph listened, tears came to his eyes. "Leave us!" he ordered his servants.

Then he wept openly. "Don't be afraid!" he said. "I am Joseph, the brother you sold. But I am not angry – and do not be angry with yourselves. God has been with me and sent me here so that your lives might be saved."

At first the brothers couldn't take it in. When they began to understand, they were overjoyed. No longer need they feel guilty about Joseph. He was safe, and had forgiven them.

"Now," said Joseph. "Go back to Canaan and tell my father I am alive. Tell him there will be five more years of famine. And bring him here to live with me."

# Jacob Goes to Egypt

Pharaoh had heard that Joseph's brothers were in Egypt. He sent for Joseph. "I'm glad your brothers have come!" he said. "Let them go back to Canaan with plenty of corn. But also send enough carts to bring the whole family here, where they can live in plenty. It doesn't matter if they can't bring all their possessions. The best of everything in Egypt can be theirs."

Gladly Joseph carried out Pharaoh's orders, and his brothers set out again. And this time not only were their donkeys loaded with corn – they each had several sets of new clothes, money in their pockets, and gifts for their father, Jacob. Behind the brothers went the long line of carts, as Pharaoh had said.

The long, slow journey seemed to take forever, but at last they reached home. Eagerly they hurried to tell their father the good news.

Jacob was a very old man now, and could hardly take it in. His son Joseph was *not* dead? The brothers explained again, and as proof showed Jacob the carts which were to take everyone back to Egypt.

Then Jacob believed. "It is enough!" he cried joyfully. "I will go to Egypt. And I shall see my son again before I die!"

So everyone prepared for the journey; and presently they set out. Jacob was placed carefully in the first cart. Behind him came the brothers, their wives and their children. Then came the servants, the camels, the donkeys, the sheep, the oxen, and some household things. It was a huge procession.

Back in Egypt, Joseph had been watching and waiting impatiently. When he heard that his brothers had reached Goshen he could wait no

longer. He ordered his chariot, and hurried to meet them.

At last Jacob's arms were round his son once more. At last Joseph could hug his father, and weep with joy and relief.

Joseph took his father and five of his brothers and presented them to Pharaoh. Pharaoh welcomed them kindly, and told Joseph to settle them in the fertile land of Goshen. Any of the men who were specially skilled could be put in charge of Pharaoh's own cattle. Jacob blessed Pharaoh in gratitude.

For some years Jacob lived happily in Egypt. But presently the time came when everyone knew he must soon die. Joseph took his two sons, Manasseh and Ephraim, to be blessed by Jacob. Manasseh was the elder, but Jacob gave Ephraim the special blessing.

"Both of them will become great," Jacob said. "But Ephraim will be the greater."

Then Jacob said to Joseph, "I am going to die. But God will be with you." And he asked for his other sons to come to him.

When they were all present, Jacob spoke his last words. "Do not bury me in this strange land. Bury me with my fathers, next to Abraham and Sarah, Isaac and Rebecca, and Leah."

Then he lay back and died.

57

Joseph wept bitterly. When the proper time of mourning was over, he went to Pharaoh's court and asked that he might be allowed to go to Canaan to bury his father.

Pharaoh gave his permission, and a long, sad procession set out. All Pharaoh's officials went with Joseph, as well as every member of Jacob's family. Only the children were left behind.

At last they reached the cave near Mamre which Abraham had bought as a burying place long ago. And there Joseph and his brothers buried Jacob, as he had asked.

Then they returned to Egypt. But Joseph's brothers were afraid. Now Jacob was dead, would Joseph take vengeance on them for having sold him as a slave?

They sent a message to Joseph. "This is what our father Jacob said. He said we were to tell you that he asked you to forgive us for the wrong we did you!"

Joseph wept when he received their message.

Then his brothers came themselves, and knelt in front of him. "We are your slaves!" they said, trembling.

"Don't be afraid!" Joseph said. "It's all right! You did mean ill, but God meant it for good. Because of your action many, many lives have been saved in this famine. Don't worry. I will still take care of you, and your children."

And Joseph and all his family remained in Egypt, in Goshen, and were known as the Israelites.

Joseph lived long enough to see his grandchildren and his great-grandchildren. And when he was very old, Joseph said to them, "Remember! One day God will bring you out of this land, into the land which He has promised. The land He promised to Abraham, to Isaac, and to Jacob."

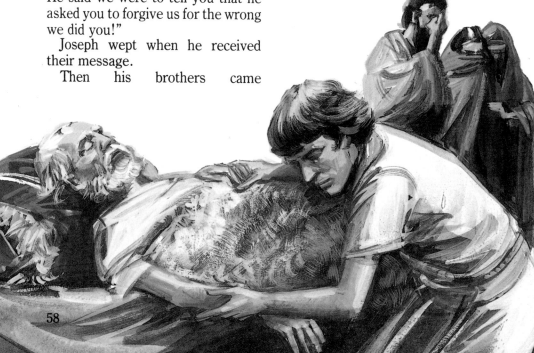

58

# The Baby in the Bulrushes

Years passed. Joseph had died. So had the Pharaoh who had been so kind to the Israelites.

Now the Pharaoh who ruled in his place began to be afraid.

"There are so many of these Israelites!" he complained. "It seems there are more of them than there are of us! If there is a war, they might join with our enemies and fight against us! We must make them work hard – turn them into our slaves. Then they'll have no strength for a battle, if one should come."

So life became hard for the Israelites. Tough taskmasters were put over them. They were forced to work in the fields, making bricks. They built the cities of Pithom and Raamses.

But Pharaoh's plan didn't work. The more the Israelites were beaten and ill-treated, the more they grew – in strength *and* in numbers. Pharaoh cried, "We *must* stop their numbers increasing!"

He ordered that every baby boy born to the Israelites should be drowned in the river. Girls could be allowed to live. They would grow up to be slaves.

The Israelites were greatly distressed; and one family could not bear to drown their baby. They decided to try to save his life. While he was tiny he slept most of the time, and it was easy to hide him

inside the house. But as he grew he slept less, and his cries became louder.

His mother, Jochebed, watched and worried. And at last she thought of a plan.

She asked God to help her. Then she went down to the River Nile and picked some of the bulrushes which grew there. Back at home, she dried the rushes in the sun, then she wove them into a basket-cradle, with a lid. She covered the outside of the basket with pitch, so that it was waterproof and would float. Next she made the inside soft and cosy with blankets.

Then came the hard part... Jochebed picked up the sleeping baby, kissed him lovingly, and laid him in the basket.

Jochebed's daughter, Miriam, had

been watching all this. Now she saw her mother cover the basket with the lid, pick up the basket, and beckon Miriam to follow her.

Secretly, they crept down to the river. Carefully, Jochebed placed the basket in the water, amongst the reeds. Miriam held her breath. With the weight of a baby in it, would the basket sink?

No. It floated perfectly, rocking gently, soothing the baby inside. Miriam's eyes filled with tears. They would have to leave him now, and go home...

But no!

"Hide nearby, and watch!" Jochebed told Miriam. Jochebed knew that every day the Pharaoh's daughter came to this part of the river to bathe. The baby would be found...and he was very beautiful...

Jochebed prayed again to God, and hoped against hope.

With fast-beating heart, Miriam crouched amongst the bulrushes, watching and waiting.

Presently she heard voices. Peeping out, she saw Pharaoh's daughter coming with her maids. Would the baby be discovered? Would Pharaoh's daughter have him drowned? Miriam clasped her hands tightly together...

Pharaoh's daughter saw the basket-cradle. "Bring that to me!" she commanded. One of her maids obeyed. Miriam watched, and felt as if she could hardly breathe...

As Pharaoh's daughter opened the lid, the baby began to cry.

"This is one of the Israelite babies," said Pharaoh's daughter, with sorrow in her eyes.

Suddenly, Miriam knew what to do. Scrambling to her feet, she ran forward. "Please – shall I find a nurse to look after the baby for you?" she gasped.

Pharaoh's daughter was surprised

at Miriam's sudden appearance, but she didn't hesitate. "Yes. Go," she said.

Eagerly, Miriam rushed away – and brought back her mother!

"Take care of this baby," Pharaoh's daughter ordered Jochebed. "I will pay you."

The baby's life saved! Herself to be allowed to look after him! And to be paid for doing it! Jochebed's heart was full of joy and thanksgiving. It was better than she had ever hoped...

Gladly, she and Miriam took the baby home. They cared for him openly, for no one could now say he should be drowned.

As he grew, Jochebed taught him about God, and told him stories of Abraham, Isaac and Jacob.

When he was old enough, Jochebed took him to Pharaoh's palace to live. Pharaoh's daughter named him Moses, and treated him as if he were her own son.

But Moses was growing up...

# Moses in the Land of Midian

Moses lived in the splendid palace of the Pharaoh, but he never forgot that he was an Israelite. As he grew up he hated to see his own people ill-treated, forced to toil as slaves.

One day as he walked through the fields, he saw an Egyptian task-master cruelly beating an Israelite slave. Furious, Moses glanced around. There was no one else nearby...

Moses struck the Egyptian, hitting him so hard the man was killed. Breathing heavily, Moses looked around again. Still no one was near, except the Israelite he had helped.

Quickly, Moses buried the task-master's body in the sand. Then he walked on, thinking his deed would stay a secret.

Next day, he saw two slaves fighting each other. "Stop that!" he cried. "Why are you hitting one of your own countrymen?"

The men paused. One of them answered rudely, "Who made you a judge over us? Are you going to kill me, like you killed that Egyptian?"

Moses was horror-struck. The slave must have told them!

"Everyone knows what I did!" he thought in panic. "Someone is sure to report it to Pharaoh!"

Pharaoh did indeed hear of it. He ordered that Moses should be killed.

But Moses escaped, fleeing to the land of Midian. There, lonely and tired, he sat down by a well to rest.

Seven daughters of Jethro, the priest of a nearby village, came to the well to get water for their sheep. Idly, Moses watched. Some shepherds came along, all men. Roughly, they told the girls to get out of the way until *their* sheep had been given a drink.

It wasn't fair! Angrily Moses sprang up. Making the men wait, he helped the girls, drawing water for them himself until all their sheep were satisfied. The girls were amazed – and delighted.

When they reached home, their father said, "How is it you're back so early today? Were the men not so rough?"

"They were the same as usual," answered the girls. "But there was someone else by the well – a man dressed like an Egyptian. He made them take their turn! He even drew water himself for our sheep!"

"Where is he now?" cried Jethro. "Surely you didn't leave him alone by the well? Go and invite him here for a meal!"

So Moses came to Jethro's home. The two men got on well together, and Moses was happy to stay with the family.

After a while, Jethro gave Moses his daughter Zipporah for a wife. Moses and Zipporah were happy. They had a baby boy. Moses became a shepherd.

But his people, the Israelites, were still in Egypt.

God had not forgotten them; and He remembered the covenant He had made with Abraham, Isaac and Jacob...

63

# Moses and the Burning Bush

Moses now lived in the wide, silent desert, caring for his father-in-law Jethro's sheep. One day, searching for pastures where the flock could graze, Moses came to Mount Horeb.

And he saw a most extraordinary thing!

On the mountainside a bush was on fire. Flames were shooting up – yet the bush didn't burn away! Cautiously, Moses moved closer to have a better look. Next moment he leapt back! A voice was speaking to him. And the voice came from the burning bush...

"Moses! Do not come any closer. And take off your shoes, for this is holy ground. I am God, the God of Abraham, and Isaac, and Jacob."

Moses shook with fear. Hastily he slipped off his sandals, as was the custom with the Israelites when they were entering a holy place.

God spoke again. "I have seen how My people suffer in Egypt. I am going to free them. And I have chosen you to lead them out of that land."

It took Moses a moment or two to take in the words. Then he cried, "Me! But I'm nobody special! No one will take any notice of what I say!"

"I will be with you," said God.

"But they will ask me Your name. What shall I say?" cried Moses.

"Tell the people the One who is called I AM has sent you."

Moses swallowed hard. "Suppose they still don't believe me?"

"What is that in your hand?" asked God.

"My rod," Moses replied.

"Throw it to the ground," commanded God.

Puzzled, Moses obeyed. Instantly, the rod turned into a writhing snake! "Aah!" cried Moses, running from it.

"Pick it up!" commanded God. "By the tail!"

Moses stopped. Pick it *up*! By the *tail*! That wasn't the way to pick up a snake – if you were foolish enough to try it at all. Pick it up by the tail, and it could whip round and strike you!

Yet that was what God had commanded...

With all the courage he had, Moses forced himself to go over to the snake – to bend down – reach out – and grab it by the tail.

And the snake turned back into a rod in his hand!

God said, "Now put your hand inside your cloak."

Moses obeyed. When he brought his hand out, it was white with the dreaded disease of leprosy.

"Now put it back again," God ordered.

And this time when Moses brought his hand out, the leprosy was gone.

"These are two miraculous signs by which you can prove I have spoken to you," said God. "If they will still not believe, this is the third sign.

Take some water from the River Nile and pour it onto the ground. It will turn into blood."

Moses stood there in front of the burning bush and imagined himself in Egypt, speaking to the leaders of his own people...speaking to the Pharaoh...

"Lord," he pleaded, "I am not good at talking to people."

"Who makes men's mouths, so that they are able to speak at all?"

cried God. "*I* will help you!"

Moses was still unhappy. "Please send someone else!" he begged.

Then God grew angry because Moses still didn't trust Him. But He said, "Take your brother Aaron with you. He shall speak for you both. And take your rod! For *you* shall perform the signs. And *you* shall lead My people out of Egypt!"

Then Moses knew he must obey God, and go to Egypt.

# Pharaoh and the Israelite Slaves

Moses had to explain to his father-in-law Jethro why he suddenly wanted to leave Midian. "Please let me go back to my own people in Egypt, to see if they are still alive," he said.

This was a reason Jethro could understand. "Go in peace," he said.

Moses prepared for the journey. But he was very anxious. Would there still be trouble for him in Egypt because of the man he had killed?

God reassured him. "All the men who wanted to kill you are dead."

So that worry was settled. But there still remained the enormous task of leading the Israelites out of Egypt...

Still anxious, Moses set out, taking his wife and sons with him. God knew how Moses was feeling, and sent Aaron to meet him in the wilderness.

The two brothers greeted each other warmly, hugging and kissing, for it was years since they had met. Then Moses told Aaron the task which God had given them to do, and the miraculous signs which Moses was to perform as proof that God was with them.

Now that Aaron was with him, Moses felt better. Together they went to the Israelites and called an

assembly of the leaders. Aaron gave God's message, and Moses showed them the signs.

The Israelites believed, and when they heard how much God cared about them, they worshipped Him. "God has not forgotten us!" they cried. "We shall soon be free!"

But first, Pharaoh had to agree to set his slaves free...

Moses and Aaron stood in front of Pharaoh. Aaron spoke. "This is what the God of Israel says. 'Let My people go, so that they can hold a feast in the wilderness, and make sacrifices to Me there.'"

Nervously, Moses and Aaron waited for Pharaoh's answer.

Pharaoh replied angrily. "Who is this God of Israel? *I* don't know Him! Why should I do as He says? I will *not* let Israel go. You're simply trying to get the slaves some time off! They already outnumber the Egyptians! Now you want them to stop work!"

Pharaoh gave orders that the Israelites should be made to work harder than ever. "Don't *give* them the straw to make bricks, as you have been doing," he commanded the taskmasters. "Let them find their own straw! But they must still make just as many bricks as before! Keep them busy! Then they'll have neither time nor energy to listen to these stories of feast days and sacrifices!"

The taskmasters obeyed Pharaoh. Now the Israelites had to search for straw; which took time. The slaves simply weren't *able* to make the same number of bricks as before, no matter how hard they tried, toiling all day in the hot sun. Then the taskmasters beat them cruelly.

The leaders of the Israelites went to Pharaoh. "Why do you treat us so harshly?" they cried.

"Because you are getting lazy," Pharaoh answered. "All this talk of sacrificing to your God! It's just an excuse. Go and get on with the brick-making!"

The Israelite leaders could see there was no mercy to be had from Pharaoh. As they left the palace they met Moses and Aaron, who had been waiting anxiously outside.

"God will judge you!" the leaders cried angrily. "You have made things much worse for us! Now we'll either die from overwork, or be beaten to death!"

Moses prayed to God. "Why did You send me here? Since I came, Pharaoh is treating the people worse than before! And You're not doing anything to save them!"

God replied, "You shall see what I will do to Pharaoh. Because of My strong hand he *will* let the people go. For I am the God of Abraham, and Isaac, and Jacob. I promised them I would give the Israelites the land of Canaan. Go and tell the people that I will keep My promise."

Moses tried to give the people God's message. But they were suffering so much they wouldn't listen.

Then God said to Moses, "I will perform signs and miracles, and the Egyptians *shall* know that I am God. Go back to Pharaoh and there do as I tell you."

# The Plagues of Egypt

Once again Moses and Aaron were standing in front of Pharaoh.

"If I am to believe you bring a message from your God, show me a sign," said Pharaoh.

This was exactly what God had foretold that Pharaoh would say. Aaron was prepared. He threw down his rod. Immediately the stick turned into a snake!

Pharaoh was not going to be impressed so easily. He sent for his magicians. They threw down their rods, and by magic turned them into snakes.

But Aaron's rod swallowed all the others!

Even then, Pharaoh wouldn't listen to Moses and Aaron.

Discouraged, disappointed, they left the palace.

God spoke to Moses. "Pharaoh is very stubborn. This is what you must do. In the morning, Pharaoh will go down to the River Nile. Wait for him on the bank, holding the rod which turned into a snake. As he comes near, say, 'The Lord God of Israel has sent me, to tell you to let the Israelites go and worship in the desert. This is how you will know He is God! I will strike the waters of the Nile with my rod, and it will turn into a river of blood.'"

Moses listened, swallowing hard. God spoke again. "Then tell Aaron to hold out *his* rod. And all the rivers, canals and ponds of Egypt shall turn into blood."

Moses and Aaron obeyed God

exactly. And it happened exactly as God had said. Pharaoh came down to the river. The water turned into blood. The fish in the river died. The water smelt *terrible*, all across Egypt. No one could drink it.

Stubbornly, Pharaoh sent for his magicians. They also turned water into blood, by magic.

"There you are," said Pharaoh, and he went back to his palace.

The Egyptian people had to dig for water along the banks of the rivers.

A week went by, and the waters were clearing. God said to Moses, "Go again to Pharaoh and give him My message. Tell him if he still refuses to let My people go, I will send a plague of frogs."

Moses and Aaron went to Pharaoh. Faithfully they repeated God's message. But Pharaoh was unmoved.

Aaron held out his rod – and up

from the River Nile came hundreds and thousands of frogs! They hopped into the palace – into the bedroom – onto Pharaoh's bed. They were *everywhere* – in all the houses – in the ovens – in the feeding troughs. Wherever the people stepped, there were frogs...

At first, Pharaoh pretended he was untroubled. He sent for his magicians. They made even *more* frogs appear.

"You see?" said Pharaoh. But really, he couldn't *stand* it. Frogs hopping out unexpectedly; frogs getting squashed underfoot; frogs *croaking*...

He sent for Moses and Aaron. "Um – my people are unhappy," he said. "Ask your God to take these

frogs away. Then I will let your people go, to offer sacrifices in the wilderness."

Moses didn't obey immediately. "*You* may fix the time when I shall pray to my God," he said. "And so that you will know it *is* God's work, when I pray, all the frogs will die – except those in the river."

Pharaoh was still pretending to be unmoved. "Pray tomorrow," he said, as if there was no hurry.

Then Moses and Aaron left the palace. The next day Moses prayed to God, and the frogs died exactly as he had said. There were piles and piles of dead frogs. The whole land smelt of dead frogs.

Yet as soon as the frogs were gone, Pharaoh changed his mind, and would not let the Israelites go.

God said to Moses and Aaron, "Strike the dust of the ground with your rod, and all through Egypt the dust shall turn into gnats."

Moses and Aaron obeyed, and gnats sprang up everywhere. They zoomed around, biting both people and animals. Pharaoh knew at once who was responsible. He sent for his magicians. But try as they might, the magicians could not make gnats appear.

"The gnats are a sign from the Lord God of Israel!" they said trembling. Yet *still* Pharaoh would not let the slaves go...

God spoke again to Moses. "Get up early tomorrow morning. Once more speak to Pharaoh as he goes to the river. Tell him if he will not let My people go, the houses of the Egyptians will be full of flies, which I shall send. But so that he will know I *am* God, there shall be no flies in the land of Goshen where the Israelites live."

And so it happened. Pharaoh would not let the people go; and on the following day swarms of flies filled his palace. All the land of Egypt was ruined by flies – there were flies on the food; flies in the drinking water; flies everywhere. But in the land of Goshen there were no flies.

Pharaoh sent for Moses and Aaron. "You may sacrifice to the Lord your God!" he cried. "But do it here, not in the wilderness!"

Moses was feeling bolder now. "No. That wouldn't be right," he answered. "Your people would be offended. They would throw stones at us. We *must* make a three day journey into the wilderness to offer our sacrifices. This is what the Lord God commands."

The flies buzzed and zoomed around Pharaoh's head. "Oh – very well!" he snapped. "You may go into the wilderness! But not far! Now pray to your God to take these flies away!"

"As soon as I leave the palace I will pray for you," Moses replied warily. "Tomorrow the flies will go. But the Pharaoh must keep *his* part of the bargain."

"Of course," said Pharaoh.

Moses left the palace safely, and prayed to God.

Next day not one fly remained in Egypt. But as soon as Pharaoh realized there were no more flies, he refused to let the Israelites go.

Once more God sent Moses to warn Pharaoh. God would send a cattle disease, so that all the Egyptian livestock would die; but the animals of the Israelites would be untouched. Once more, Pharaoh refused to listen; and once more God did as He had said.

Still Pharaoh would not let the Israelites go.

Then God told Moses and Aaron to take handfuls of soot from the fire and, in front of Pharaoh, throw the soot into the air. When Moses and Aaron obeyed, boils broke out on all the people of Egypt. The magicians suffered especially badly from the boils. Yet still Pharaoh would not let the Israelites go.

Then God sent Moses with another message for Pharaoh. Moses spoke. "So that you may know His power, the Lord God will send a great storm. The people and the animals of Egypt should all get under cover, or they will be killed."

By now, some of the Egyptians believed God *would* do as He said. These people hurried to get all their families and animals indoors.

But some people took no notice. They stayed out in the open as usual.

When the storm came, with mighty crashes of thunder and fierce bolts of lightning, hail accompanied it. It was the worst storm Egypt had ever known, and every living thing out in the open was killed. Yet in Goshen there was no storm at all.

Pharaoh sent urgently for Moses and Aaron. As the lightning flashed, and the thunder rolled, Pharaoh cried, "I know I've done wrong! Pray to your God! No more storms like this! Please! You and your people can go! At once!"

Moses was still wary. "When I am outside the city I will pray to God. The storms will stop, so that you may know God's power. But I can see you still do not *really* believe in Him."

Moses left the palace. Once outside the city he prayed as he had promised. Immediately the rain, the thunder and the lightning stopped. There was calm.

But when Pharaoh realized the storm was over he would not let the people go.

Moses was desperate. God comforted him. "Do not get too upset. I am performing these miracles so that you will be able to tell your children's children how I treated the Egyptians. Then they will know I am indeed Lord. Now go to Pharaoh again. Warn him that if he does not let My people go I will send a plague of locusts."

So once more Moses and Aaron stood in front of Pharaoh, giving him God's message. The leaders of the Egyptians were afraid. "How much more must we put up with?" they cried. "Let the people go and worship their God. Don't you see – Egypt is being ruined!"

Pharaoh asked warily, "Who will go and worship your God in the wilderness?"

"Every one of us," replied Moses.

"No!" cried Pharaoh angrily. "Only the men may go." And he had Moses and Aaron thrown out of the palace.

So God sent the locusts. The ground was black with them. They ate every leaf and every fruit in all the land of Egypt.

Once more Pharaoh begged Moses and Aaron to have the plague removed. Once more God removed it. But still Pharaoh would not let the Israelites go.

Then God sent darkness over the land of Egypt for three whole days. Only the Israelites had daylight.

In fear, Pharaoh sent for Moses. "Go!" he cried. "Every one of you!"

"We must also take our animals," said Moses.

"No!" stormed Pharaoh. "Get out of my palace! If I ever see you again you shall die!"

"Very well!" retorted Moses. "I will never come to the palace again!"

Now God prepared to bring the worst plague of all on Egypt...

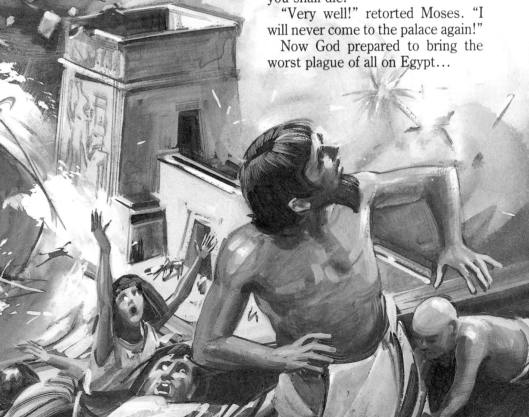

# The Passover

God said to Moses, "After *this* plague, Pharaoh will not only let you go – he will throw you out of Egypt altogether. But you must first give him warning of what I mean to do."

So – in spite of the way in which the two had parted – Moses once more stood in front of Pharaoh.

"This is the message from the Lord God of Israel," said Moses. "At midnight all the first-born children in every family in Egypt shall die. The first-born animals shall die, too. But none of the Israelites shall die in this way. You shall see that God treats the Egyptians differently from the Israelites."

Pharaoh listened to the dreadful news, but still he would not let the people go.

Moses called together all the leaders of the Israelites. There was a message from God for them also. "You must kill a lamb – one that is big enough to make a meal for your whole family. Dip a bunch of herbs into the lamb's blood, and mark your door-posts with it, both sides and at the top. No one must go outside before morning. You shall roast the lamb, and eat it with unleavened bread and bitter herbs. And even as you eat, you shall be ready to leave quickly. You must have your shoes on your feet, and your staffs in your hands. God is going to strike down the Egyptians. But when the angel sees the blood on your door-posts he will pass over your door. Death will not come to your household. And you shall remember the passover every year, as a covenant between you and God for ever. And you shall tell your children, and your children's children, how the Lord God saved all our families."

The people worshipped God. Then they went away to carry out their instructions.

At midnight, every first-born child in Egypt died, from Pharaoh's own child to the child of the lowliest prisoner in the jail. There was a great cry from every Egyptian household. Pharaoh sent for Moses and Aaron.

As light dawned, Moses and Aaron hurried to the palace.

"Go!" cried Pharaoh, when they stood before him. "Every one of you can go, *and* your flocks and herds! Get out from amongst my people, and go and worship your God!"

And the Egyptian people, in fear, also urged the Israelites to leave. "If you don't, we will *all* be dead!" they cried.

Hastily, the Israelites gathered up their belongings. They had been making bread, but they didn't even wait for the dough to rise before they set out.

So the huge host of men, women and children, with their flocks, their herds, and as many possessions as they could carry, came safely out of Egypt. They were free!

But their rejoicing did not last long.

# The Red Sea

Travelling day and night, the Israelites reached the edge of the wilderness. There was no time to be lost, in case the Egyptians came after them. God led the way, in a pillar of cloud by day and a pillar of fire by night. He led them around towards the Red Sea by the desert road.

Back in Egypt, Pharaoh and his people realized the Israelites really *had* gone. Now there were no slaves to do the work...

"Why did we let them leave?" the people cried.

"We shall get them back!" Pharaoh declared. He chose six hundred chariots, the best in all Egypt, and he set out after the Israelites with his horses and his men.

The Egyptian army travelled much faster than the Israelites, who had young children and animals with them. The Israelites had almost reached the Red Sea when they looked up – and saw the sight they had been dreading. The Egyptians were coming.

"Weren't there any graves in Egypt?" the people cried to Moses in fear. "Why did you bring us out here to die? Why didn't you leave us alone? It was better to be slaves in Egypt than to die in the wilderness!"

"Don't be afraid!" said Moses, trying to calm the people. "The Lord God will fight *for* you, if you will only let Him!"

Moses prayed urgently to God.

God answered, "Why are you talking to Me? Tell the people to keep moving forward!"

Move forward? The sea was in the way!

God was still speaking. "Stretch out your rod over the waters. The sea will divide, and the Israelites will walk across on dry land. The Egyptians will try to follow. Then you *and* they shall see My power!"

Now the pillar of cloud moved from in front of the Israelites to behind them. It came between the Israelites and the Egyptians, bringing darkness to the Egyptian side so that they set up camp for the night.

But Moses told *his* people to keep moving. Then he stretched out his rod over the sea as God had commanded. The Israelites watched in awe. The waters *were* dividing...

They started to cross – fearfully at first, then growing bolder. All night long the procession of people and animals walked and stumbled across the dry bed of the sea, with high walls of water on either side of them.

Suddenly, the Egyptians realized the Israelites were escaping. Quickly they harnessed their horses. At speed they raced their chariots across the ground, on to the sea bed. They were catching up!

As day dawned, God looked at the army of the Egyptians. They were too close! They must be hindered!

God made the wheels fall off the chariots. As the Egyptians struggled in the sand, they gasped, "Let's get away from these Israelites! Their God is fighting for them!" But they were stuck fast on the sea bed and the last of the Israelites was safely across.

Then God said to Moses, "Stretch out your rod again, so that the seas will come together."

In excitement and fear, Moses obeyed. As he held up his rod the seas came crashing down. The Egyptian army turned in panic, trying to get back to land. But it was useless...every single one of the Egyptians was drowned. And every single one of the Israelites was saved, completely unharmed.

Then the Israelites knew their God was great. They believed in Him, and in Moses, and they sang and danced in triumph and praise.

But once again, their happiness did not last...

# In the Wilderness

The great crowd of Israelites, with their animals and possessions, were travelling through the wilderness, hoping to reach the land which God had promised them. But they were desperate.

For three days they had found no water. Their mouths were dry, their throats parched. They longed above everything for a drink of cool, clear water.

At last they came to a place called Marah.

"Look!" they cried. "There is water here!" Thirstily they knelt to drink at the pools, but next moment they were spitting the water from their mouths. In rage and disappointment they shouted at Moses. "The water is bitter! It tastes horrible! No one could drink that! What are we to drink?"

Moses prayed to God. God told him to throw a certain piece of wood into the water. As always, Moses obeyed, and at once the bitter water became sweet and good. Gratefully the Israelites drank.

God made a covenant with them. "If you keep My laws, I will not send to you any of the plagues which I sent to the Egyptians."

The Israelites travelled on. They came to Elim, where there were twelve springs of water and seventy palm trees. There, in the shade, they camped to rest.

Soon they travelled on again. And once more they complained to Moses. "We're hungry! Why didn't you leave us in Egypt? At least there we had food! Why did you bring us

out into this desert to starve?"

Then God said to Moses, "I will rain food from heaven for them. They must collect it fresh each morning, and they must collect only enough for one day. I shall test them, to see if they are ready to obey My laws. On the sixth day they may gather enough bread for two days."

Moses and Aaron gave the good news to the people. "This very evening you will know that the God who brought you out of Egypt can be trusted. And in the morning you will see how glorious He is."

They explained the rules about collecting the food. "And remember!" Moses finished. "When you grumbled, you weren't grumbling at *me*, but at God Himself!"

The day seemed long as the Israelites waited to see what sign God would send them.

Just before dusk, flocks of small brown birds – quail – came flying low across the ground. The quail landed on the camp. There were so many, the ground was covered with them. They were very good to eat. Rejoicing, the people collected them. Soon from all over the camp came the smell of meat roasting. That night the people ate a good meal.

In the morning, when the dew had dried up, the ground was covered with tiny white flakes.

"What is it?" asked the Israelites, half afraid. They'd never seen anything like it before.

"That is the food God has sent," Moses explained. "Collect it as He commanded."

80

Most of the people obeyed, but some were lazy. "If we collect enough for two days, we won't need to get up early tomorrow," they whispered. So they gathered twice as much as they needed.

But by next morning maggots were in the food, and it smelt *terrible*.

Moses was angry. "You *know* the rules God made!" he said.

Then the people kept the rules. But on the sixth day, Moses reminded the people, "God has said there won't be any food from heaven tomorrow. Cook some that you collect today, so that it will keep."

Again, most people obeyed. Yet even after all their experience of God some people went out on the seventh morning looking for food.

God was angry. He spoke to Moses. "How long will this disobedience go on? I sent food for six days so that on the seventh day everyone may rest from work. No one is to go out on the seventh day!"

At last all the Israelites did as they were told. Every evening they ate meat, and in the morning they ate the bread food. It was delicious – thin and crisp with a flavour of honey. The Israelites called it manna, and God told Moses and Aaron to put some of it into a jar, and keep it to show the Israelites not yet born.

So the Israelites did not starve in the wilderness, but came at last to the borders of Canaan. Once more they could not find water...

They shouted at Moses, "Why did you bring us out of Egypt, to make us die of thirst in this place?"

Moses lost patience. "Why are you blaming *me*? I have *told* you – it is really God you're blaming!"

But the people were too angry to listen.

Moses said to God, "What am I to do with them? They look angry enough to kill me!"

"Walk on in front," said God. "Take some of the leaders with you, and carry your rod – the same rod which you had in Egypt. I will meet you by the rock at Horeb. Strike the rock with your rod, and water will flow from it. Then the people may drink."

Moses obeyed. Soon the Israelites were drinking clear, cool water. But Moses still felt angry. Would the people *never* stop doubting God, and His presence with them?

# The Battle with the Amalekites

The Israelites were camping at Rephidim when suddenly they were attacked by a fierce tribe – the Amalekites.

After a short skirmish, the Israelites had to prepare for a long battle next day. Moses wondered what best to do. He was old now, and no warrior. They needed someone young, strong, and a skilled fighter to lead the Israelites in the battle.

After more thought, he sent for Joshua, son of Nun. "Joshua," he said, "choose whichever men you want, and lead them against the Amalekites tomorrow."

Joshua's face lit up. This was a great honour! And yet – he couldn't quite prevent the thought – the Amalekites were strong, and well trained...

Moses explained the whole plan. "I will go up to the top of the hill and stand there holding up the rod which God has blessed so much in the past. From the hilltop I shall have a good view of the battle. And I know God will help you."

Joshua nodded. He went away and carefully picked the best fighters.

Next morning he marched them out, ready to face the enemy.

Moses climbed to the hilltop, taking with him his brother Aaron, and a man called Hur. As the Amalekites made the first charge, Moses lifted the rod, holding it high as he had promised.

From their viewpoint the three men could see that the battle was going this way and that. Whenever Moses' arms ached and he lowered the rod, the Amalekites began to win. Whenever Moses held the rod high, Joshua's men gained command.

Aaron and Hur realized what was happening. They found a large stone and brought it for Moses to sit on. Now they could hold up his arms *for* him, with no strain on their own. So Moses was able to keep the rod lifted high; and by evening the Amalekites were defeated.

And God said to Moses, "Write this whole story down – and be sure to read it to Joshua!"

Moses obeyed. And he built a special altar to God on the hillside, and worshipped Him there.

# The Ten Commandments

The Israelites left Rephidim and came into the Sinai Desert. They camped at the foot of Mount Sinai, and Moses climbed up to the top to speak to God.

God said, "I am going to make a very special covenant with the Israelites. If you obey My words you will be My special people. My chosen nation."

Excitedly, Moses hurried back down the mountain to give the people God's great message.

"Whatever God commands, we will obey," the people promised eagerly.

God was pleased. "On the third day I will come down to Mount Sinai in a cloud," He told Moses. "The people will see the cloud and know that I am with you. They will trust you. Tell them they must prepare themselves. You must bless them. During the next two days they must wash their clothes so that everything is very clean. And tell them they must on no account set foot on the mountain, for anyone who even touches it will die. Not until the ram's horn sounds may they go up the mountain."

So Moses blessed the people; and they washed their clothes and were very clean; and they waited expectantly for the third day to come. On the morning of the third day thunder rolled and lightning flashed over the mountain. A thick cloud covered the top of it, and a trumpet sounded loudly. The Israelites shook with fear.

Moses led the people to the foot of the mountain. There they all waited. Then the mountain trembled and the trumpet sounded, even louder than before. The mountain was covered with billowing smoke. And God called to Moses.

Moses climbed the mountain, and went into the cloud.

God told Moses the ten commandments, saying, "I am the Lord your God who brought you out of the land of Egypt. You must have no God other than Me. You must not worship statues, pictures or images, or anything which you have made yourselves. If you do not obey this law, I will punish not only you, but your children and your children's children.

"You must not use God's name carelessly, or without good reason.

"Remember the Sabbath day, the seventh day, and keep it holy. On six days you may work, but on the seventh day you and all your family must rest. Remember – I, the Lord, made the world in six days; but on the seventh day the Lord rested. The Lord blessed the seventh day, and made it holy.

"Treat your father and your mother with honour and respect.

"Kill no one.

"Do not sleep with another man's wife, or another woman's husband.

"Do not steal.

"Do not tell lies, or give wrong evidence against anyone.

"Do not long for anything which belongs to someone else."

Down below, the people saw the storm and the smoke. They ran back. From a distance they called to Moses in fear. "*You* speak to us! We will listen! But don't let God Himself speak to us, or we shall die!"

"Don't be afraid!" Moses comforted them. "God only wants you to do right."

Again Moses went into the cloud where God was, and God gave him more rules for the Israelites to keep.

"If there has been a fight, take a life for a life, an eye for an eye, a tooth for a tooth.

"If you find your enemy's donkey straying, return it to him.

"Do not be unkind to a foreigner. You know how it feels to be a foreigner, because of the time you spent in Egypt."

God gave many more rules to Moses. And Moses came down to the people, and told them.

"We will obey!" the people promised again. Then Moses wrote down all that God had said, and built an altar at the foot of the mountain. And he set up twelve pillars. The pillars stood for the twelve tribes of Israel.

Moses made a sacrifice to God. Then he read the laws to the people, and said, "The Lord has made a covenant with you."

Now the Israelites needed a very special container in which to place the written laws...

# The Ark of the Covenant

God said to Moses, "Come up to the mountain top. I will give you tablets of stone on which I have written the commandments."

Moses called to Joshua to come with him. He told the Israelite leaders to wait at the foot of the mountain. "While we are gone, Aaron and Hur will be in charge," he said.

Then Moses and Joshua climbed Mount Sinai. Cloud and fire covered the top of the mountain. For six days Joshua and Moses waited in the cloud. At last God called to Moses. But before God gave Moses the tablets of stone, there was something else which needed to be said.

The Israelites were to build a chest, or Ark; also a Tabernacle, or place of worship. God told Moses exactly what offerings could be made by every Israelite who wanted to contribute. Rich gifts of gold, silver or bronze; and gifts which the poorer people could manage – goat skins, olive oil. Gifts of acacia wood; of blue, purple or scarlet yarn; fine linen; and many other things.

The Ark was to be made of acacia wood. It was to be about one metre long, and just over half a metre wide and high. The Ark was to be covered with gold inside and out. Four rings were to be made. Two rings would be on one side, two on the other. Through the rings poles were to be slipped – poles also made of acacia wood covered with gold. The poles must never be taken out of the rings, so that the Ark could always be lifted up and carried.

The written laws were to be kept in the Ark, which would be known as the Ark of the Covenant.

God described more details of the Ark, and instructed that it should be kept in the Tabernacle. He also described the Tabernacle. It was to have a curtain hanging in it. The curtain would divide the Holy Place from the Most Holy Place. The Ark would be kept in the Most Holy Place.

Then God described what the priests of the Tabernacle should wear. He had even chosen the men who should make all these things.

When God had finished speaking, He gave Moses the two tablets of stone. But Moses had been on the mountain for forty days and forty nights, and the Israelites were growing tired of waiting for him to come down...

*Exodus 32 : 1–32; 34 : 1–4, 29*

# The Golden Calf

At the foot of the mountain, the Israelites waited…and waited…

They saw the clouds covering the mountain top. They heard the thunder, saw the lightning. And still Moses had not returned…

The people spoke to Aaron. "You will have to *make* us a god to go in front of us. This man Moses, who brought us out of Egypt – well, who *knows* what's happened to him? It seems he never will come back."

All these years, in Egypt and in the wilderness, it had been Moses who talked with God; Moses who then told Aaron what God wanted them to do. Without his brother, Aaron felt lost.

Perhaps Moses had fallen on the mountain. Perhaps he had been killed… The people were restless. They might become violent. Aaron remembered there had been times when even Moses had been afraid for his life because of the people's discontent…

Forgetting that when the people had been unhappy Moses had always prayed to God for help, Aaron made a decision on his own.

"All right. Bring me all your gold earrings and necklaces," he said.

When they obeyed, Aaron melted down the gold over a hot fire. Then he made it into the shape of a calf.

"There is our god!" cried the people. "That's the god who brought us out of Egypt!"

When Aaron heard what they were saying he was afraid. Quickly, he built an altar in front of the calf. "Tomorrow we will make a sacrifice to the Lord God," he said.

Next morning the people got up early and made burnt offerings. But afterwards they held great feasts of eating and drinking, and they worshipped the calf.

Up on the mountain, God spoke to Moses. "Go down at once! The people have made themselves an idol! They are kneeling in front of it!

They are saying it brought them out of Egypt! I shall destroy them all! Only you will be saved!"

Deeply distressed, Moses pleaded with God, trying to think of a reason why God should not destroy the Israelites. "Please don't be so angry with them! Don't let the Egyptians say, 'Their God took them out of Egypt so that He could destroy them in the wilderness!' Please remember all the promises You made to Abraham, to Isaac, and to Jacob! Their children would be more than anyone could count; and would reach the promised land!"

God listened to Moses and He decided to let the Israelites live.

Moses slipped and slithered hastily down the mountainside, carrying the two tablets of stone.

Joshua was waiting anxiously for him on the slope. "Listen!" Joshua cried. "There is war in the camp!"

"That is not the sound of war," Moses answered grimly. "It is the sound of singing and dancing."

Panting, he got far enough down the mountain to see the camp. And he saw the golden calf...

Moses was furiously angry. He threw down the tablets of stone. They shattered into pieces at the foot of the mountain.

Then he whirled into the camp, seized the golden calf and hurled it onto the fire. When it was melted he ground it to powder, scattered the powder onto water, and forced the terrified Israelites to drink it.

Then he rounded on Aaron. "Why did you do it?"

"They told me to," Aaron said, trembling. "They thought you were probably dead. I asked them for their jewellery, and when they gave it to me I threw it on the fire and it turned into a golden calf."

Moses could see that Aaron simply wasn't *able* to control the people. This was why God had chosen Moses, not Aaron, to lead the people...

Moses brought order to the camp. Then, with mixed feelings, he climbed the mountain once more. Once more he pleaded with God for forgiveness for the people. For forty days more Moses stayed on the mountain top. This time *Moses* wrote the commandments on tablets of stone.

When he came down the mountain this time, the Israelites were waiting for him. They saw that his face was shining; for he had seen God's glory.

# Departing from Sinai

The Israelites had promised once more that they would obey God. Now it was time to leave Sinai and move on towards the promised land. This time the Ark of the Covenant was carried in front of them, and the cloud of the Lord was over them. And whenever the Ark was lifted up, Moses said, "Rise up, Lord, and let Thine enemies be scattered." And when it rested, he said, "Return, O Lord, unto the many thousands of Israel."

So the Israelites journeyed on, and as usual began to grumble. "Can't we have more meat to eat? We remember all the fish we had in Egypt – and it was free! And we had melons and cucumbers; leeks, onions and garlic. Now we never have anything but this manna! Day after day after day! We can't eat any more of it! Not one more mouthful!"

God grew angry; and Moses spoke to Him resentfully. "Why did You make me leader of these people? They're not *my* children! Where can *I* get meat for them? It's all too much for me. I wish You'd let them die, right now!"

God had sympathy for Moses. "You're doing too much," he said. "Too many people are bringing you their disputes to settle."

Moses sighed. He did indeed feel tired.

"Bring Me seventy of the leaders of the people," said God. "I will tell them to help you with the task of

leading the Israelites." And then He said grimly, "The people shall have meat! Not for one or two days, but for a whole month, until they are sick of it! This will happen because they have not trusted Me."

"What?" cried Moses. "There are six hundred thousand men here! Even if we kill every single animal we have with us there won't be enough meat for every day of a whole month!"

"Is My arm too short?" God demanded. "You shall see whether or not what I say *will* happen!"

And God made a wind blow from the sea, bringing on it hundreds and thousands of quail. For two days and a night the people gathered up the birds, to cook them and eat them. But the meat made the people ill, and many of them died.

For a while there was no more grumbling about manna...

Still the journey continued. Moses' sister Miriam and his brother Aaron began to be jealous of him as he led the way. "Hasn't God spoken through *us*? Why does He only talk to Moses?" they demanded.

Moses had often wondered the same thing. He'd never thought he was anything special...

But God was very angry with Miriam and Aaron.

"I speak only through Moses because he is the only one I can trust! I can speak clearly to him. How dare you speak against him?"

And God made Miriam ill, so that she had to be on her own, outside the camp, for seven days.

Moses begged God to heal her, and after the seven days she was quite well again.

As soon as she was back in the camp the Israelites moved on again, still travelling towards their promised land.

Would they *never* reach it?

# Twelve Spies Explore Canaan

God spoke exciting words to Moses. "Choose twelve men, one from each of the twelve tribes of Israel. They are to go on a secret mission to spy out the land of Canaan – the land I have promised to give you."

At last! The Israelites were nearing the promised land!

The twelve men would need to be brave, strong and skilful if they were not to be discovered by the Canaanites. Moses picked them carefully; amongst them was Joshua, son of Nun.

Moses told them exactly what it was necessary to know about Canaan and its people if the Israelites were to attempt an attack. "And try to bring back some fruit," he instructed finally.

The twelve men set out. The rest of the Israelites waited as patiently as they could in their camp at Paran. For forty days they waited. Then they saw the men returning.

By then, every one of the Israelites knew which men had left the camp, where they had gone, and why. Eagerly, the people crowded round, crying, "Tell us! What's Canaan like?"

The twelve men had had a successful mission, and gave a full report.

"It's a very rich land, with good harvests. Look what we brought back! Grapes, figs and pomegranates. It's a land which flows with milk and honey! But – "

The Israelites, who had been getting ready to celebrate, stopped to hear more.

"The cities are large, and well defended!" one of the spies said, trembling. "And the *people*! They're

*huge*! Like giants, almost! We felt like grasshoppers beside them!"

The people all began to talk at once.

Caleb, another of the spies, silenced them. "Listen! Although the cities are strong – and although the people are powerful – we should certainly make our attack! Because God is on our side! We can fight – and win!"

But the other spies said, "No! We could *never* win a battle against the Canaanites!" And they spread discouragement among the people, so that the Israelites were not willing even to try.

The men shouted angrily at Moses and Aaron. "It would have been better if we'd died in Egypt! Why did God bring us here, just to die in a battle and have our wives and children captured?"

Then everybody wept. And some said, "Let's find another leader! One who will take us back to Egypt!"

Joshua stepped forward to stand beside Caleb. The two men tore their clothes as a sign that what they had heard was blasphemy against God. Then Joshua tried to reason with the people.

"The land of Canaan is well worth fighting for! Do not disobey God! And don't be afraid! We will beat those Canaanites! They have no protection which can match the power of our God!"

But the Israelites were too worked up to listen. Some of them picked up stones. Seeing this, many more were ready to throw stones at Caleb and Joshua.

God could let the dispute go no further. In a cloud of glory He appeared at the Tabernacle so that all the Israelites could see His majesty. He spoke to Moses. "How long will these people refuse to trust Me? In spite of all they have seen Me do? I *will* destroy them all!"

Moses pleaded, "If You kill them here the Egyptians will say You were not *able* to bring Your people into the promised land. I know You are slow to anger, and full of love, and that You forgive sin and disobedience..."

Once more, God listened to Moses, then said, "Very well. I will forgive them, and they shall live. But not one of the people who were in Egypt shall ever reach the promised land – only their children shall do so. Now – all turn back, into the wilderness. You shall live there for forty years. One year for each of the forty days. Of all the men here, only Joshua and Caleb shall reach the promised land."

The Israelites were bitterly sorry for the way they had behaved. Some of them even made an attack on Canaan *without* God's help; but it failed, and they were thoroughly defeated.

For forty long years the Israelites wandered in the desert wilderness. But at last, the time drew near to its end.

# Moses Dies

"I'm too old now to lead you," Moses told the Israelites. "Also, God has said I shall never reach the promised land. You must have a new leader."

Moses called Joshua, son of Nun, to come forward. In front of everyone, Moses spoke to him. "Joshua – be brave and strong, for you must now be the leader. God Himself will go in front of you, and be with you. He will never leave you, never forsake you. You must not be afraid. And you must never lose heart!"

Joshua listened steadily. And God Himself made a promise to him. "*You* will bring the Israelites into the land which I have promised them. And I Myself *will* be with you."

For the last time, Moses wrote down the laws which God had given to the Israelites, and the book was placed by the Ark of the Covenant. Then Moses wrote a song, as God told him to. It told the story of the past, and reminded everyone of the power of God. Moses taught the song to the Israelites, so that they would always remember their history.

Now Moses knew he was near to death. But before he died, God told him to climb Mount Nebo, and there look across the land of Canaan spread out below.

"That is the land which I promised to Abraham, to Isaac and to Jacob," God said. "I wanted you to see it before you go to your forefathers."

And there Moses died; and the people mourned for him. There would never be another man like Moses.

But Joshua was their new leader, full of strength and wisdom. Moses had blessed him, and the people listened to him.

And Joshua told them it was time to prepare to enter the promised land.

# Joshua Sends Out Spies

Joshua sent two men on a secret mission. "Find out how strong the city of Jericho is," he ordered.

The two men decided on their method. They would pretend to be ordinary visitors to the town, and find somewhere to lodge overnight. Then they would be able to see everything.

They entered Jericho quite openly, and went to the house of a lady called Rahab. On the way, they noted Jericho's strong walls and well guarded towers.

"It's more of a fortress than a town," they said to one another, gloomily.

Rahab let them in. But they had been recognized!

A messenger rushed to the King of Jericho. "Some of the Israelites are here, spying out the land!" he panted. "They are in Rahab's house!"

In anger and fear, the king sent men to capture the spies. It was already dark as the king's men reached Rahab's house. They banged on her front door, shouting, "Bring out the Israelites! We know you have spies in there!"

Trapped! thought the Israelites desperately.

But to their amazement, Rahab was beckoning to them. Her face was pale with fear, but swiftly and silently she led them up to the roof and hid them under stalks of flax which she had laid out earlier that day to dry in the sun.

There she left them, and hurried down to open the door to the king's men.

"It's true, some men *did* come," she said. "But they left at dusk because they knew the town gates would soon be shut. I don't know which way they went, but if you go after them quickly you could surely catch them!"

"They'll have gone towards Jordan!" cried the king's men, and set off in pursuit.

Up on the roof, the Israelites heard the noise and shouting fading into the distance. They lay still in their hiding place and presently Rahab crept up to them.

"They've gone," she whispered. "They'll be outside the gates by now. I will tell you why I saved you. We've all heard that your God has given you this land of Canaan. We're all afraid of you, because we know how powerful He is, and how He dried up the Red Sea so that you could cross safely. Now I beg you – when you attack the city, please don't harm me or

my family, or our possessions! Remember, I have saved your lives."

The men looked at one another in the starlight.

"We will see that you are all saved," they promised. "But on one condition. You must not say one word about us to the king."

"Not one word," Rahab agreed.

Her house was built on the town wall. She let down a rope from the outside window so that the spies could slide down it and get away.

"Go and hide in the mountains for three days!" she advised, in a low voice. "The search will be over by then."

And they said, "We shall keep our promise to you. When the Israelites come, you must tie a piece of scarlet cord in this window. Bring your whole family into your house. And as long as none of you go outside, you will not be harmed."

"I will do it!" she said.

The minute they had gone she found a piece of scarlet cord and tied it up at the window, taking no chance of not being ready.

The spies reached the mountains and hid for three days, until the king's men had given up and gone back to the city.

Then the two spies made their way back to Joshua, and gave their report. "God has given the city into our hands! All the people are terrified of us!"

Gratefully, Joshua asked God just how the city might be captured.

# Jericho Falls

Every gate into the city of Jericho was tightly closed and bolted. The people who lived in the city were terrified. They knew the Israelites were about to attack.

But Joshua was not at all sure how to go about it. The Israelites were not trained fighting men, as were the men of Jericho. And the walls of Jericho were very thick and well fortified...

Then God spoke to Joshua. "I will deliver Jericho, its king and all its fighting men into your hands. This is what you must do."

And God gave Joshua exact instructions.

Joshua listened with growing amazement. This was indeed a new way to attack a city! But he trusted God; so he gave the orders to the people, and whatever they thought, the people obeyed.

Every day for six days they marched round the city of Jericho. The armed guard went first. Then came the Ark of the Covenant, carried by the priests. Seven more priests, blowing trumpets of rams' horns, walked in front of the Ark. Then came the rest of the people.

"You must be silent, not giving

your war-cry until I tell you," Joshua warned the people. So the only sounds were the rams' horns and the tramp, tramp, tramp of marching feet, echoing eerily over the city of Jericho.

On the seventh day the Israelites got up at dawn and started their march around Jericho. But on this day they marched round seven times. The seventh time, as the Israelites completely encircled the city, the priests blew loudly on the trumpets, and Joshua cried, "Shout! The Lord God has given you the city!"

Then the people yelled their war-cry, and the walls of Jericho fell down!

The hordes of Israelites swarmed into the city, destroying everyone and everything in it, except the silver and gold and other valuables, which Joshua had ordered must be put into the treasury of the house of God; and the things which belonged to the gods of the people of Jericho.

And Joshua said to the two spies, "Quickly! Go to the house of Rahab and her family. Bring them safely out of the city. They can stay with us, in our camp."

So Rahab's family were saved, as the men had promised; but the rest of Jericho was burned to the ground.

And the Israelites knew that God was with Joshua, as He had been with Moses.

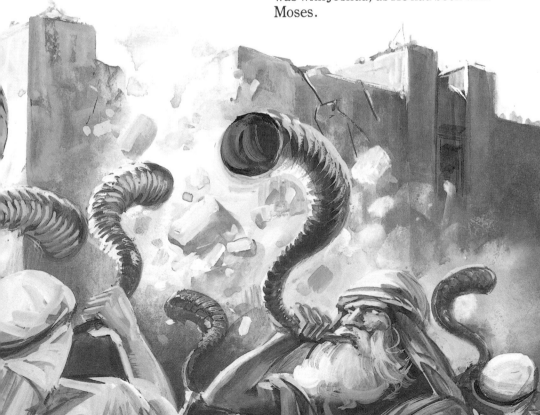

# Joshua Conquers Canaan

Jericho had fallen, but the rest of the land of Canaan wasn't conquered yet. Joshua had to decide on the next step in his campaign. He knew that the hard years in the wilderness had made the Israelites stronger. He could see that – with no memories of the easier life in Egypt – these people had the spirit of adventure which God needed in people who were to work with Him. Joshua was sure the Israelites were ready to fight.

But he did *not* know that one man – Achan – had disobeyed orders. In the earth under his tent, Achan had buried a bar of gold, some silver, and a beautiful cloak, which he had stolen from the treasures of Jericho.

Joshua sent men to spy out the city of Ai. "Easy!" they cried, when they came back. "You'll only need two or three thousand men. There are hardly any people in Ai."

So Joshua sent three thousand men – and they were defeated so soundly they *ran* from the city, with the men of Ai chasing after them.

Joshua could hardly believe it. He threw himself down on the ground in front of the Ark of the Covenant.

"Lord God, why did You bring us to this side of the River Jordan? Everyone will hear about this defeat. They will band together and attack us. We shall all be destroyed. Then who will be left to honour Your name?"

God answered. "What are you doing, flat on your face? Stand up! One of the Israelites has stolen. The people have lied. The covenant between us is broken! That is why your men were defeated! I was not with you. And I shall not be with you until the man who has stolen is punished, and the treasures are returned."

Then God told Joshua how to discover the guilty man.

Joshua called the Israelites together. Grimly he told them what had happened, and why they had been defeated. Achan listened, quivering with fear. Joshua went on speaking. The people were to prepare themselves; for tomorrow God would speak, and the man who had stolen would be found out.

All night, Achan worried. In the morning Joshua called for the twelve tribes of Israel to come forward, one by one. With God's help, he picked out the tribe of Judah. Achan was one of the tribe of Judah...

From the tribe of Judah, Joshua picked out the clan of the Zerahites. Achan belonged to that clan. He watched Joshua coming closer and closer...

From the clan of the Zerahites Joshua picked out the family of Zimri.

Achan was part of that family.

By now, Achan was helpless with fear. Sternly, Joshua started to question each man in Zimri's family. God had guided Joshua to the right man. Achan was discovered.

"Tell the truth before God!" Joshua ordered.

Achan confessed. His secret hoard was dug up, and he was put to death.

Joshua was upset. But God said to him, "Don't be afraid or discouraged. Attack Ai once more. This time I will be with you; and you will triumph."

So Joshua planned carefully, and gave orders to his army. Most of them were to hide near Ai, while he took a small group of men with him to make an attack.

As Joshua attacked, all the men of Ai came rushing out, expecting to chase the Israelites away as they had done before. But even as Joshua's group turned and ran, the rest of his army were entering the city, which had been left defenceless.

When the men of Ai stopped to glance back, they saw smoke rising from the city. They realized they had been tricked, and that Joshua's army was burning down the city. They turned and raced back to the rescue, but it was no use; Joshua's group now turned and chased *them*. They were caught between the two parts of Joshua's army, and they were defeated. Joshua's plan had worked perfectly.

Joshua built an altar to God, and offered a sacrifice of thanksgiving. Then he read the laws of Moses to the Israelites. The covenant was re-made, and God was with them again.

Joshua had many more adventures, but in the end he overcame the whole of the land of Canaan.

He divided the land amongst the twelve tribes of Israel, as God ordered, and for a while there was a rest from war.

The Israelites behaved as usual. Sometimes they remembered God, and things went well for them. But sometimes they forgot God, and disaster followed...

# God Chooses Gideon

would this have to go on? Where *was* God?

Suddenly a voice spoke to him. "God is with you, mighty warrior."

Mighty warrior? *Him*! Gideon jumped, and turned to look. A man was sitting watching him. Was the man making fun of him – calling him a mighty warrior when he was hiding in fear? And as for saying *God* was with him...

Gideon spoke angrily. "God has deserted us! He has simply handed us over to the Midianites!"

The man replied, "Go and save Israel. I am sending you."

Gideon was an Israelite, young and strong. Yet as he threshed the wheat belonging to his family he was hiding in a winepress. He was afraid that if he threshed in the open, the wheat would be stolen by the Midianites.

Joshua had died years before. Now many of the Israelites worshipped false gods, and God had allowed the fierce tribe of the Midianites to overcome Israel.

But as Gideon threshed, he was angry. The Israelites were almost starving. Didn't God *care*? How long

Then Gideon realized this was no ordinary man. It was an angel, with a message from the Lord God. And what a message! Save Israel?

"Me?" cried Gideon. "How can I save Israel? My clan is the weakest in all the tribe. And I'm the least important member of my family!"

God spoke through the angel. "*I will be with you. You will be able to defeat the Midianites as if they were just one man.*"

Gideon tried to think straight. "If what you say is true, please give me a sign! Will you wait here a minute?" he begged.

"I will wait," promised the angel.

Gideon rushed away, and came back with an offering of meat and bread.

"Put them on that rock," instructed the angel.

Trembling, wondering what would happen, Gideon obeyed.

The angel stretched out the rod he was carrying and touched the food with its tip. Instantly, flames of fire sprang up. The food was burnt to nothing, and the angel disappeared.

Gideon was terrified. "I have seen the face of the Angel of the Lord!" he cried. And he expected to die at once.

God answered him. "Don't be afraid! You're not going to die!"

That night God told Gideon how to start the work of saving Israel. He was to destroy the false altar which Gideon's father had set up in the market-place. Then he was to build a new altar.

Gideon swallowed hard. His father would be very angry. And not only his father. The townspeople would be furious. They might even kill Gideon. Yet Gideon wanted to obey God...

He thought about it. He didn't dare destroy the altar in daylight. But it might be managed under cover of darkness...

It was not yet light. Gideon called ten of his servants. They crept down to the market-place. As quietly as they could they pulled down the false altar to Baal. In its place they built an altar to the Lord God, and Gideon made a sacrifice on it as God had commanded. Then they crept home.

When the townspeople woke in the morning they saw what had happened. They were *furious*. "Who did it?" they yelled. And they wouldn't give up their investigations until they discovered it was Gideon, son of Joash.

The townspeople turned on Joash. "Bring out your son! We shall kill him!"

Gideon quivered with fear. Would his father hand him over?

But Joash loved his son dearly. "What?" he cried, thinking fast. "Are you trying to save a god? If Baal really is a god, surely he can defend himself? Let *him* come down and kill my son!"

The angry mob listened. If they acted *themselves*, it would seem as if they thought Baal could do nothing.

"All right," they muttered, "we'll leave it to Baal to punish him."

They waited to see what would happen.

Gideon was relieved. He knew Baal had no power at all. And sure enough, he remained completely unharmed. The story soon spread.

When men from all the tribes of Israel heard that Gideon had been chosen by God to be the new leader, they came together to follow him. The sight of so many men ready to trust him almost overwhelmed Gideon. He begged God to send him another sign. God gave him two special signs. Then Gideon knew that the task of leader really had been given to *him* and that God would be with him.

He began to think of a plan of attack. How could the Midianites be defeated?

# Gideon and the Midianites

Gideon had decided on a battle plan. He and his thirty-two thousand men were camped around the well at Harod. The place had been wisely chosen, for the spring which rose there flowed down the hill in a stream, providing plenty of water for an army.

God spoke to Gideon. "You have too many men. If I let you overcome the Midianites with this huge army, the Israelites will say they did it by themselves, without needing my help. Tell anyone who is afraid that they can go home."

Gideon could hardly believe what he heard. This would indeed be a strange way to speak to an army! But he obeyed. The men listened in silence. There was a pause, while they looked at each other out of the corners of their eyes. Was anyone going to admit to being afraid?

Suddenly, one man began to move away, then another, and another, until huge crowds of men were hastening back towards home. Gideon watched in amazement. Twenty-two thousand men left...

Now Gideon understood more of God's meaning. It would have been impossible to control such an enormous number of frightened men in battle. They would have been more of a hindrance than a help. Any victory would have been due to God, but no one would have believed it.

Gideon looked at the ten thousand men that remained. Ten thousand men of courage would be enough...

But God said, "There are still too many."

Still too many? Gideon felt anxious.

"Take the men down to the water to drink," said God. "I will show you which ones to choose."

Puzzled, Gideon ordered his men to go down to the stream. As they reached the water's edge Gideon watched them closely. Most of the men knelt, heads down, to lap the water with their tongues. Only three hundred knelt upright, scooping up the water in one hand.

"Those are the men to choose," said God. Then Gideon realized why. These men were alert, on guard even while they drank. The others had forgotten the enemy in their thirst.

But only three hundred? Against the whole army of the Midianites?

"With these three hundred, I will give the Midianites into your hands," God promised.

So Gideon told the other men to go back to their tents. But he was very frightened.

God understood. That night He said to Gideon, "Take your servant, Purah, and go under cover of darkness to the Midianite camp. Listen to what they are saying. You will gain courage."

It was a relief to be up and about, rather than tossing and turning, trying to sleep. Gideon called to Purah, and together they made their way over the hills to the enemy camp.

At first sight of it in the starlight, Gideon was astounded. The valley was thick with tents. Even the camels were too many to be counted. This army was to be defeated by three hundred men?

Grimly, Gideon crept down to the edge of the camp; and exactly as he sneaked up to listen outside a tent, one of the Midianites inside was telling a dream to a friend.

"I dreamed a loaf of barley bread fell on the camp; and it hit this tent so hard the tent collapsed."

The other Midianite spoke in fear. "The loaf of barley bread stands for the army of Gideon, son of Joash. Their God fights for them! We shall all be destroyed!"

Gideon felt a surge of joy. The Midianites were in no mood to win a battle! He praised God. Then, swiftly, he and Purah returned to their own camp.

"Get up!" Gideon shouted to his three hundred men. "We are attacking at once! God will give us the victory!"

He divided the men into three groups. To each man he gave a trumpet, and an empty jar with a torch inside it. The men looked at Gideon in amazement. Could he be serious? What kind of battle was this to be?

"Follow my lead!" Gideon ordered. "We will surround the camp in the darkness. When I and my group blow our trumpets, you must blow yours, and shout, 'For God and for Gideon!'"

Tense with excitement, the small band of men crept down towards the Midianites. Splitting into three

107

groups, they took up their positions surrounding the camp.

On the signal from Gideon, they all blew their trumpets and smashed the empty jars. Holding up the torches in their left hands, they yelled their battle cry: "For God and for Gideon!"

The shouting, the trumpets, the sound of the jars being smashed and the lights of the torches startled the Midianites awake. In the darkness, noise and confusion of the tents, each man believed the other was one of the Israelites whose attack they had been dreading. The Midianites began to kill each other. Gideon's astonished army stood firm as escaping Midianites rushed away from the camp in all directions.

When light dawned there were only a small number of men left to fight. Gideon's army was victorious, as God had promised.

The Israelites were delighted, and wanted Gideon to rule over them.

Gideon refused. "No. The Lord God will rule over you."

And as long as Gideon was alive there was peace in the land. The Israelites worshipped the true God.

But Gideon died. There were more wars, more leaders. The Israelites had many enemies. Among their enemies were the Philistines. Because the Israelites were again doing wrong, God allowed the Philistines to overcome them.

For forty years the Israelites suffered under the Philistines. But God was about to choose the man who would begin to free them.

# Samson and Delilah

Samson was a man chosen by God to be the person who would begin to free Israel from the Philistines.

Samson was immensely strong, and had a furious temper. He was always in trouble, either with his own people or with his enemies, the Philistines. For years the Philistines plotted to capture him, but so far, using the strength given to him by God, Samson had always escaped.

At last, the Philistines realized the only way they would ever catch him would be by trickery. So they watched, and waited; and one day they learnt that Samson had fallen in love with a lady named Delilah.

"Now's our chance!" said the Philistines. They promised Delilah large sums of money if she could discover what made Samson so strong.

Delilah was no true friend of Samson, or of the Israelites; and she was greedy for the money. So she asked Samson about his secret.

"How could anyone possibly tie *you* up?" she asked, pretending to be playing. For a while Samson teased her with wrong answers. Each time, Delilah told the Philistines what he'd said; and each time, the Philistines had men hiding in the room, ready to spring out and capture Samson as soon as Delilah had tied him up. But each time Samson broke the bonds easily, before the men had shown themselves.

But Delilah kept on asking, and in the end, Samson told her. "My strength lies in my hair, which has never been cut. If my head was shaved, my strength would leave me."

Quickly, Delilah sent yet another message to the Philistines. Secretly they came, bringing her promised reward with them. Then, while the Philistines hid nearby, Delilah coaxed Samson to sleep with his head in her lap. And while he slept, a man cut off all Samson's hair.

Then Delilah cried, "Samson, wake! The Philistines are upon you!"

Samson jumped to his feet, thinking his strength would save him yet again. But his strength was gone. Then Samson realized that his head had been shaved.

The Philistines blinded him, put him in chains, and took him to the prison. There they set him to heavy work at the grinding mill. Dejected, humbled, Samson struggled with the task.

But while he was in prison, his hair started to grow again...

Some time later, the Philistines held a celebration. It was partly in honour of their god Dagon, and partly because they had captured Samson at last. In the middle of the feast, they called for Samson to be brought, so that they could taunt him.

In shuffled the once proud Samson, totally blind, a boy leading him by the hand. Amid the jeers of the crowd, Samson was forced to perform. But he managed to whisper to the boy, "Put me near the pillars that hold up this building, so that I can lean on them."

The boy did so. Samson could tell that the temple building was crowded with the rulers of the Philistines and at least three thousand more men and women. Some were even on the roof. Samson prayed, "God, give me my strength just once more."

He reached towards the two main pillars which held up the temple. He put his right hand on one pillar, and his left hand on the other, and said, "Let me die with the Philistines!"

Then, with a mighty effort, he pushed the pillars apart – and down crashed the building, killing the rulers and everyone else.

And Samson died too, in the middle of his enemies.

# Naomi, Ruth and Boaz

At the time when the judges were ruling in Israel there was a famine in the land. A man called Elimelech, who had been born in Bethlehem, took his wife Naomi and his two sons, Mahlon and Kilion, to live in the country of Moab. And Elimelech died there, leaving Naomi a widow.

Her sons married two Moabite girls, Orpah and Ruth. But then Mahlon and Kilion also died.

The famine was over and Naomi wanted to return to her own people. So she and her daughters-in-law set out on the journey back to Bethlehem.

Before they had gone far, Naomi stopped. If she took Ruth and Orpah to Bethlehem, *they* would be far from their own people. Naomi knew how lonely *that* felt; so she said, "You must each go back to the home of your mother. You've been very good to me, and I hope you'll soon find new husbands in your own land."

The girls looked lovingly at Naomi. "No!" they cried. "We'll come with you."

But in those days a woman without a family to protect her would have a very hard life. Naomi spoke as firmly as she could through her tears. "I'm never going to have any more sons who would be your husbands! You *must* go back."

They were all crying now. Weeping bitterly, Orpah kissed Naomi goodbye, and started off towards home. But Ruth clung to her mother-in-law.

"Don't ask me to leave you!" she sobbed. "Nor to return from following after you! For wherever *you* go *I* will go. Where you live, I will live. Your people shall be my people, and your God, my God. Wherever you die I will die, and there shall I be buried. Nothing but death shall separate us."

Then Naomi kissed Ruth, and hugged her. And the two of them went on together.

At last they reached Bethlehem. The people who had known the family years before stared at them. "It is really you, Naomi?" they asked, hardly recognizing her.

"Don't call me Naomi," she answered. "Call me 'Mara' – 'bitter' – because my husband and sons are dead."

Ruth tried to comfort her mother-in-law. They both felt very lonely. But Naomi did have *some* relatives in Bethlehem. One of them was a man named Boaz, who owned some fields nearby.

It was the time of the barley harvest. Ruth said, "We must have food. Let me go out to the fields and pick up the grain which the harvesters leave behind on the ground. Then we will be able to make bread, and eat."

"Very well. Go," said Naomi.

So, with the other people who were too poor to get extra corn any other way, Ruth began to glean.

Unknowing, she chose to work in the field which belonged to Boaz. It was hard work. Gleaners had to bend low to see the grain, and it could take all day in the hot sun to fill even a small sack. By evening the gleaners' backs were aching painfully, and their eyes could hardly see.

When Ruth had been toiling for some hours, Boaz came by. He called a greeting to the harvesters. Then he noticed Ruth.

113

"Who is that girl?" he asked his foreman.

"Her name is Ruth," the man answered. "She came back from Moab with Naomi, your cousin. Early this morning she asked if she could glean here. She's hardly stopped to rest all day."

Boaz called to Ruth to come to him. Nervously she approached. Would he send her away?

No! "Don't go to any other fields. Stay in mine," said Boaz. "And if you are thirsty, drink from my water jars. I'll tell the men not to bother you."

Ruth was very grateful. "Why are you being so kind?" she asked. "I'm a foreigner here."

"I've heard how good you are to my cousin Naomi," Boaz answered. "May God bless you because of it. Come and share our meal with us."

Thankfully, Ruth obeyed. She had been feeling very hungry. But as soon as she had eaten enough, she went back to work.

Boaz watched her for a moment. Then he said to his men, "Let her take as much grain as she wants. Drop some for her to pick up."

Ruth gleaned all day. In the evening she threshed the wheat she had gathered into flour. She took the flour home to Naomi.

Naomi was amazed. "However did you get so much?" she asked. "Where did you glean?"

"In the field belonging to Boaz," Ruth replied.

"He is one of our close relatives," Naomi answered thoughtfully.

In those days, if a man died it was usual for his brother – or closest relative – to marry the widow, and take responsibility for her and for the dead man's land.

Boaz was not the brother of Mahlon or Kilion. He was not even Ruth's closest relative. But as the days went by he grew to love her. He wanted to marry her.

Before he could do that, he had to settle things with the man who *was* her closest relative.

Boaz worked out a plan. Then he went to speak to the man. "Do you want to buy the piece of land which belonged to Elimelech?" he asked. "It is your right as closest relative. If *you* don't want it, I'll buy it."

"I do want it," said the man.

Boaz had expected this. "If you buy the land, the law is that you must also marry Ruth so that the field stays in Elimelech's family," he said.

The man thought again. "Then I won't buy it," he said. "It would get in the way of the rights of my own children."

So, in front of witnesses, Boaz bought the land. Now he was not only free to marry Ruth – it was the law that he should.

Boaz and Ruth were married. They had a son called Obed. In time, Obed had a son called Jesse. And Jesse had a son called David. David was to become King of Israel, a great man.

But first, there were many more years while the judges ruled Israel. Years during which the boy Samuel was born...

# Samuel in the Temple

There were two Israelite women – Hannah and Penninah. They were both married to the same man – Elkanah. (It was the custom in those days for a man to have more than one wife.) Penninah had lots of children; but Hannah had none, and this distressed her very much.

Every year, Elkanah and his whole family went to the Temple at Shiloh. There they worshipped God, and made a sacrifice to Him. Elkanah always gave portions of the meat to Penninah and her children; but he always gave twice as large a portion to Hannah because he loved her very much, and knew how she felt about having no children.

Penninah knew, too. And every year she made things much worse for Hannah by teasing her cruelly, until Hannah got so upset she couldn't eat.

"What's wrong?" Elkanah asked tenderly. "Aren't I worth more to you than *ten* children?"

But still Hannah wept, and refused food. Later, when she went to the Temple, she prayed desperately to God.

"Lord God, if You will only let me have a baby son I promise I will give him back to You. He shall serve You all his life."

Eli the priest noticed her. When he heard her story, he spoke kindly. "Peace be to you. May the Lord God give you what you ask."

Hannah felt better. She even felt hungry enough to eat some food.

The family returned home to Ramah; and before too long Hannah did indeed have a baby boy. She was overjoyed. She named him Samuel, and loved him very much. But she hadn't forgotten her promise to God…

115

That year, when Elkanah and the family went to Shiloh, Hannah and the baby stayed at home.

"He's too young to leave me yet," she said, cradling Samuel in her arms.

"Do whatever you think is best," Elkanah answered gently.

Another year went by. Hannah watched her baby growing bigger. Able to walk. Able to run. Beginning to talk... Sometimes her heart ached. But she never faltered in her resolve. And next year, when the time for the sacrifice came round, Hannah and Samuel went to the Temple at Shiloh with the others.

Elkanah made the sacrifice. Then, with fast-beating heart, Hannah carried her tiny boy over to where Eli the priest stood. Elkanah was beside her, but it was Hannah who spoke.

"Do you remember me?" she asked Eli. "I'm the woman who prayed so hard for a child. This is the boy God gave to us. Now I give him back to God."

So Hannah left Samuel with Eli the priest, to grow up in the Temple; and she and Elkanah returned to Ramah.

At first they missed Samuel very much; but they saw him every year when they made their visit to Shiloh. Hannah always took new clothes for him; and Eli always blessed Hannah and Elkanah, and asked God to send them more children. Before too long, Hannah had three more boys, and two girls, so she was happy.

Eli was very glad to have Samuel. His own two sons were wicked, and no comfort to him.

As Samuel grew up, he listened as Eli taught him about God; and he helped more and more in the work of the Temple.

One night, the boy was lying on his bed in the Temple, near the Ark of the Covenant, when he heard a voice call his name.

"Samuel!"

Samuel had been almost asleep. Now he started awake. He sat up. Who had spoken? In the dim light of the lamp which was always kept burning he peered around.

There was no one to be seen. It must have been Eli calling him. Eli was old now, and almost blind. Maybe something was wrong... Samuel sprang up, and ran to Eli's bedside. "Here I am!" he panted. "You called me!"

Eli was puzzled. "I didn't call you," he said. "Go back to bed."

Perhaps he had been dreaming... Samuel went back and lay down.

"Samuel!"

The voice again! Samuel scrambled to his feet, and ran in to Eli. "Here I am! You *did* call me!" he cried.

"No," said Eli, still not properly awake. "I *didn't* call you! Go and lie down!"

Slowly, Samuel made his way back, and lay down. He was wide awake. He lay there in the near darkness. And the voice came again.

"Samuel!"

Samuel got up slowly. Slowly he went to Eli. Taking a deep breath, he said, "Here I am. You *did* call me."

Now Eli was fully awake too. And

he realized what was happening. God Himself was calling Samuel.

"Go and lie down," Eli said gently. "And if you hear the voice again, say, 'Speak, Lord. Your servant is listening.'"

Once more, Samuel lay down in the Temple near the Ark of the Covenant.

Tensely, half excited, half afraid, he waited. And God spoke.

"Samuel!"

Samuel found his voice. "Speak, Lord. Your servant is listening," he said.

Then God gave Samuel a message for Eli. It was such a sad message that as Samuel listened he wanted to cry. He didn't go rushing in to tell Eli. He lay still.

In the morning he got up and started work, trying to keep out of Eli's way. But Eli called him over. "Samuel, my son! What did God say to you?"

Then Eli saw the look on the boy's face. "Don't be afraid to tell me," he said gently.

So Samuel repeated the message. Eli's family were to be punished because of the wickedness of Eli's two sons.

"God knows best," Eli answered quietly. "Let Him do whatever seems right to Him."

As Samuel grew older, all the Israelites knew that God was with him, and they listened to his words.

But before long, the punishment of Eli's family – and the Israelites – was to begin.

117

# The Philistines and the Ark of the Covenant

The Israelites were again fighting with the Philistines; but this time, because of the wickedness of the Israelites, God allowed the Philistines to overcome them.

"Let us take the Ark of the Covenant into battle with us!" cried the leaders of the Israelites when their defeated army came straggling back. "The Ark will give us victory!"

So men went to Shiloh to get the Ark; and Eli's two sons were among the priests who came back with it.

When the weary Israelites saw the Ark of the Covenant being carried into their camp, they gave a great shout of gladness.

Over in their own camp, the Philistines heard it. "What's going on over there?" they asked, trembling. A defeated army did not usually shout in triumph...

The Philistines sent spies out. The spies came back, saying, "A god has come into the camp of the Israelites!"

Then the Philistines were even more afraid. They said, "We must fight harder, or the Israelites will make us their slaves."

So the Philistines attacked with all their might. Thousands of Israelites were killed, including Eli's sons. And the Ark of the Covenant was captured...

A messenger ran from the battlefield to Shiloh. His clothes were torn, and dust was on his head. As soon as the townspeople saw him, they guessed the battle was lost. When they heard the whole truth, there was a tremendous commotion.

Eli was quite blind now. He had been sitting anxiously in a chair by the side of the road, waiting for news of his sons. When he heard the noise, he asked, "What is it? What's happening?"

The messenger hurried over to the old man. "I've just come from the battlefield," he said.

"And?" Eli asked.

The messenger swallowed hard. "Israel was defeated. Your sons are dead. And the Ark of the Covenant has been captured."

When Eli realized what the man had said he was so upset that he fell over and died.

The triumphant Philistines had carried the Ark into the temple of their god Dagon, in Ashdod.

But when they came back in the morning, Dagon had fallen flat on his face in front of the Ark!

119

The Philistines stood him up again. But next morning, not only was Dagon lying flat on the ground – his head and his hands were broken off! And the people of Ashdod began to be ill. They begged their rulers to take the Ark away.

So the Ark was moved to Gath. The people of Gath became ill. They were terrified, and sent the Ark to Ekron. But the people of Ekron saw it being brought into the city.

"Don't bring it here!" they cried. "We shall all die! Send it back to the Israelites!"

The panic-stricken Philistines asked their priests how they should return the Ark.

"You must send it with an offering to show you are sorry," the priests replied. So the Philistines placed the Ark in a cart, with special gifts of gold in a box beside it. They harnessed two oxen to the cart, and set it off along the road towards Beth Shemesh where the Israelites were.

The people of Beth Shemesh were harvesting in their fields. Suddenly, they saw a driverless cart coming down the road. And when they looked again, they realized the Ark of the Covenant was in the cart. As they watched, spellbound, the cart stopped beside the field of Joshua.

Then the Israelites ran to it. They lifted out the Ark, and the gold, with great rejoicing.

When the watching Philistines saw that the Ark was safely back, they returned to Ekron, breathing sighs of relief.

The Israelites made a sacrifice of thanksgiving to God. When Samuel heard the news, he said, "If you are *really* ready to serve the Lord God, destroy all your false gods."

The Israelites obeyed. Before long, the Philistine army again attacked. But now God was on the side of the Israelites. The Philistines were soundly defeated, and for many years there was peace.

Then the Israelites grew restless...

# The Israelites Demand a King

Samuel was growing old; too old to go on ruling over the Israelites. So he appointed his two sons in his place. But his sons were unjust, and took bribes.

The people complained. "We want a king to rule over us!" they declared.

Samuel was distressed. He prayed to God about it.

"Tell them," said God, "if they *do* have a king he will treat them harshly. They will cry to Me for help, and I will not listen to their cries."

Samuel gave God's message to the people, but they paid no attention. "We want a king!" they repeated stubbornly. "Besides, if we have a king we shall be like all the other nations."

Samuel told God what the people said.

"Very well!" said God. "We shall *give* them a king!"

# Saul

Saul, an Israelite of the tribe of Benjamin, was tall, young and handsome. His father was named Kish. At the time the Israelites were demanding a king, Kish said to Saul, "Our donkeys have strayed away. Take one of the servants and go and look for them."

Saul obeyed. He and the servant walked miles searching for the animals, without success. After three days, Saul said wearily, "Let's go back, or my father will be more worried about us than he is about the donkeys!"

"Wait!" said the servant. "I've heard of a holy man who lives in a town near here. Let's see if he can advise us which way to go."

"All right," said Saul. So they set off to find the holy man – and the holy man was Samuel.

Only the day before, God had said to Samuel, "The man whom you must anoint as King of Israel will come to you tomorrow. He will be from the tribe of Benjamin."

Now Samuel stood in the gateway of the town. And as soon as Samuel caught sight of Saul coming towards him, God said, "This is the man."

Samuel wondered how best to give Saul this extraordinary news.

Quite unsuspecting, Saul came straight up to Samuel. "Will you tell me how to get to the house of the holy man?" he asked.

Samuel answered quietly, "I am the man you are looking for. Come and have a meal with me – and don't worry any more about the donkeys that were lost three days ago. They have been found."

And while Saul still gazed at him in astonishment, Samuel said, "*You* are the man the people of Israel have been wanting."

"What?" cried Saul. "But I come from the smallest tribe in Israel! And my family is of no importance even in *our* small tribe!"

"Come," smiled Samuel. Saul and his servant went with him. They shared a meal with about thirty people, and Samuel ordered that Saul be given a special portion of meat. Afterwards, Samuel took Saul up to the roof of his house. The day had been hot. Now they sat in the cool light of the stars and talked together.

When Saul grew sleepy, Samuel gave him a bed, up there on the roof.

Saul woke refreshed. Next day, he and his servant set out for home. Samuel went with them as far as the edge of town. There the servant was sent on in front.

Quietly and solemnly, Samuel anointed Saul's head with oil in the ceremony used by kings throughout the years. And Samuel told Saul other signs by which Saul could know he really *was* the man chosen by God to be King of Israel.

Saul set off along the road with his thoughts whirling in his head. But by the time he reached home, God had spoken to him. And his behaviour was so different, his family wondered what had happened to him. But Saul didn't tell them.

Then Samuel called the Israelites together. "You wanted a king," Samuel said. "Now God will show you who it is to be."

One by one, all the tribes of Israel came forward; but no one was chosen, until they came at last to the tribe of Benjamin. They reached the family of Kish. Saul was chosen – but he was nowhere to be found!

The people asked God, "Where is he?"

"He's hiding amongst your possessions," answered God.

Then the people ran and found him, and brought him out. As Saul stood in front of them, unsure whether to be proud or embarrassed, he was taller than anyone else there.

"See the man whom God has chosen!" cried Samuel. "There is no one like him!"

"Long live the king!" shouted the Israelites.

Then Samuel explained to everyone exactly what the powers of a king were, and what rules should be kept. And he wrote everything down, so that there might be no misunderstandings.

So Saul became king, and started to rule over the Israelites. And Samuel warned the people, "Remember what great things God has done for you! Love and serve God faithfully. For if you keep doing wrong, you *and* your king will be overcome."

# David, Jesse's Son

At first Saul ruled well, and kept God's laws. He had a son, Jonathan, whom he loved dearly.

But after some years, Saul grew proud. He began to do as *he* wanted, and then made excuses to Samuel.

"Your kingdom won't last," Samuel warned him sadly, "because you keep disobeying God."

And sure enough, God said to Samuel, "How much more time are you going to waste being sad about Saul? I no longer want him to be king. Go to Bethlehem, to the house of a man called Jesse. I've chosen one of his sons to be the next king. You must go and anoint the boy."

"If Saul discovers I've done that, he'll kill me!" cried Samuel. It was no more than the truth.

God said, "Go to Bethlehem, but take a calf with you. Tell the people you've come to make a sacrifice."

Samuel loved and trusted God. So he took the calf as God had commanded. When he reached Bethlehem the elders of the city came out to meet him, with fear on their faces.

"Why have you come?" they asked, trembling.

"I come in peace," Samuel reassured them. "I'm going to offer a sacrifice to God here."

Then he sent a message to Jesse, asking him to bring his sons to the sacrifice.

Jesse and seven of his sons hurried to wash themselves and put on clean clothes, as was the custom before making a sacrifice. Then they came to Samuel.

One at a time, Jesse ordered his sons to stand in front of the holy man. When Samuel saw Eliab, the eldest, he thought, *this* must be the one. For Eliab was very handsome.

"No," said God. "You are looking only at the outside of a person. *I* look at his heart. What a person believes – how he feels and acts – *that* is more important than the way he looks. I have not chosen Eliab."

The next son stood in front of

Samuel; and the next; until all seven had stood there. But still God made no sign.

Samuel was puzzled. Then he had a thought. "Have you any more sons?" he asked.

Jesse stared at Samuel in surprise. "Only David," he replied. "He's the youngest. He's out looking after the sheep."

"Send for him," Samuel ordered.

Presently David arrived, flushed and panting. He was handsome, with eyes full of courage.

"This is the one," God said to Samuel. "Anoint his head with oil."

Samuel obeyed. David's father and brothers watched in amazement. Did this mean David was to be a follower of Samuel?

Samuel did not explain. David went back to tending the sheep. But from that day, God's spirit was especially with him.

And soon, God's plan for David was going to start working out...

# David Meets Saul

Sickness had begun to torment King Saul's mind. Sometimes the sickness made him feel utterly sad and hopeless. At other times it made him angry and violent.

Saul's servants noticed that music could soothe him, and would often cure him for a while.

"Sir," they said, "why not appoint a musician to your court? Then he could play to you whenever the sickness comes upon you."

"Find me a musician!" Saul ordered. "But he must play *well*!"

The servants began to search for such a person. Then one of them cried, "Sir, I know of a musician! He sings his own songs and plays the harp. *He* plays well! He is a brave young man who would make a very good warrior for your army! And the spirit of God is with him! He is one of the sons of Jesse of Bethlehem."

"Send for him!" commanded Saul.

Messengers rushed to Bethlehem. "King Saul wants to see your son David!" they told Jesse. Jesse was puzzled. His youngest son *again.*

Once more, David was called in from tending the sheep. Hurriedly, he was told the news. Almost before he could take it in, David found himself being hustled into clean clothes for the journey, while Jesse rushed about to find what gifts David could take for the king.

Soon David set off with the messengers and the gifts – a donkey loaded with bread, a skinful of wine, and a young goat.

"Where's your harp? Don't forget that!" cried a messenger.

"It is here!" smiled David. He always had his harp with him.

When they all arrived at court, David was taken to the king. Saul liked the look of him at once. "You shall be one of my armour bearers," Saul announced. And he sent a messenger to Jesse asking that David be allowed to stay for a while.

After that, David lived partly with Saul's men, and partly at home, caring for the sheep.

But whenever the sickness came upon Saul, David was sent for. Quickly he came; and he played his harp until the beautiful sounds calmed Saul's tormented mind.

But trouble was coming for the Israelites…

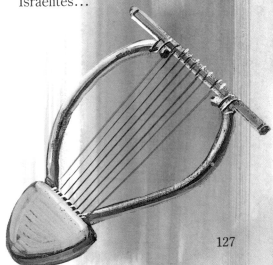

127

# David and Goliath

The army of the Philistines had marched into the land of the Israelites, intending to occupy it. King Saul gathered his army to repel the Philistines, and now the two armies were camped on either side of a valley. Neither army wished to start the battle, because whoever attacked the other would be at a disadvantage, having to fight uphill, an easy target for the spears and arrows which the enemy would hurl down.

It seemed as if the armies would be there for ever...

Then one day, out from the Philistine camp strode a huge man, over three metres tall, called Goliath. He was protected by heavy armour and he carried a huge spear. He bellowed a challenge across to King Saul's army.

"If any man can defeat me single-handed, we will be your slaves. But if I defeat *him*, *you* shall be *our* slaves!"

His voice echoed around the mountains; and far from taking up his challenge, King Saul's men turned and ran for their tents.

King Saul offered a reward of immense riches, and marriage to a princess, to the man who would fight Goliath. But no one volunteered. Every day, Goliath hurled his challenge across the valley; every day Saul's men cowered in a silence of fear and anger.

In Saul's army were three of David's older brothers. David was at home at that time, looking after the sheep. But his father Jesse called to him. "I want you to go and see how your brothers are getting on and bring me word from them. Take them this food and these presents."

Gladly David set out. It was an eleven kilometre walk, but he kept going until at last he could see the tents of King Saul's army.

Just as he reached the camp, the army was ordered to battle positions. Eagerly, David left the gifts with the keeper of supplies, and ran to find his brothers.

Before he could do more than greet them, Goliath strode out from the Philistine army, and yelled his challenge.

David waited, expecting someone to spring forward to reply. Instead, the Israelites turned and ran.

David couldn't believe his ears and eyes. "Who *is* this man who challenges the army of God's people?" he cried. "If no one else will fight him, *I* will!"

"You!" cried his brothers. "We know how you love to show off! You only came to watch the battle! Go home and look after the sheep!"

David flushed angrily; but he had learnt self-control. He answered quietly, "Can't I even speak?"

He talked to more of the soldiers, and some of them went to tell the king what David was saying.

Saul sent for David.

David stood in front of the king. His heart beat fast, but he spoke steadily.

"No one need be afraid of Goliath. *I* will fight him."

"You!" cried Saul. "You're only a boy! He's a trained fighting man!"

"I am a *shepherd* boy," David answered. "When a bear came to carry off a lamb, I killed it. Another time I had to kill a lion. God saved me from the lion and the bear; and God will save me from this Philistine."

So King Saul said, "Very well. Go, and the Lord be with thee." And the king put his own armour on David, and gave him a sword.

Clank, clank! David tried to walk. He could hardly move – the armour was so heavy. And he'd never been trained to fight with a sword. He struggled out of the armour, and put on his own shepherd's tunic. Then he took his rod, and his shepherd's sling – the sling from which he'd often twirled stones to drive wild animals away from the sheep. Then he went out to face Goliath.

A silence fell over the whole valley. David's brothers watched, hardly daring to breathe.

Calmly, David walked down to the little stream which flowed through the valley. Bending down, he carefully picked out five smooth, round stones from the water's edge.

Then he stood up and spoke clearly. "I am ready."

Goliath strode forward. Then he saw David. "You! A boy! You dare to challenge *me*! And am I a dog, that you come to fight me with a stick? I'll cut you into pieces and give you to the birds and beasts to eat!"

David replied steadily, "I come in the name of God. He is with me. I will kill you, Goliath! And everyone will know that the God of the Israelites is the one true God!"

Furious, Goliath rushed forward. But David placed one of the stones in his sling, and whirled the sling around.

Straight as an arrow flew the stone, striking Goliath's forehead with full force. Down fell the giant, flat on the ground. David ran forward, took Goliath's own sword, and cut off the giant's head.

When the Philistines saw their champion was dead, they turned and ran. With a great shout, King Saul's army pursued them. The Philistines were chased out of the country, and defeated thoroughly.

And after that day, King Saul took David to live in the palace all the time.

And for a while, David was happy there. But more trouble was coming.

# David and Saul

David's life had changed completely. He was treated as if he were King Saul's own son. And Saul's son Jonathan – far from being jealous – became David's greatest friend.

Whatever Saul asked David to do, David did well. Whenever he led his men in battle against the Philistines, the Israelites won. At first, Saul was pleased. But soon he noticed how popular David was becoming. The Israelite women sang a song: "Saul has killed thousands in his fights; but David has killed tens of thousands!"

When Saul heard those words, he was furiously jealous. "I suppose soon he'll be wanting my kingdom!" he fumed.

Next day, the sickness came upon him. As always, David was sent for.

He began to play his harp, hoping to soothe Saul. Saul sat watching him, and dark, angry thoughts grew in Saul's mind.

He remembered how everyone had praised David far more than they had praised him. Perhaps David really *might* be the man God had chosen to be king in Saul's place... The thought was too much. Without warning, Saul sprang up and hurled a spear at David, meaning to pin him to the wall.

David was taken completely by surprise; but even so, he was too quick for Saul. He leapt to one side. Twice Saul hurled a spear. Twice

David escaped by leaping aside. Then panting, watchful, David stood, ready to dodge yet again.

But Saul realized he could never harm David that way. He would need a plan. He ordered David to leave him; and David obeyed.

Saul made David captain over more than a thousand soldiers, thinking that when David led the soldiers into battle he would be killed. But David was *not* killed. He fought bravely, and won many honours; and God was with him. David behaved so wisely and well that the people loved and praised him more than ever.

So Saul pretended to be friendly towards David; but inwardly his hatred and fury grew. Then his daughter Michal fell in love with David.

"I can use this as a trap!" schemed Saul.

He sent his servants with a message to David.

"The king is pleased that his daughter loves you," said the servants. "You can marry her, and become his son-in-law."

"What?" cried David. "I'm only poor! I can't marry a princess!"

Secretly delighted to hear that David had answered exactly as he had expected, Saul sent another message.

"The king says you may marry the princess, if you will pay the price."

"What price?" asked David, puzzled. Saul *knew* he had no riches of his own.

"The price is the lives of one hundred Philistines," said the servant. "You must kill them yourself, in the next battle."

"I accept," said David.

Saul was overjoyed. Surely David would be killed *now*! Surely *no* man could kill one hundred others, single-handed, in one battle, with little or no time to rest...

But David *did* kill the hundred Philistines.

Inwardly raging, Saul was forced to honour his promise, and David and Michal were married.

Saul made plan after plan to trap David, but each time David escaped unharmed – once with the help of his wife Michal.

Saul could hide his anger no longer. He went to Jonathan. "Catch David and kill him!" he ordered.

But Jonathan was David's friend, and would never harm him. Getting away unseen, Jonathan hurried to warn David.

"My father wants to kill you! Tonight you must go into hiding. I'll speak to my father about you, and come and tell you what he says."

So David hid.

Next morning, Jonathan went to Saul and asked, "Why do you want to harm David? He has served you well and faithfully."

Saul listened as Jonathan pleaded, and his anger melted away. Saul made a promise. "As surely as our God is alive, David will not be killed by me."

Gladly Jonathan ran to tell David and bring him back to Saul. For a short time the friends were happy, as they'd been before. But soon war broke out again. David fought as well and bravely as ever. Again the people shouted his praises. And Saul – far from being grateful to David – felt the old hatred return.

This time, Saul's anger was so terrible, all his servants ran away. Only David was unafraid. Remembering that his music had often been able to calm the king, David took his harp and began to play. But it was no use. Mad with rage, Saul seized a spear and once again tried to pin David to the wall. David leapt aside, and the spear went deep into the wall just beside him. David knew he must get away.

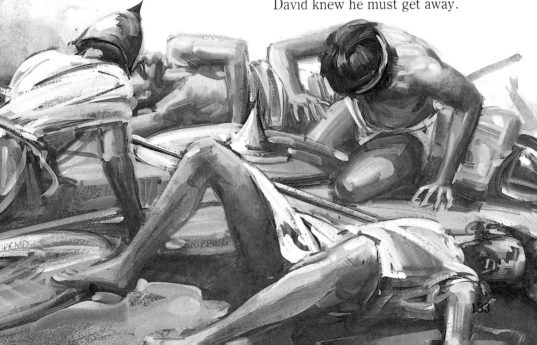

# David and Jonathan

Saul had David hunted from place to place. After many months, David grew tired and weary. He went to meet Jonathan.

"Why is your father trying to have me killed?" he asked.

"He's not!" cried Jonathan. "He *promised*! Besides, he never does anything without telling me! Why should he hide this? It isn't true!"

But David answered, "Your father knows we're friends. He doesn't want to upset you. But I tell you truly there's only one step between me and death."

David was so certain, Jonathan agreed to do whatever his friend thought best.

The next day was a special festival, when David was supposed to dine with the king. Instead, David would hide near a field where Jonathan often practised with his bow and arrows. Meanwhile, Jonathan would dine with Saul. If the king grew very angry because David was missing, Jonathan would know for certain that Saul *was* still plotting.

"Who will tell me what happens?" asked David, afraid to trust *anyone*.

"I will tell you myself," Jonathan replied. "We'll have a secret sign. I'll shoot the arrows to land near your hiding place. Then I'll send a boy to fetch them back for me. If I call out to him, 'Look! The arrows are this side of you!' then you'll know everything

is safe. But if I call out, 'Look! The arrows are over there! They've gone past you!' you must escape quickly!"

So it was arranged. Jonathan dined with the king, and on the second day, Saul asked where David was. As they spoke about him, Saul's face grew purple with rage, and he hurled a spear at *Jonathan*!

Jonathan knew that David was right. Sadly, he went to the field, taking a boy with him, and shot an arrow. When the boy went to fetch it, Jonathan called out, "Look! Hasn't the arrow gone past you? Hurry! Go quickly!"

And David understood the secret message.

Jonathan told the boy to take the arrows back to the town. Then David came out of hiding. He wouldn't leave without saying goodbye to his friend.

They were both very sad. They knew there was nothing but danger ahead, and they might never see each other again. David must go at once. Jonathan could only remind him that they would always be true friends.

For as long as Saul lived, the king made no peace with David; although twice David had Saul at his mercy and yet spared his life.

Finally, Saul fought his last battle with the Philistines. Jonathan and Saul's two other sons were killed in the battle, and Saul was badly wounded. In great distress, and rather than have the Philistines kill him also, Saul took his own sword, and fell on it. As he was dying, he asked an Amalekite to give him the final blow.

When David heard the news, he mourned bitterly for his friend Jonathan; and he was also sad about Saul. He wrote a song about it. "How are the mighty fallen! Tell it not in Gath, lest the daughters of the Philistines rejoice. Saul and Jonathan were lovely and pleasant in their lives, and in death they were not divided. They were swifter than eagles, they were stronger than lions! How are the mighty fallen in the midst of the battle! I am distressed for thee, my brother Jonathan; thy love to me was wonderful. How are the mighty fallen!"

In due time David was made King of Israel in Saul's place. One of his first tasks was to capture Jerusalem from the Jebusites. He made it the capital city of Israel, and called it 'The City of David'. He had the Ark of the Covenant brought there, and there was a great feast, with singing and dancing. David wanted to build a Temple so that the Ark might be kept in it. But God said, "No. Not David, but one of his sons shall build the Temple in Jerusalem."

All this time, David had not forgotten his friend Jonathan. "Are *none* of his family left alive?" he asked.

"Jonathan's son still lives," his servants answered. "He is called Mephibosheth, and he is a cripple. He cannot walk properly."

David sent for Mephibosheth, and for Jonathan's sake gave back to him all the land which had belonged to Saul. And Mephibosheth lived at the palace with David, and was kindly treated.

After more exciting years, David had grown old, and knew he was about to die. He sent for his son Solomon. His voice was weak.

"I am going the way of all things on earth," he said. "You must be strong. Do as the Lord God says. Walk in His ways. Lead the people of Israel to do right in His eyes. Then the Lord God will keep His promises to Israel. Be wise, my son, and show yourself to be a man."

David gave a few more instructions to Solomon. Then, wearily, he lay back on his pillows and fell asleep. And in his sleep, he died.

Solomon became king.

During David's long life he had written many songs. Some of David's songs, called psalms, are still sung today. They are written in the Book of Psalms, in the Bible.

# A Psalm of David

The Lord is my shepherd, I shall not want.
He maketh me to lie down in green pastures;
  He leadeth me beside the still waters.
He restoreth my soul; He leadeth me in the paths of
  righteousness for His name's sake.
Yea, though I walk through the valley of the shadow
  of death, I will fear no evil; for Thou art with me;
  Thy rod and Thy staff they comfort me.
Thou preparest a table before me in the presence of
  mine enemies; Thou anointest my head with oil;
  my cup runneth over.
Surely goodness and mercy shall follow me all the
  days of my life; and I will dwell in the house of
  the Lord for ever.

# Solomon's Wisdom

Solomon found himself ruler over thousands of people. He felt he could never cope with it. People kept bringing problems to him which he was expected to solve. And his father David was not there to advise him...

Solomon tried to follow his father's instructions, and keep God's laws; although his people still made sacrifices in various high places because there was no Temple built yet.

One day, Solomon himself went to Gibeon to offer a sacrifice. That night, as he lay sleeping, God came to him in a dream. "Solomon," said God, "what gift would you like to have from Me?"

"Oh," cried Solomon, "give me wisdom! I am so young! I don't know how to give the right answers when people bring me their problems! I don't even know how to rule Your people wisely!"

God was pleased. "You haven't asked to be rich, or to have a long life. You haven't even asked that I give you victory over your enemies! Because you have asked for wisdom I will give it to you. You shall be wiser than anyone ever was; no one shall ever be as wise as you again. And I will give you the honour and wealth which you did not ask for. And if you keep My laws, I will give you a long life as well."

Solomon stirred in his sleep, woke up, and opened his eyes. Had it just been a dream?

In the morning he went back to Jerusalem to offer a sacrifice in front of the Ark of the Covenant. Then he held a great feast for all the members of his court.

Two women asked for an audience with him. One of them carried a baby in her arms.

"My Lord Solomon!" cried the other, in great distress. "This woman and I live in the same house. I had a baby. Three days later, *she* had a baby. During the night, her baby died because she lay on him. There was no one else in the house and I was asleep. She took my baby and put her dead baby beside me. When I woke up, I went to feed my son – and saw that he was dead. I cried and cried. But when the morning light came, and I looked at him, I could see it wasn't my baby at all. *She* had him!"

"No!" cried the other woman, hugging the baby to her. "She's lying! *Her* baby died! This one is mine!"

Bitterly they argued in front of Solomon. Here was a problem!

"One of you is lying," said Solomon. "The baby cannot belong to both of you. Tell me the truth!"

"I am telling you the truth!" cried both women.

Solomon searched desperately in his mind for an answer to the problem. And a thought came to him…

"Bring a sword!" he ordered. There was a puzzled silence in the court. Everyone watched as a soldier came forward with a sword.

"Now," said Solomon. "It shall be cut in half. You can have half each."

"No!" screamed the first woman. "That would kill the baby!"

But the other woman nodded. "It is fair. Neither of us should have him. Divide him in two!" And she laid the baby at Solomon's feet. The soldier lifted the sword...

Sobbing, the first woman pleaded desperately. "No! No! Give the baby to her! Don't kill him!"

The soldier looked at Solomon.

Solomon spoke. "Give the baby to the first woman. She is his real mother. Only his real mother would give the baby away rather than see him hurt."

Still sobbing, the woman took her baby and held him close. And all the people marvelled at Solomon's wisdom.

Then Solomon knew that God's promise had not been just a dream. It was true.

Solomon continued to give wise judgements. By the time he had been king for four years he had become as rich and powerful as God had said. People of all nations came to listen to him, and ask for help with their own problems. And each one brought gifts.

Solomon wanted to show his love for God. It was time to start building the Temple, where God could be worshipped, and where the Ark of the Covenant could be kept in safety and with honour.

140

# Building the Temple

The work of building the Temple was started. Solomon wanted only the finest craftsmen to work on it, and only the best materials to be used. To get them, he sent messengers to all parts of Israel and beyond.

Materials began to arrive. Sweet-smelling cedar wood from Lebanon was used for the walls and ceilings. Pine trees were sawn into planks for the floors. All the stone used was hewn and shaped in the quarries, so that no sound of iron tools should disturb the peace of the Temple Courts, even while they were being built.

The Temple was about thirty metres long, ten metres wide, and fifteen metres high. It had three levels. It had an inner room, called the Holy of Holies, or Most Holy

Place. In the inner room was the altar.

Two cherubim were carved from wild olive wood, and overlaid with gold. They were placed so that their wings would be outstretched over the Ark. All the walls were beautifully carved, and in the inner room they were overlaid with gold. The altar was made from cedar wood overlaid with gold. By the time the Temple was finished, all the inside surfaces were overlaid with pure gold.

Solomon sent to Tyre for a man called Hiram. Hiram was especially skilled at working in bronze. Solomon gave him instructions, and Hiram built two huge columns of bronze to stand at the entrance to the Temple. Each one was about eight metres high, and beautifully carved. The columns were given names. The one on the south side was called Jakin – which probably means 'He (God)

establishes', and the one on the north side was called Boaz – which probably means 'In Him (God) is strength'.

For seven years the work of building the Temple went on. At last it was finished. The Temple had been built to the glory of God; and it was very beautiful.

Solomon brought all the treasures which had belonged to King David and placed them in the Temple. Then, offering a sacrifice, the priests lifted up the Ark of the Covenant on its two poles and carried it to the place prepared for it in the Holy of Holies.

And all the people rejoiced and were glad.

But Solomon's reign was not over yet.

*1 Kings 9 : 26, 27; 10*

# The Queen of Sheba

Solomon had a large navy, with ships which sailed to many ports; and so his fame spread. News of his wisdom reached the court of the Queen of Sheba. For a while she listened to the tales told of him. Then, "Rubbish!" she declared. "No man could be so wise!"

"Indeed, the stories are true!" her attendants persisted.

"I shall go and see for myself," announced the queen. And she did, travelling across the desert with a great number of servants, bringing with her many splendid gifts of gold, precious stones and silks.

143

Her arrival in Jerusalem was magnificent. Solomon, dressed in his most beautiful robes, sat on the throne in his palace awaiting her. In she swept, wearing silks and damask, splendid with pearls and rubies. A long line of slaves carrying the gifts came behind her.

The two rulers greeted each other. Then the queen began to test Solomon, asking him many questions, trying to catch him out.

But Solomon answered every one of the questions wisely. There was nothing he did not know.

Presently he led the way to his banquet hall, where a great feast had been prepared. The herbs in the food were as rare as any the Queen of Sheba had ever tasted; and perfumes as rich as those of her own court scented the air.

Then Solomon took her to the entrance to the Temple. She looked at its magnificence and cried, "Enough! I was wrong! Everything I heard about you is true. Blessed be the Lord your God who has shown you such favour! Surely God must love Israel very much, to give it a king such as you!"

She gave Solomon many gifts, and in exchange he gave her anything she asked for. It was a splendid and satisfying visit.

The Queen of Sheba and her attendants returned home. But Solomon's wealth continued to grow, as yet more people heard of the wisdom which God had given him, and came to ask him questions – each one bringing gifts. Solomon's army grew to twelve thousand horsemen and one thousand, four hundred chariots. In Jerusalem he made silver as plentiful as stones.

Through the gift of wisdom, God had made Solomon a very great king. But perhaps Solomon had become *too* great...

# Solomon's Reign Ends

Solomon became very proud. He stopped remembering God, and began to worship false gods.

God was very angry. "For as long as you live, I will keep My promise," God said to him. "Israel shall remain one nation. But when you die, the people shall divide into two nations. And the two tribes of the south shall be at war with the ten tribes of the north."

For forty years Solomon reigned over Israel, and it *did* remain one nation. Then Solomon died...

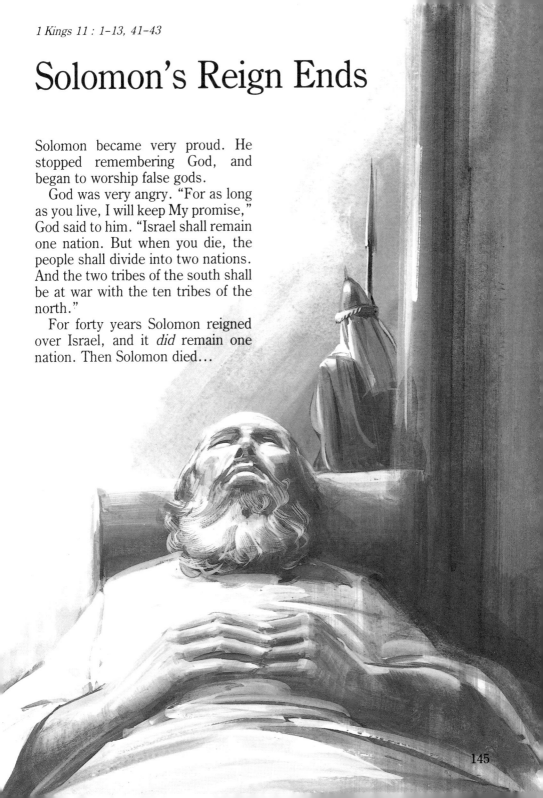

# Elijah, the Ravens and the Widow

Now Israel was divided into two kingdoms. Both were ruled by wicked kings. But Ahab, one of the kings of the ten tribes of the north, was the worst. Most of the people in Ahab's kingdom forgot about God, and began to worship Baal.

But one man, Elijah, remained faithful; and God gave him a message for Ahab.

Bravely, Elijah stood in front of the king. "I am the prophet of the *true* God," said Elijah. "And I tell you, unless I say so, there will be no rain nor dew in this country for the next few years." Then he rushed hastily from the palace before the furious Ahab could have him arrested.

"Go and hide in the Kerith Ravine, near the River Jordan," God commanded. "I will send the ravens to feed you there, and you will be able to drink from a brook."

It was not the time to stand and argue. Glancing warily from left to right, Elijah hurried to the hiding place. But *ravens*! How could *ravens* feed him? Was he to catch and kill them?

No. That evening, as Elijah sat hungrily by the brook, ravens came flying towards him. They were carrying bread and meat in their beaks! The birds dropped the food, and Elijah ate. Every evening and every morning, for as long as Elijah hid there, the ravens came with food.

But after a while, because there had been no rain, the brook dried up.

"Now what?" thought Elijah. "I shall die of thirst!"

But God had a further plan. "Go to Zarepah. I have ordered a widow there to feed you."

Elijah set off for Zarepah. Sure enough, as he reached the gates of the town he saw a widow there, gathering sticks for a fire. Thirsty and hungry, Elijah spoke. "Please will you bring me some water so that I may drink?"

The widow turned at once to fetch it. Elijah cried, "And please will you bring me a small piece of bread?"

She paused anxiously. "Truly, I have no bread! All I have left is one handful of flour and a little oil. I'm gathering these sticks so that I can cook the last meal for myself and my son. After that, we shall starve to death."

This was a strange reply from someone whom God had promised would be able to feed Elijah. Yet God could surely be trusted...

"Cook your meal," said Elijah, "but first make me a little cake. Afterwards make some for yourself and your son. For the Lord God of Israel promises that your barrel of meal shall not be empty, nor shall the jar of oil, until the day when He shall send rain on the land again."

The widow could hardly believe Elijah's words; but she obeyed him.

And sure enough, when she took flour from the barrel there was always some left. And so it was with the oil. She, Elijah and her household had food for many days.

When Elijah had been living in the house for a while, the widow's little son became so ill he stopped breathing. The widow cried out to Elijah, "Did you come here to show me I had done wrong and to kill my son?"

"Give him to me," Elijah answered in distress. He carried the boy up to the room where he was staying, and prayed desperately. "My Lord God, have You brought evil on this woman by killing her son? Let his life return to him, I beg You!" Then Elijah laid the boy on the bed. He stretched himself over the boy three times. And God heard Elijah's cry for help. The boy began to breathe again!

Joyfully, Elijah carried him downstairs to where the mother was weeping. "He's alive!" cried Elijah.

Not daring to hope, the woman raised her head.

"There!" Gently, Elijah placed the boy in her arms.

For a moment she gazed at the boy. Then, softly, she spoke to Elijah. "Now I know you are a man of God. And the message you bring from Him is the truth."

Soon Ahab was to make the same discovery.

# Baal

After three years God said to Elijah, "Go again to Ahab to give him My message."

Bravely, Elijah obeyed. "God will send rain," he told Ahab. "But first you and all your people, and your priests, must meet me on Mount Carmel."

If Ahab wanted rain, he would have to obey. Angrily, he sent orders out to all the people.

Soon a great crowd was assembled on Mount Carmel.

Elijah spoke. "How much longer will you take to make up your minds?" he cried. "You cannot have two gods! Either Baal or the Lord God of Israel is the true God! Choose!"

The people gazed at him. No one moved or spoke.

Elijah tried again. "I'm the only one here who serves the Lord God. Over there stand four hundred and fifty priests of Baal. Let them choose two young bulls. They will prepare one for sacrifice. I will prepare the other. We will lay the sacrifices on two separate altars. We will light no fire under either of them. Then you pray to Baal and I will pray to the Lord God. The god who answers with fire shall be the one true God."

The people shouted, "Yes! Yes!" The priests of Baal dared not refuse the challenge.

The two bulls were killed and prepared for sacrifice. The priests of Baal stood around their altar. "O Baal! Hear us! Send fire!" they prayed.

Everyone waited. Nothing happened. The priests of Baal began to jump and dance around their altar, calling to Baal.

Nothing happened. At midday, Elijah began to mock them. "You'd better call louder! He *is* a god – isn't he? Maybe he's gone on a journey! Or

maybe he's asleep! You'll have to wake him up!"

Furiously the priests of Baal continued their cries. They cut themselves with knives until their blood ran. They knocked down the second altar as they leapt about. But still there was no sign that Baal could hear them.

When evening came, with still no sign, Elijah said to the people, "Come close." They gathered around him. He went to the altar which had been broken down, and built it up, using twelve stones, one for each of the tribes of Israel. Then he dug a deep trench all around the altar. He arranged the wood for the fire and placed the sacrifice on the altar. Then he amazed the people.

"Bring four barrels of water, and pour it over the sacrifice!" he commanded. Pour on *water*! How could a fire burn if everything was soaked with water?

Yet they dared not disobey. Elijah stood waiting. Three times they poured water over the sacrifice. The water ran down and filled the trench all round the altar.

When everything was thoroughly soaked, Elijah spoke to God. "Lord God of Israel, God of Abraham, of Isaac and of Jacob, let it be known today that You are the one true God and I am Your servant, so that the people may turn from their false gods, and worship You!"

As he finished speaking there was a mighty flash of flame. With a great roar the fire burned up the sacrifice, the altar – even the water in the trench. Nothing remained.

The people fell on their faces, crying, "The Lord is God! The Lord is God!"

The priests of Baal had been spellbound with fear. Now they tried to run.

"Don't let them get away!" cried Elijah. "With their lies they have brought great evil on you!"

When all the false priests had been put to death, Elijah spoke to the people again. "Go home, and eat and drink! I can hear the sound of rain! The drought and the famine will end!"

Ahab went off for a meal; but Elijah climbed to the top of the mountain. There was still no rain. He said to his servant, "Look out to sea! Are there any clouds coming?"

Six times the man looked. Nothing. But the seventh time, when he'd almost given up hope, he cried, "There *is* a cloud! It's about as big as a man's hand!"

"Run!" Elijah commanded. "Tell Ahab if he doesn't set off at once, his chariot will be overwhelmed by rain!"

Now the sky was black with clouds. The wind began to blow. Rain pelted down. Ahab drove off in his chariot, hastening back to his palace and Queen Jezebel.

Excitement filled Elijah, and power from God came to him so that he tucked his cloak up into his belt and ran all the way back. And he reached the palace ahead of Ahab and his chariot!

But his excitement was soon to change...

# Jezebel and Elijah

Still shaken by the happenings on Mount Carmel, King Ahab told the story to his wife Jezebel.

Jezebel had worshipped Baal. When she heard that Baal's priests had been killed, she sent a furious message to Elijah. "*You* have had the priests killed. *I* shall kill *you!*"

Elijah fled. He took his servant with him as far as Beersheba. Then he went on alone, into the desert. Exhausted, he sank down under a juniper tree. "I can't take any more, God!" he groaned. "Let me die."

Miserably, he fell asleep. Presently, a gentle touch on his shoulder startled him awake. An angel stood beside him. "Eat your meal!" said the angel.

Meal? Elijah looked around. There, just beside him, was bread, newly baked on a fire of hot coals. The bread smelt delicious! Also beside Elijah stood a jar of cool water.

Elijah ate and drank. Slightly comforted, he slept again.

A second time the angel prepared a meal for him. "Eat," said the angel, "or you won't have strength for your journey."

Elijah obeyed. Then he travelled on until at last he reached Mount Horeb. Here was a cave where he could take refuge.

All night Elijah slept in the cave.

In the morning God spoke to him. "What are you doing here, Elijah?"

Didn't God *know*? The words burst from Elijah. "I've done my very best, working for You! The Israelites have killed all Your other prophets! I'm the only one left! And now they're trying to kill me!"

"Go and stand on the mountain," said God. "I am going to pass by."

Leave his hiding place? And God was going to pass by? Elijah trembled.

He heard a great, powerful wind tear past the cave. But God was not in the wind.

A rumbling earthquake shook the ground nearby. But God was not in the earthquake.

A fire sprang up. But God was not in the fire.

After the fire and the noise, there was a silence. And in the silence Elijah heard a still, small voice.

Then Elijah pulled his cloak around him and went to the entrance of the cave.

"What are you doing here, Elijah?" the voice asked again.

Quietly, Elijah repeated his earlier reply.

God said, "Go back. Your work for Me is almost finished. Anoint Hazael as King of Syria. Anoint Jehu as King of Israel. And then anoint Elisha, son of Shaphat, to be My prophet after you."

Greatly heartened, Elijah set out. He found Elisha, and dropped his cloak over Elisha's shoulders as a sign that Elisha was to follow him. And Elisha went with Elijah, to become his servant. Then God gave Elijah another task...

# Naboth's Vineyard, and the Departure of Elijah

King Ahab wanted the vineyard next to his palace; but its owner, Naboth, refused to sell it.

Queen Jezebel was furious. Although Naboth was completely innocent, she bribed some judges to declare him guilty of speaking against both King Ahab and God. Naboth was stoned to death. Triumphantly, Ahab took possession of the vineyard.

But God sent Elijah to give him terrible news. "Your son shall die where Naboth died. Jezebel shall die also, and her body will be eaten by wild dogs."

The message came true. More messages were given to Elijah by God, and faithfully delivered, until at last Elijah knew his work on earth was done.

"I'll never leave you!" Elisha declared, in deep distress.

Elijah knew the two of them *must* be parted. "What can I give you before I go?" he asked gently.

"Give me your spirit." Elisha choked back the tears. "Give me a double portion!"

This was what a father usually gave to his eldest son.

Elijah said, "If you see the miracle which is about to happen, you will know God has chosen you to be His prophet; and you will have what you ask."

Suddenly, a chariot and horses of fire appeared. Elijah was lifted into the chariot and carried up into the sky. And Elisha *did* see it.

"My father!" he cried, in desperate sorrow. Then he bent and picked up Elijah's cloak, which had fallen to the ground. He put it on. Elisha knew that the spirit of Elijah was in him. He set out to continue Elijah's work for God. And he heard of a man called Naaman, who needed him.

# Naaman is Healed

Naaman was a great man, commander of the King of Aram's mighty army. But now he had caught the dreaded disease of leprosy, and it seemed there was no hope of a cure.

But Naaman's wife had a young slave girl who had been captured and brought from Israel.

"If only my master would go to the prophet Elisha, he could be healed!" the girl said earnestly.

It was worth trying. The King of Aram gave Naaman a letter to take to

the King of Israel, begging for help.

The King of Israel read the letter, and was terrified. "I can't cure leprosy! The King of Aram is trying to pick a quarrel with me!" he cried.

Then Elisha said, "Send Naaman to *me*."

Soon Naaman's horses and chariots arrived at the door of Elisha's house. Elisha sent out a message. "Go and wash seven times in the River Jordan, and you will be healed."

"What?" cried Naaman in fury. "Aren't our own rivers better than the *Jordan*? I thought Elisha himself would come out and heal me!" And he faced towards home.

But Naaman's servants persuaded him to try doing as Elisha had said. And Naaman was cured.

Humbly he went back to Elisha. "Now I know that your God is the true God, and I will worship Him," he vowed.

"Go in peace," smiled Elisha.

After a long life serving God, Elisha died.

Time passed. Many kings ruled in Judah. The people did not worship the true God, and hard times befell them. Jerusalem was destroyed. The people were taken as captives to Babylon. They were very unhappy.

But God had not forgotten them. Among the Israelites brought to Babylon was a boy called Daniel...

# Shadrach, Meshach and Abednego

Nebuchadnezzar – King of Babylon – picked out some of the clever, handsome children from amongst his captives, and ordered that they live in the palace and become members of his household. Four of these were Daniel, Shadrach, Meshach and Abednego.

The four boys were friends; and as they grew up they never forgot God. So when Shadrach, Meshach and Abednego were ordered to worship the golden statue which Nebuchadnezzar had had built, they refused. They worshipped God, no one else.

Nebuchadnezzar was furious. He ordered that they be securely tied up and thrown into a fiery furnace – a furnace so hot, the heat killed the men who threw them in! Yet Shadrach, Meshach and Abednego stood unbound and unharmed in the midst of the flames.

Nebuchadnezzar was overcome with awe. "I see *four* men walking in the fire," he whispered, "and the fourth looks like God's own son."

He called the three to come out of the fire; and not one hair on their heads was even singed.

Nebuchadnezzar ordered that in future no one was to speak against the God of Israel; and the three men were given important jobs in Babylon.

Soon Nebuchadnezzar died. His son Belshazzar became king. And Belshazzar gave a great feast, where something extraordinary happened...

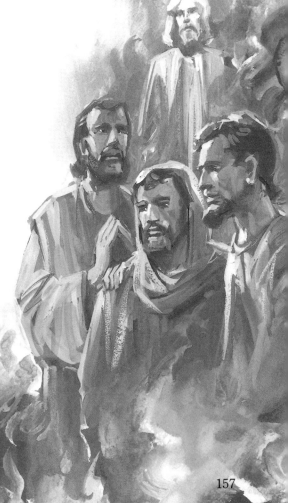

157

# Belshazzar's Feast

The feasting was going on merrily when suddenly King Belshazzar turned pale with fear. A hand was writing a message on the wall.

Terrified, the king cried, "Whoever can tell me what this message means shall become third ruler in the land!"

All the wise men attempted to explain the message, but failed. Then the queen remembered Daniel. *He* had sometimes interpreted dreams and riddles for Nebuchadnezzar...

Daniel was sent for. Refusing all the rewards offered by Belshazzar, Daniel quietly told him the meaning of the writing on the wall. God had judged Belshazzar's deeds and found them unworthy. Belshazzar's kingdom would fall and be divided amongst his enemies, the Medes and Persians.

Daniel's words came true. That same night the Medes attacked Babylon. Belshazzar was killed, and Babylon overcome.

But Daniel's work for God was not over.

# Daniel

King Darius, king of the mighty Medes and Persians, needed someone to be chief ruler in Babylon. He chose Daniel, whom he knew to be brave, wise and honest.

The other rulers were furious. "We'll get rid of him!" they whispered jealously. And they worked out a trap to catch Daniel.

The Medes and Persians worshipped many gods, but Daniel worshipped only the God of Israel…

With fast-beating hearts, the rulers approached the king.

"O King, live for ever!" they cried.

"All the rulers have agreed you should make a law saying that for thirty days no one should pray to any god or man except you. And if anyone disobeys the law, he should be thrown to the lions."

King Darius was flattered. The rulers must think him a great king, if they wanted this law. Of course, he *was* a great king… He smiled and nodded.

The rulers hadn't finished. "This law should be written down immediately!" they declared. They held their breath as they waited for a reply.

King Darius nodded again. "Very well."

Gleefully, the rulers watched him write; for once a law of the Medes and Persians was written down, it could never be altered.

The law was made known. As soon as Daniel heard it, he knew it was a trap set for him. He must either give up his daily prayers to God, or be thrown to the lions.

With his head held high, he walked down the road towards his home. He could feel enemy eyes watching him…

159

He could save his life by not praying to God for thirty days…He could save it by praying secretly in his head…He could try to find a hiding place, and pray there…

No. He strode into his house. Upstairs he went, to the front room where he always prayed. Steadily, he opened the windows which faced towards Jerusalem, his own country, so far away.

And he prayed to God to help him.

His enemies in the street below saw him, and knew their plan had worked. Triumphantly, they rushed back to the king. Once in front of him they controlled themselves, and spoke softly.

"King Darius, live for ever! Did you not make a law saying anyone who prayed to any god or man except you these thirty days should be thrown to the lions?"

"Yes I did," Darius agreed.

Then they said, "Daniel, who is one of the Jews captured and brought to Babylon years ago, takes no notice of your law. He still prays to his God, three times a day."

Then King Darius saw the trap which had been laid. Greatly distressed – for Daniel was a favourite of his – he tried to find a way out. All day he tried. But it was no use. He himself had written the law down, and it was unchangeable.

That evening, the rulers came back and reminded him that the law must be carried out. So the king consented, and Daniel was brought to the edge of the lions' den.

Below, the hungry lions paced backwards and forwards, roaring. Steadfastly, Daniel waited.

And the men threw him in.

160

The king cried out, "Daniel, may the God to whom you are so faithful save you!"

Then, hardly able to bear it, Darius watched as the huge stone was rolled into place over the entrance to the den. The king had to seal the stone with his own ring, so that everyone would know if the stone had been moved in a rescue attempt.

Then King Darius made his way back to the palace. All night he was tormented by his thoughts, not sleeping, not eating. At the very first sign of dawn, he hurried back to the lions' den.

Then he stopped short. What would he see? Had his friend been torn to pieces? Fearfully, he made himself call out. "Daniel! Has your God saved you?"

He waited, hardly daring to hope. Then strong and clear came Daniel's voice. "O King, live for ever! I am safe. God did not let the lions harm me."

Overjoyed, King Darius ordered, "Get Daniel out!"

Awed, the men who had thrown Daniel into the den now lifted him out. Sure enough, he was completely untouched by the lions. After a joyful greeting, King Darius ordered that Daniel's accusers should be brought and thrown into the lions' den themselves.

They were; and before they even touched the floor of the den the lions sprang on them, and tore them to pieces.

Then King Darius wrote to all the people in his kingdom. "I command that everyone should respect Daniel's God. For He is great, and will last for ever."

*Story taken from Ezra 1; 3; 4; 5; 6 and Nehemiah 1; 2; 3; 4; 6; 8*

# Rebuilding the Temple and Walls of Jerusalem

Many years after Jerusalem had been destroyed, Cyrus, King of the Persians, issued a proclamation. God had ordered him to see that the Temple was rebuilt in Jerusalem. And Cyrus was freeing all Jews who had been captured as slaves.

With great rejoicing, thousands of Israelites – or Jews – made the long journey back to their own land of Judah.

There they began to repair the city of Jerusalem; and after many months more they started to rebuild the Temple. Throughout the reign of Cyrus enemies tried to hinder them. But when Darius became king he ordered that they should be allowed to work without harassment.

At last the Temple was finished. It was splendid. But still Jerusalem had no mighty walls around it to defend it.

Nehemiah, cup-bearer to the King of Persia, was troubled about this. He got permission from the king to have the walls rebuilt, and he inspired the Jewish people to persevere with the task in spite of all the difficulties put in their way by their enemies.

Finally, with God's help, the work was completed. The walls stood triumphant.

God continued to care about the people He had created, and to be hurt by their disobedience. And He looked at the wicked city of Nineveh, and knew He must find someone to take a message of warning to its people…

# Jonah and the Whale

God spoke to Jonah. "Jonah, I want you to go to the city of Nineveh and tell the people there they are so wicked that their city is going to be destroyed."

"Me?" cried Jonah. He imagined himself giving such a message. The people would probably *kill* him! No, no! He couldn't go! Anyway, God was kind and merciful. Surely He'd never destroy a whole city!

"I must get away!" thought Jonah. "If I stay here, God will know I'm disobeying Him! I'll get a ship..."

So Jonah hurried down to the port of Joppa, and there found a ship about to sail for Tarshish. The very thing! Quite the opposite direction from Nineveh.

Hastily, still afraid God might stop him, Jonah paid his fare to the captain and went below. Now he should be safely out of God's sight...

Relieved after all his worry, Jonah lay down and went to sleep.

The ship set sail. Suddenly, a great storm blew up. The crew were terrified. They all knelt and prayed to their gods, but still the ship tossed violently on the huge waves. They threw the cargo overboard to lighten the ship, but things were no better.

Making his way below to check the hold, the captain discovered Jonah, still sleeping soundly.

"Wake up!" The captain shook him. "We are in deadly peril! Pray to your God! Maybe *he* will save us!"

Jonah struggled awake, trying to realize what was happening. The sailors had already decided Jonah must be the reason for the storm. As he clambered up on the deck, they shouted through the noise of the wind and the waves, "Who are you? Where are you from? What is your country?"

"I'm a Hebrew," Jonah answered. "I worship the God who *made* the sea and the earth. And I was trying to run away from God..."

The crew were even more terrified. "What can we do?" they cried.

"Throw me overboard," said Jonah. "Then the sea will be calm."

The sailors looked at one another. Throw a man overboard? Was there no other way? "We'll row for the shore," they said. They settled

themselves, and heaved on the oars with all their strength. But the storm grew even worse.

Then the sailors cried, "O Lord, please don't blame us for killing an innocent man!" And they picked Jonah up, and threw him into the sea.

Immediately, the storm died away. The sailors were very much afraid. They offered a sacrifice to God, and promised to serve Him.

Meanwhile, Jonah was sinking under the water, sure he would drown. But God sent a huge fish, like a whale, which swallowed Jonah in one gulp! Coughing, spluttering,

Jonah tried to get his breath back. He was in total darkness. He was *inside* the whale.

But he was alive. He began to pray to God. He realized how stupid he'd been to think there was anywhere God couldn't see him. He saw that even though he'd disobeyed God, God had saved his life. And he was grateful.

For three very miserable and

uncomfortable days Jonah lived inside the whale. Then, at God's command, the whale gave a great cough – and out came Jonah, onto a beach!

As he blinked in the light and took in great gulps of fresh air, God spoke to him again. "Jonah, go to Nineveh. Give the people My message."

This time Jonah couldn't get there fast enough. When he reached Nineveh, he gave the people God's message. To Jonah's surprise, they believed him at once. They took him to the king. The king also believed Jonah, and commanded that everyone in the city should pray to God for forgiveness. To show they were truly sorry for their wickedness they should take off their fine clothes, and wear sackcloth. And they were not to eat or drink.

When God heard their prayers and saw how sorry they were, He forgave them, and did not destroy Nineveh.

Jonah was *furious*! "I *knew* that's how it would be!" he declared. "I went through all this for nothing!" And he went into the desert, sat down, and sulked.

God made a bushy plant grow up behind him, to give him shade. But the next day, when Jonah was still sitting there, God commanded a worm to attack the plant.

The plant withered and died. Jonah was sorry for it, and angry that it had died so soon. But as the sun's rays beat down on him, and the hot scorching wind blew over him, he began to feel so ill himself that *he* lay down and wanted to die.

Then God spoke gently to Jonah. "You felt sorry for the plant when it died so soon – yet you didn't plant it, and you hadn't taken care of it. Think how much more sorry I would have been to destroy the people of Nineveh and their animals; for I made them, and I love them. Do you *really* think I should not have let them live?"

*Micah 6 : 8*

# Words from Micah

Some words written by the prophet Micah:
"He (God) has shown you, O Man, what is good;
and what does the Lord require of you but to do justly;
to love mercy; and to walk humbly with your God."

# THE
# NEW
# TESTAMENT

# The Angel Gabriel Visits Mary

For Mary, the day had begun just like any other. Mary lived in the small town of Nazareth, in Galilee; and she was looking forward to getting married to Joseph, the local carpenter. Joseph was honest and kind; strong, yet gentle. She loved him very much.

Mary was sitting day-dreaming when suddenly she looked up. Startled, she saw an angel – Gabriel – standing close by. He spoke. "God is with you! You have found favour with Him."

Mary was terrified. What did this mean?

The angel said, "Don't be afraid, Mary! God loves you! You are going to have a baby son. You must name Him 'Jesus'. He will be great; and He will be called the Son of the Most High. God will give Him a kingdom – the throne of His forefather, David. And this kingdom will *never* end."

Mary tried to calm herself; to understand.

"But how can I be going to have a son? I've never yet slept with a man…"

"The spirit of God will come upon you; and the power of the Most High will overshadow you," Gabriel answered. "And the child which shall be born will be the Son of God. Elizabeth, your cousin, is also going to have a child, although she has grown old and people said it was impossible. With God, *nothing* is impossible."

Mary listened. All her life she had loved and trusted God. Now, she took a deep breath. "I will do anything which God asks of me," she said quietly. "Let this happen, just as you have said."

The angel left her. Mary sat for a while, trying to take in the tremendous news… Elizabeth! The angel had mentioned Elizabeth…

Hastily, Mary started to prepare for a journey. She would go and visit her cousin.

# Mary Visits Elizabeth

Elizabeth was married to a man called Zacharias (sometimes written Zechariah), a priest of the Temple Church. Elizabeth had often prayed for a son. Now, as Mary came into the house and greeted her, Elizabeth was full of joy; for she had just felt her baby move inside her.

"How blessed I am!" she cried. "The mother of the Son of God has come to see me! And you, Mary, are blessed indeed!"

Mary could see it was true – Elizabeth was going to have a child; and her cousin's words helped her to accept what was happening to herself. The two women hugged each other.

Elizabeth cried, "Let me tell you about my baby! Zacharias was in the Temple one day when the angel Gabriel came and told him I would have a baby son, whom we must call

John. Our son is going to be special, Mary! When he grows up, he is to tell the people to be ready; for their Saviour, the Messiah, is coming!"

As Mary listened breathlessly, Elizabeth went on. "Zacharias wouldn't believe what the angel told him – we're both so old! So the angel made Zacharias dumb! He can't say a word! He has to make signs when he wants anything – or write on this tablet. But it's *true* about the baby! What God promises, He will do!"

And Mary said softly, "My soul praises the Lord God, and my spirit rejoices in Him. He has done great things for me, and holy is His name."

Mary stayed with Elizabeth for about three months before returning to Nazareth. In due time Elizabeth's baby was born. Her friends and relatives thought she would name him Zacharias, after his father.

"No!" Elizabeth insisted. "He is to be called John!"

"But why?" cried her relatives. "No one else in our family is called John!"

They made signs to Zacharias about the name, sure he would agree with them. Zacharias pointed to his writing tablet. They handed it to him, and watched eagerly as he wrote.

He held up the tablet; and they were astonished. Zacharias had written, "His name is John".

And suddenly, Zacharias found he could speak again. He began to praise God. Soon, everyone in Judea had heard the story, and were full of wonder.

"What *will* he be when he grows up?" they said. "Surely God is with this child!"

But Mary's baby was yet to be born...

# Joseph and Mary

When Joseph heard that Mary was expecting a child, he was puzzled and distressed. But he loved her too much to break with her. He decided he would have to hide her away, so that no one would know she was to have a baby before the two of them were married. The Israelites thought this was a disgraceful thing to happen.

But God sent an angel to Joseph, in a dream. "Joseph, son of David," said the angel, "do not be afraid to take Mary to your house as your wife. God's Holy Spirit has come upon her. She will have a son. You must name Him Jesus, which means 'Saviour', because He will save the people from their sins."

Then Joseph was reassured; and he and Mary began to make preparations for the baby. They expected it would be born at home in Nazareth.

But one day, when they knew the birth would be soon, Joseph came hurrying in with worrying news.

The Roman ruler, Caesar Augustus, wanted to know exactly how many people were living under Rome's command. So everyone was ordered to go to the place where they had been born, to be counted. Wives would go with husbands.

And Joseph had been born in Bethlehem, in Judea. More than one hundred and fifty kilometres away…

# No Room

There was no help for it. Joseph and Mary packed what they thought they would need for the journey into bundles. Mary made sure she had put in some warm swaddling-clothes for the baby. Then, with Mary riding on a donkey, she and Joseph set out for Bethlehem.

The road was long and hard. There were many other people making the same journey. With sinking hearts Mary and Joseph realized that the small town of Bethlehem would be full to overflowing. Where would they find lodgings?

Unable to hurry, they came to

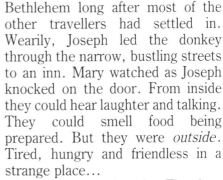

Bethlehem long after most of the other travellers had settled in. Wearily, Joseph led the donkey through the narrow, bustling streets to an inn. Mary watched as Joseph knocked on the door. From inside they could hear laughter and talking. They could smell food being prepared. But they were *outside*. Tired, hungry and friendless in a strange place...

Joseph knocked again. The door was thrown open. The innkeeper stood there. "No room! No room!" he said, and started to bustle away.

"Please!" Joseph's voice stopped him. "Is there *nowhere* we can rest?"

The innkeeper paused. This time he looked past Joseph at Mary; and he was very sorry for her.

"The inn is full," he said. "But there is the stable. The lady would at least be sheltered there – if you don't mind being in with the animals."

"Anywhere!" said Mary gratefully. She knew the baby would be born very soon.

And so it was that God's son was born in a stable in Bethlehem. And Mary wrapped Him in soft, warm swaddling-clothes, and laid Him tenderly on the sweet-smelling hay in the manger; because there was no room for them in the inn.

Then Mary and Joseph tried to rest. But soon the baby was to have His first visitors...

173

# The Visit of the Shepherds

On the hills around Bethlehem, shepherds kept their sheep. The work could be exciting and dangerous. Not only did the shepherds have to lead their flocks along steep, narrow paths to the patches of grazing land – they had always to be on the watch for wild animals which might attack the flock.

Even at night the shepherds stayed with the sheep, wrapping themselves in their thick, warm cloaks, and sleeping fitfully in the open air by the camp fire.

On the night Jesus was born in Bethlehem the shepherds were out on the hillside as usual. It was a clear, quiet night. The only light came from the stars and the dull glow of the fire. The only sounds were the soft bleating of a sheep, or the restless movement of a lamb.

And then all at once, a bright, glorious light began to fill the sky, surrounding the shepherds with its brilliance.

Sleepily rubbing their eyes, they were suddenly wide awake – and terrified! What was happening?

Petrified, they hid their faces in their cloaks and lay shivering on the

ground. And they heard the beautiful voice of the Angel of the Lord.

"Do not be afraid! I have good news for you, and all the people. For unto you is born this day in the city of David a Saviour which is Christ the Lord. And this shall be a sign unto you. You will find the baby wrapped in swaddling clothes, lying in a manger."

Now, as the shepherds dared to look, they saw the whole sky filled with angels, singing, "Glory to God in the highest, and on earth, peace. Goodwill towards men."

Then the light faded, and the music of the angels died away. Once more there was starlight, and silence.

The shepherds sat up, trying to take in what they'd seen and heard. The city of David. That meant Bethlehem. Was there truly a baby born in Bethlehem that night who was the Christ, the Messiah, the Saviour?

The shepherds scrambled to their feet. "Let us go to Bethlehem at once, and see the baby!" they cried. Leaving one man on guard, the others raced along the paths, stumbling in the darkness, stubbing their toes, not bothering; only wanting to prove this news was true.

Reaching Bethlehem, they paused, panting for breath. Which way now? Bethlehem seemed to be silent, asleep. There were many mangers – animal feeding boxes – in the town. Everyone who owned a donkey would have a manger for it.

The shepherds began to walk along the streets, looking for signs that someone was awake. They came to the inn. There, from the stable, a dim light was showing.

The shepherds stood still, looking

at one another, hardly daring to hope. Then, trembling again, they peeped inside.

And in the manger, wrapped in warm clothes exactly as the angel had said, lay Baby Jesus, with Mary and Joseph watching over Him. Softly the shepherds knelt to worship.

They told Mary and Joseph about the message of the angels. And on their way back to the hillside, as dawn broke and people began to be about, they told the good news to everyone they met.

And Mary remembered all these things, and thought deeply about them.

And when the time had come according to the laws which Moses had written down, Joseph and Mary prepared to take Baby Jesus to the Temple in Jerusalem.

# Simeon and Anna in the Temple

In Jerusalem lived a man called Simeon. Simeon was old, but God had promised him he would not die until he had seen the Messiah – the Saviour for whom the Jewish people were longing. So Simeon waited, and prayed; and at last God said to him, "Go to the Temple *today*, Simeon. Today you will find the Messiah there."

Trembling with excitement, Simeon made his way as fast as he could to the Temple Courts. He peered around at the throng of people. Which one was the Messiah?

Then Mary and Joseph came into the Temple Courts, carrying Baby Jesus. And Simeon *knew*.

Shakily, the old man went up to Mary. "Please – may I hold Him? " he begged. Simeon's face shone with excitement and love. Mary handed the baby to him.

Then Simeon praised God. "You have kept Your promise, Lord. Now let Your servant depart in peace. For I have seen Your salvation with my own eyes – the salvation which is for everyone. The light which shines here shall shine for all nations; and it will bring glory to the people of Israel."

Mary and Joseph listened in amazement. Simeon blessed them. He said to Mary, "This child will alter the lives of many. But some people will speak against Him; and your own heart will be pierced with sorrow."

Gently, he handed the baby back to her. And a very old lady, called Anna, who never left the Temple, came up to them at that moment.

"This is the Messiah!" she cried. She thanked God; and told the people there, "This is the Saviour!"

Then Mary and Joseph carried out the ceremony of presenting the Baby Jesus to God, which the law demanded. And they made their offering of two turtle doves, as a thanksgiving. They couldn't afford the lamb and the dove which richer people would offer.

Then they took the tiny baby back to Bethlehem, to rest for a while.

But more surprise visitors were to come.

# The Wise Men and the Flight into Egypt

King Herod sat in his palace in Jerusalem and knew nothing of the angels, or the shepherds, or the extraordinary things which had been happening to Mary and Joseph. Until one day, wise men from a land far away in the east asked for an audience with him.

Politely, the wise men bowed low. But their words filled Herod with horror. "Where is the new baby king?" the wise men asked. "As we studied the sky, we saw His star rise in the east; and we have come to worship Him."

New baby *king*? To replace himself? Herod went pale. He ordered his chief priests and lawyers to search in their books. "Discover where this new king is to be born!" he said.

After a while they replied, "In Bethlehem of Judea!"

Craftily, Herod took the wise men to one side. "Go to Bethlehem," he said. "Search carefully for the child. When you've found Him, come back and tell me. *I* want to worship Him, too."

Unsuspecting, the wise men left the palace. They looked up – and saw the star. The same star they had seen in the east. It went ahead of them, leading them to the place where the Baby Jesus was. There it stopped.

And there the wise men found Mary, and Joseph, and the baby.

Mary and Joseph watched in astonishment as these splendid travellers from a foreign land knelt and worshipped the baby. They

179

watched as the wise men searched amongst their treasures and brought out rich gifts for Him – gold, frankincense and myrrh. Gold was a present given to kings. Frankincense was burnt on the altar of the Lord God. And myrrh – Mary and Joseph shivered a little. Myrrh was used to help preserve the bodies of people when they died.

It was late now. The wise men rested for the night. And God sent them a dream.

"Do not go back to King Herod! He means to harm the child! Go home another way!"

So in the morning the wise men departed, and obeyed God's instruction to keep away from Herod.

Then Joseph, too, had a dream. An angel appeared to him. "Get up!" the angel said. "Take the boy and His mother, and escape into Egypt. Stay there until I tell you it is safe to return. For Herod means to kill the child."

Joseph woke with a start. He took a moment to realize what had happened. Then, hastily, he got up, stumbling in the darkness.

"Mary! Mary!" he whispered urgently. "Wake up! We must take the baby and get away. At once!"

He told Mary about his dream. Soon the donkey was saddled, their few possessions were bundled up, and the sleepy baby was wrapped warmly.

Then they set out in the starlight. They hurried along the streets of Bethlehem, with only the clip clop of the donkey's hooves breaking the silence.

Would they escape?

180

*Matthew 2 : 16–23; Luke 2 : 41–52*

# The Boy Jesus

God's warning *had* come in time. Joseph, Mary and the Baby Jesus reached Egypt in safety. But when Herod discovered he had been outwitted by the wise men, he was furious. In rage and fear he ordered that every boy living in or near Bethlehem, aged two and under, was to be killed.

There was great weeping and mourning; but Herod rubbed his hands, satisfied that no baby king now existed to threaten his throne.

Meanwhile, in Egypt, Jesus was alive and unharmed. He grew bigger, watched over, loved and taught by Mary and Joseph.

At last King Herod died; and the angel appeared again to Joseph in a dream. It was safe to return.

So Mary, Joseph and Jesus came to Nazareth in Galilee. And there they lived, in one of the small white houses with a flat roof; and Joseph took up his work as a carpenter again.

When Jesus was old enough, He went to school in Nazareth. He learnt to write – making the letters with His finger in the dust, to begin with. He learnt how to read from the scrolls. And He asked a lot of questions.

On the Sabbath day He went to the Synagogue with Joseph. Mary went as well; but she sat with the other women, as was the custom.

As soon as Jesus was old enough He began to listen very carefully to all He heard in the Synagogue. And He had more questions to ask...

Every year Joseph and Mary went to the Temple in Jerusalem for the Feast of the Passover – the time when Jews remembered their escape from Egypt, years before. When Jesus was twelve years old, they took Him with them; for this was also the custom.

There were many other people on the road. Some were from Nazareth. All were going in the same direction. How exciting to be going so far! And to *see* Jerusalem, the city of which Jesus had heard so much!

But most exciting – and wonderful – was to go into the Temple itself; to take part in the special ceremonies; and to listen to the wisdom of the scribes and teachers there.

When the festival was over, Joseph and Mary set out for home. They were with a large group of people from Nazareth. As usual, the women and children walked in one part of the group, the men and older boys in another. So neither Joseph nor Mary worried that Jesus wasn't beside them. Each thought He was with the other one.

All day they travelled; but when darkness began to fall, and people were setting up camp for the night, they realized He had been with neither.

Mary and Joseph began to enquire amongst their friends and relatives – slightly irritated at first; then getting more and more anxious. No one had seen Jesus since they left Jerusalem.

Pale with worry, Joseph and Mary tried to think. Could Jesus have come to some harm along the road? It was unlikely. Wild animals and robbers wouldn't attack a crowd of people. That was one reason why they all travelled together if they could. Jesus wouldn't have wandered off alone. Even if He had, someone would have seen Him go.

No. There was only one answer.

He must still be in Jerusalem. Somehow, He had been left behind.

Deeply distressed, Mary and Joseph hastened back to the city. But it was still full of people. Where to search?

For three days Mary and Joseph scoured Jerusalem. At last, almost without hope, they entered the Courts of the Temple. What twelve-year-old boy would want to spend time *there*?

Next moment, Mary and Joseph stood still in amazement. There was Jesus – sitting amongst the most clever men in Jerusalem. Talking to them. Asking them questions. And clearly, the men were astonished at the kind of questions He asked, and the amount He understood.

After a moment, Mary rushed forward. "Son! Why have You behaved like this? We've been searching everywhere!"

Jesus was surprised. "Why were you searching? I thought you would know I was here – in My Father's house."

Joseph and Mary looked at Him, unable to understand. "Anyway – come home with us now," they said.

Jesus obeyed immediately.

They went back to Nazareth, and life went on as usual. But Mary remembered all that had happened, and often thought about it as she watched her son grow into manhood.

And Jesus Himself knew He must soon leave home, and start on the task for which He had come.

His cousin John had already begun.

# John the Baptist

John, son of Elizabeth and Zacharias, grew up seeing much of life in the Temple in Jerusalem where his father was a priest.

But John soon felt that the Temple, with all its rules and regulations, wasn't the place for him. So as soon as he was old enough, he left.

He went into the desert to live by himself. And there, God spoke to him. And John believed God's words. The Messiah – the Saviour – was coming soon; and it was John's task to tell everyone. To get the people ready to listen to the Messiah, when He *did* come.

183

# The Baptism of Jesus

Straightaway, John started to preach to the people.

"Get ready for the Kingdom of God to come soon! Own up to the wrong things you have done! Show that you are sorry by living a better life! And come and be baptized!"

'Baptized' meant being 'washed' – being dipped in the water as a sign that the wrong things in a person's life were being washed away, ready for the new life to begin. It was because he baptized people that John was given the name 'John the Baptist'.

Soon, people in the towns were talking about John.

"He wears clothing made from camel hair, with a leather belt round his waist! He lives in the desert all the time, and eats locusts and wild honey! And you should *see* his hair! And he's preaching a new message!"

184

The more they heard, the more curious they grew. And soon crowds of people were coming out to see John.

They came because they were curious; but they stayed to listen. Many of them believed John's message; and those people John baptized in the River Jordan.

Some people wondered if John were the Saviour, the Messiah the Jews had long been waiting for. John told them he was not.

"I baptize you with water," he

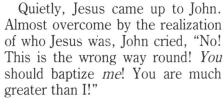

Quietly, Jesus came up to John. Almost overcome by the realization of who Jesus was, John cried, "No! This is the wrong way round! *You* should baptize *me*! You are much greater than I!"

Jesus answered softly, "This is the way *God* would have it done."

So Jesus and John went together into the River Jordan; and John baptized Jesus.

Jesus' baptism was different from everyone else's, because He had done no wrong things which needed to be washed away. And as He came back onto the bank, it seemed as if the sky was opened, and the spirit of

said, "but someone is coming who is much more powerful than I am. I'm not fit even to untie His sandals. He will baptize you with fire, and with the Holy Spirit."

Jesus heard about his cousin John's preaching, and came from Galilee to be baptized.

When John saw Jesus, he felt God speaking to him. "Look!" he cried. "That's the One. *He* will take away the sins of the world!"

God in the shape of a dove came down to Him.

And God's voice was heard. "This is My beloved son, in whom I am well pleased."

Then Jesus was full of the Holy Spirit. And He knew He must go into the wilderness for a while, to be by Himself, and prepare for the work which He had come to earth to do. But it was not easy for Him in the wilderness...

# Jesus in the Wilderness

For forty days and forty nights Jesus was in the wilderness. He ate nothing. He spent a long time thinking deeply about the power which God had given Him, and how He should use it.

At the end of forty days He was very hungry. And Satan tempted Him. "Look at these stones! If You are *really* the Son of God, You could turn these stones into bread!"

Bread! How Jesus longed for it! But He knew His power had not been given to Him to use for Himself.

"It is written in the Scriptures, 'Man shall not live by bread alone, but by God's words also'," He answered.

Then Satan, seeing that he had lost *that* time, tried again. He took Jesus to Jerusalem, to the highest ledge of the Temple. "If You are *really* the Son of God," whispered Satan, "throw Yourself off this ledge!" And craftily, Satan spoke some words from Scripture himself. "It is written, 'God will order His angels to take care of You. They will hold You up, and not let You even bruise Your foot on a stone'."

Jesus knew that if He did throw Himself down from this height, and yet remain unhurt, people might well flock to become His followers. But it would be for the wrong reason – because they thought Him some sort of magician; not because they had heard and understood His true message from God.

Steadily, Jesus refused this easy way to impress the crowd. He answered, "But it is also written, 'Do not tempt the Lord thy God'!"

Satan was defeated again; but he would not give up yet. He led Jesus to a very high place.

"Look!" he whispered. "You can see all the kingdoms of the world from here! All authority over the world – all the splendour of the world – has been given to me. If You worship me, I will give it to You."

But Jesus answered, "Get thee behind Me, Satan! It is written, 'Thou shalt worship the Lord thy God; and Him *only* shalt thou serve!'"

Then Satan gave up for the moment; waiting until he could seize his chance again.

And angels came to Jesus, and took care of Him.

Then Jesus went back to Galilee; and all through the countryside people began to tell each other about Him, and the things He said and did.

And they wanted to see and hear more...

# Jesus' Disciples

Except in His own village of Nazareth, the people of Galilee crowded round Jesus to listen to Him wherever he went.

One day, four fishermen – Simon, Andrew, James and John – were on the shores of Lake Gennaseret gloomily cleaning their nets, while their empty boats bobbed on the water behind them. They went out fishing at night, because that was usually the best time to catch fish. But last night they'd caught nothing...

Now, as they worked on the nets, they heard a commotion. Looking up, they saw Jesus coming. Crowds of people were following Him, pushing and jostling each other as they tried to get close to Him. The fishermen watched anxiously. Was someone going to get hurt?

No. Jesus had noticed the boats at the water's edge.

"Simon," He said, "may I borrow your boat?"

Simon sprang to his feet. Jesus was asking him for help! Gladly he agreed. Jesus stepped into the boat. The people on shore watched. Was Jesus taking the chance to get away from them?

No. Jesus asked Simon to row a short distance out from shore. Then He sat down, and began to speak to the people.

Now everyone could see and hear. The crowd settled down to listen. The four fishermen listened, too.

When Jesus had finished teaching the people, He looked at Simon.

"Sail out to the deep water there, and let down your nets," He said.

Simon hesitated. "Master, we've been fishing all night! We haven't caught a thing! The fish don't seem to be here... But I'll do as You say."

Andrew, Simon's partner, waded out and climbed into the boat as well. They sailed over to the place which Jesus had pointed out. Not knowing whether to hope or not, they let down a net.

From their own boat, James and John watched...

Suddenly there was a great tugging on the net. Simon and Andrew began to haul it in. The net was full of fish – so many fish, the net began to break!

"Help!" Simon cried to James and John. James and John quickly rowed across. Now they were all desperately trying to get the fish on board – almost more fish than they had ever *seen* before! So many fish, both boats were almost sinking under the weight of them!

Simon looked at Jesus – and suddenly he was afraid. "Master!" he said. "I'm not good enough for You to be with me! Please go!"

But Jesus answered, "Don't be afraid, Simon. From now on, you will catch men, not fish!"

And Simon understood. Jesus meant *him* to help in the work of telling men about God's message...

As quickly as they could, Simon, Andrew, James and John landed their boats safely on the shore. Then they left everything, and followed Jesus to become His special helpers – His disciples.

Jesus needed more disciples. He saw Matthew, a tax-collector, sitting at his table collecting taxes.

To Matthew's amazement, Jesus stopped to speak to him. Jesus was a Jew. Most Jews hated tax-collectors. Not only did they cheat by taking more money than was due; they worked for the Romans, who had occupied the country and now ruled it.

But Jesus said, "Follow Me!"

Jesus wanted *him*! *Wanted* him! Matthew could hardly believe it! Gladly he jumped up, leaving everything as the others had done. Then he had a thought.

"Jesus!" He hardly dared speak the words. "Jesus – would You come to a party at my house? If – if I invite other tax-collectors?"

He held his breath, sure that Jesus would refuse. But Jesus smiled. "I will come!" He said.

Matthew raced away to make the preparations, and soon a huge party was going on at his house.

Some of the Pharisees – Jews who were very strict in the way they kept the laws of Moses – saw it. They were shocked. They thought there was only one right way to behave – theirs. And every other way was wrong. Now, they said to the disciples, "How can your leader possibly eat with people like that? Tax-collectors, and people who don't keep the law! Why does He do it?"

Jesus overheard them. "People who are well don't need a doctor!" He said. "I came to give God's message to everyone, not just to talk to respectable people! Go and read the Scriptures, where it says God wants kindness to be shown – not animals to be sacrificed!"

The Pharisees had thought *they* were the ones who knew the Scriptures... Furiously, they moved away.

Jesus chose other disciples, until finally He had an inner group of twelve – Simon Peter; Andrew; James; John; Philip; Nathaniel, or Bartholomew; Matthew; Thomas; James, son of Alphaeus; Thaddeus; Simon the Zealot; and Judas Iscariot.

Some of His disciples were with Him at a wedding party. A party which turned out to be very special...

John 2 : 1–11

# The Wedding at Cana

There was a wedding at Cana, in Galilee. Jesus' mother, Mary, was one of the guests, and Jesus and His disciples had also been invited. The party was going splendidly, with laughing and talking, eating and drinking. And then Mary came over to Jesus. She whispered anxiously to Him. "Jesus – the wine has all gone! There's none left!"

The host and hostess would be very ashamed. Running out of wine! They would remember it with shame every time they remembered the wedding...

Jesus spoke gently. "Why are you telling Me? The time for Me to use My power hasn't come yet."

But Mary was absolutely certain Jesus would help His friends. The servants were standing by; and Mary said to them, "Do whatever He tells you!"

Jesus looked around. He saw six huge stone jars standing in the corner of the room. The jars would hold about a hundred litres of water, and were there so that people could wash their hands and feet as they came into the house.

"Fill those jars with fresh water!" Jesus said to the servants, who had been looking at Him expectantly.

They obeyed, getting water from the well and filling the jars to the brim.

"Now," said Jesus, "offer it to the man in charge of the feast."

The servants looked at one another. Offer *water*? They looked again at Jesus, and decided to do as He said. Hardly daring to breathe, they watched as the man took a sip. The host watched, also...

"Well!" said the man. "Most people serve their best wine first, and keep the worst until last – when people have already had so much to drink they'll hardly notice the taste. But *you* have kept the best wine till last!"

The water had been turned into wine; and there was plenty of it.

The host hesitated. Then he began to smile. Everyone smiled, and laughed; the party went happily on.

Jesus had performed His first miracle in Cana of Galilee. His disciples saw it; and they began to trust Him completely.

Soon Jesus would perform other miracles...

# The Man Who Couldn't Walk

There was a man who was paralysed, so that he couldn't walk. He lived in Capernaum; and he was deeply unhappy. His friends thought he was miserable because he couldn't get about and had to beg for a living. And so he was. But it wasn't only that. He knew he'd done many wrong things in his life; and it was thinking about *them* that made him so unhappy.

One day as he lay miserably on his mat-bed, four of his friends came rushing up. "Jesus is in Capernaum!" they cried. "He's healing sick people!"

"What good is that to me?" grumbled the man. "I can't go and ask Him to heal *me*! You *know* I can't walk!"

"You don't *have* to walk!" cried his friends. "Look – we've brought ropes..."

Quickly, they tied a rope to each corner of the mat-bed.

"What are you doing?" cried the man, as they lifted him.

"It's all right!" they reassured him. "All *you* have to do is lie still. We'll carry you to the house where Jesus is."

Along the road they went, with the four friends puffing and panting, and the man who couldn't walk spending half the time afraid they would drop him, and the other half wondering about Jesus. Would Jesus really be able to cure him? He'd been so wicked... Jesus probably wouldn't want to have anything to do with him...

They reached the street they were looking for. It was easy to tell which house Jesus was in. There was a huge crowd of people round the doorway, all trying to hear what Jesus was saying to the Pharisees and lawyers inside the house.

"Excuse us!" said the four friends. "Please! Let us get through! This man needs to be healed!"

It was no use. No one would give way. They'd had enough trouble getting space for themselves.

"We'll have to give up," said the man who couldn't walk. "You'd better take me back." And he wanted to cry.

His four friends looked at him, then at each other. No! They

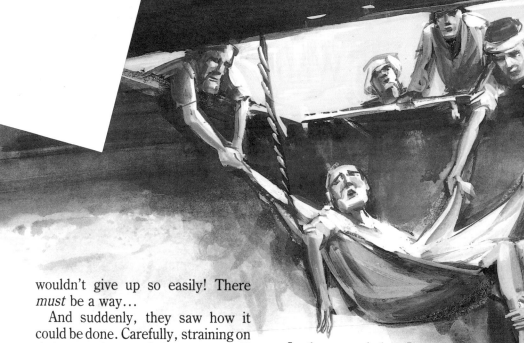

wouldn't give up so easily! There *must* be a way...

And suddenly, they saw how it could be done. Carefully, straining on the ropes, they carried the man – still on his bed – up the outside stairs and on to the flat roof of the house.

"What are you *doing*? What's the use of all this?" cried the man. He was very much afraid of falling. His four friends were too busy to answer. Before anyone could tell them to stop, they were lifting off some of the roof tiles to make a hole. A hole large enough for the bed to go through...

The friends peered over the edge of the hole. Yes. Down below they could see Jesus. He was surrounded by the Pharisees and lawyers who had come from all parts of Galilee – even from Judea and Jerusalem – to listen to Him.

"Right!" whispered the friends. Slowly, cautiously, they began to lower the man who couldn't walk down through the hole they had made. The man clung on to his bed, and hoped he wasn't going to fall...

In the room below Jesus stopped talking. He looked up at the extraordinary sight. The Pharisees and lawyers looked up, too. They were horrified. How dare anyone behave like this?

The four friends went on lowering the man into the middle of the crowd; and landed him right in front of Jesus.

Jesus looked up at the faces of the friends. He could see they were certain He had the power to heal the paralysed man. Then He looked down at the man. And the man looked up at Jesus. And Jesus could see the misery and fear in his eyes; and He understood. He spoke gently.

"My friend – the wrong things you have done are all forgiven."

Jesus was calling him 'friend'! And forgiving him...

The Pharisees and lawyers thought, "*What*? He's forgiving *sins*? Who *is* this man? He speaks

194

blasphemy! Only God can forgive sins!"

Jesus knew what they were thinking. He turned to look at them. "Which is easier?" He asked. "To say 'your sins are forgiven', or to say 'get up and walk'?"

They were silent.

Jesus went on. "So that you can know I have the power to forgive sins – " He turned towards the paralysed man again. "I say to you – get up. Pick up your bed; and *walk*!"

There was a hiss of whispered surprise from the watching crowd. This man hadn't walked for *years*, if *ever*! Now Jesus was telling him to pick up his bed...

But the man who lay on his mat-bed wasn't bothering about the crowd, *or* the Pharisees. He could feel strength flowing into him! He moved his legs... Moved his *legs*! The legs that had been paralysed and helpless for so long! He sat up. He struggled to his feet. He wobbled a little. Then – "Praise God!" he cried. His face aglow with joy, he bent to roll up his bed. Next moment, he was pushing his way through the crowd. The people stepped back in awe to let him pass.

The four friends came rushing down the stairs. Exultantly, they greeted the man. Then, praising God, he went home. And everyone who saw him was full of awe.

"We've seen something amazing happen here today," they said to one another.

Other amazing things were to happen...

195

# The Roman Centurion's Servant

Most Jews hated the Roman soldiers who had overcome their country and now occupied it. But in Capernaum there was one Roman soldier whom they liked and respected.

He was a Centurion; in charge of a hundred men; strong; a good leader. He was also kind and considerate. When the Jews' Synagogue became too old for them to use, he even had a beautiful new one built for them. He was concerned about *everyone's* welfare.

The Centurion had a servant whom he valued very much. The man was a willing, faithful worker, and served his master well. But one day the servant was taken ill. All the usual remedies were tried; but nothing worked. The Centurion could see his servant was close to death.

The Centurion had heard about Jesus, and knew that He had healed many people – even ones who were dying. But Jesus was a Jew. He probably wouldn't want to help a Roman.

Desperately, the Centurion wondered what to do. And he had an idea.

The chief rulers and elders of Capernaum were his friends. Surely they would speak to Jesus *for* him! Hastily, he went to ask them. And because of the feeling they had for the Centurion, the elders went to Jesus.

"Please," they begged, "come and heal the servant of this Centurion! He's a good man, and has been very kind to us. He respects the fact that

we are Jews. He even built a new Synagogue for us."

"Of course I'll come," said Jesus; and they set out together.

But back at home, the Centurion was feeling dreadful. How could he possibly have asked Jesus to take all the trouble of coming to the house? It was worse than going to Jesus himself!

The Centurion went hot all over at the thought. He still felt he couldn't speak to Jesus himself; but he had to do *something*...

Some of his friends were nearby. Quickly, he spoke to them. "Please – take a message for me!"

Seeing how upset and anxious he was, his friends agreed. They listened as he told them what to say.

"Hurry!" he urged.

They hurried; and they met Jesus just along the road.

"Lord!" they cried. "The Centurion says please don't trouble to come right to the house. He feels he doesn't deserve to have You visit him. He doesn't even think he's a good enough person to speak to You. He says, if You'll just say the word, he knows his servant will be healed. He's used to giving orders himself. If he tells a soldier to go, the soldier goes. Or if he says stay, the soldier stays. And his servants obey him, as well. So he knows Your word will be enough."

Jesus was utterly amazed. He turned round to the crowd of people who were following Him, as usual. "Listen!" He said to them. "I haven't found anyone else who trusted Me as much as that – not even amongst the Jews."

And when the Centurion's friends went back to the house, they found his servant was quite well again.

Crowds of people continued to follow Jesus about, but sometimes He felt He just *had* to get away...

# The Storm on the Sea of Galilee

Nearly all day Jesus had been talking to the crowds of people who had gathered to listen to Him.

"How can I tell you what the Kingdom of God is like?" He said. He thought for a moment. "It's like a mustard seed – the smallest of all the seeds you plant. Yet when you *have* planted it, it grows and grows until it's the largest plant in the garden. It's so big, the birds can perch in its branches, and be shaded from the heat of the sun."

The people listened. And He went on; telling them stories, explaining everything more carefully to His disciples later. They were trying desperately to understand His teaching.

By the time evening came, Jesus was weary; but still the crowds did not leave. It was no use trying to walk away from them. They simply followed Him… Jesus had been talking to them near the shores of the Sea of Galilee. Now, as He looked round, He noticed the fishing boats on the shore. And He saw what to do.

"Let's sail over to the other side," He said to His disciples. They had been anxious for Him, and wanted Him to be able to rest.

"Yes!" they agreed gladly. Not stopping to change their clothes – not even stopping for a wash – they all climbed into a boat, and set off.

Jesus went to one end of the boat, and lay down, resting on a cushion. Softly the waters slapped at the side of the boat. Softly the sail flapped in the wind. Gently the boat rocked up and down… The disciples talked quietly amongst themselves. And Jesus fell asleep.

But then a sudden storm blew up. The boat began to toss violently. The disciples struggled to get the sail down. The boat was near to

capsizing! Huge waves rose up and crashed down into it. It was almost swamped! The disciples were terrified! Yet still Jesus slept...

A wave lifted the boat high, then tossed it down. The disciples could bear it no longer. They scrambled down to the end of the boat where Jesus was sleeping.

"Master! Master!" Their voices could hardly be heard above the noise of the wind and waves. They touched Him on the shoulder. "Master! Wake up! We're in dreadful danger! We're likely to drown! Don't You care?"

Jesus woke. He looked at the frightened faces peering down at Him. He felt the tossing of the boat, the wind, the water. And He got to His feet.

The disciples clung to anything they could get hold of, and watched Him. What was He going to do? What could *anyone* do, in a storm like this?

Jesus stood up, straight, unafraid. And He *spoke* to the storm. "Peace! Be still!"

Immediately the wind died down. The waves sank back. The water was calm and smooth.

Jesus turned to look at His disciples. "Why were you afraid? Didn't you *know* you were safe, while I was here?"

The disciples gazed at Him in awe. And they whispered to each other, "Who *is* this man? Even the wind and the waves do as He tells them..."

The boat sailed on. Everyone landed safely on the far shore. But Jesus did not stay long on that side of the lake.

# Jairus' Daughter and the Sick Woman

It was morning. Jesus and His disciples were sailing back across the Sea of Galilee.

They looked towards the place where they were going to land. There was a crowd of people there, waiting for Jesus.

As Jesus stepped ashore they thronged around Him, welcoming Him, pleased they'd guessed correctly about His return. Then – suddenly – a man called Jairus came pushing through the crowd. His face was white and tense with anxiety.

Jairus was an important man – a ruler of the Synagogue – but now, in desperation, he threw himself down at Jesus' feet.

"Please!" Jairus cried. "Come to my house! My daughter is dying! She's only twelve years old! Please come!"

Gently, Jesus helped Jairus to his feet. "Of course I'll come," He said. They set out at once. Jairus wanted to run, but the crowds crushed around and hemmed them in. Thrusting his way through, Jairus turned to see if Jesus was following.

Jesus had stopped! He was standing still! He said, "Who touched Me?"

The people looked at Him in amazement. His disciple, Peter, said, "Master – all round You the people are pushing and touching You."

"Someone touched Me in a special way," Jesus insisted. "I felt power going out of Me."

Trembling, a woman knelt at His feet. "I touched You," she confessed. "I've been ill for twelve years, and no one could help me. But I knew if I just touched the hem of Your robe, I would be healed. And –" she added, her face beginning to light up – "I *am* healed! I know it!"

Jesus looked at her with great kindness. "Because you had faith in Me, you have been made well," He said. "Your faith has made you whole. Go in peace, and be free from your suffering."

Jairus stood, fretting and fuming. Why didn't Jesus *hurry*! There was no time to be lost!

But just as Jesus moved on again, Jairus saw some men coming from his house. A chill went through him. The men pushed their way through the crowd to him.

"Your daughter is dead," they said. "Don't trouble Jesus any more. It's too late."

Grief threatened to overwhelm Jairus. But Jesus had seen and heard. "Don't be afraid," He said. "Trust Me. Your daughter will be healed."

Then Jesus began to walk quickly towards Jairus' house. Jairus followed, hardly daring to hope. And yet... He *did* trust Jesus...

When they reached the house a

crowd of people was there already. Everyone was crying and wailing because the child was dead.

"Hush," said Jesus. "She *isn't* dead. She's only asleep."

"What?" they said. And they began to laugh at Him. Asleep, indeed! As if they couldn't tell whether or not a person was dead! She *had* died.

Jesus sent everyone out of the room except three of His disciples – Peter, James and John – and the girl's mother and father. Jairus clasped his hands together, looking down at his beloved daughter's face. Surely she *was* dead...

Quietly, Jesus went to her. He took hold of her hand. "Child – wake up!" He said gently.

The five people watching stood transfixed; for the girl who had been dead was starting to breathe again.

She stirred a little, opened her eyes, looked up at the faces of her father and mother – and at the face of Jesus.

And she sat up!

Next moment, she was standing up, perfectly well again. Still her parents gazed – not moving, not speaking.

Jesus smiled at them. "Give her something to eat!" He said.

The words were so everyday, so practical, that everyone began to come back to normal. Jairus hugged his daughter, while her mother rushed to get a meal ready. The girl had been so long without proper food, she must be starving!

Jesus looked at the three of them with great love in His eyes. "Don't tell anyone what happened here today," He said.

And He and His disciples left.

# Feeding the Five Thousand

Jesus had sent His disciples out into the villages nearby. They were to heal the sick, and tell everyone about God's Kingdom, while Jesus continued alone.

Now the disciples had returned, to report all that had happened. It had been exciting, but very tiring. Jesus, too, needed to rest for a while. But so many people kept coming to them for healing, or to talk, or to listen – Jesus and His disciples couldn't even have a meal in peace.

At last Jesus said to the twelve, "Come with Me. We'll go to a quiet place, to be by ourselves."

They went down to the shore, got into a boat, and set sail for the small town of Bethsaida. But someone had seen them go. Quickly, the message spread. People from the towns all around ran swiftly to get to the place where Jesus must land.

Jesus saw them waiting for Him; and He felt a great love and pity for them. They seemed to need Him so much. He couldn't bear to try to get away from them again...

He landed; and He and the disciples climbed a short way up a hillside. Now the people could see and hear Him better. He talked to them, telling them more about God and His Kingdom. He healed the sick people. And He told stories for the children.

The day passed. It was late in the afternoon, but the crowd was as huge as ever. The disciples began to worry. They imagined all these people trying to get home in the dark – stumbling over the rough ground, with no light other than from the stars. And they would be hungry, for they hadn't eaten all day... Surely Jesus hadn't noticed how near it was to evening...

They went to Him. "Master," they said, "this is a very lonely place, and it's going to be dark soon. Tell all these people to leave *now*, so that they can get food for themselves, and find somewhere to stay the night."

Jesus looked at their anxious faces. "*You* give them food to eat," He said.

"What?" cried Philip, one of the twelve. "It would take eight months of a man's wages to be able to buy enough bread to feed them all! Do You really mean us to spend that much money?"

"Find out how much food we have here already," said Jesus.

The disciples enquired amongst the people. And presently, Andrew came to Jesus, leading a small boy. "This boy has five small barley loaves and two small fishes," said Andrew. "That's all we've been able to find." He looked around hopelessly. "What use is *that*, amongst a crowd this size?"

Jesus said, "Tell everyone to sit down in groups. Groups of hundreds, and fifties."

The disciples looked at one another; then they obeyed. Soon, the people were sitting on the grass on the hillside. About *five thousand* people...

The boy watched. Jesus took the five small barley loaves, and gave thanks to God for them. Then He gave the loaves to the disciples to share out amongst the people...

Then Jesus took the fishes, gave thanks to God for them, and gave *them* to the disciples to share out.

And there was enough for everyone to eat as much as they wanted!

When the people were so full they couldn't eat another mouthful, Jesus said to the disciples, "Go round and gather up any leftovers, so that nothing is wasted."

The boy was amazed. The disciples, too, were amazed. For as they collected the scraps of food there was enough to fill twelve baskets...

Jesus saw how tired the disciples looked. "Go back to the boat, and go on ahead of Me," He said. "I'll tell the people it's time for them to leave."

Gladly, the weary disciples obeyed. But the people were not ready to be sent away. They were talking excitedly amongst themselves.

"Surely Jesus is the Prophet we have been waiting for! Let's make him our king!"

Jesus knew what they were saying; but it was not God's will for Him that He be king. Under cover of the near-darkness He left them, and made His way alone further up into the hills. There He began to pray.

Meanwhile, His disciples had gone down to the seashore...

# Jesus Walks on the Water

It was almost dark. The fishing boat lay waiting at the edge of the water. Some people stood close by,

watching as the disciples came towards it. They were surprised to see the disciples without Jesus.

The twelve climbed into the boat.

"Should we wait for Him?" one of them asked.

"No. He told us to go on without Him," the others replied. They were longing to get to bed.

They started to row. It was quite dark now. A strong wind was blowing against them, and the sea was rough. Wearily, the disciples pulled on the oars. It would have been hard going even if they had been fresh. Now, the journey seemed endless. They had been rowing for some time, but even so, tossed about on the waves, they had travelled little less than five kilometres.

The moon was trying to shine through the clouds. And then – quite suddenly – they looked. There was Jesus coming towards them, *walking on the water...*

The disciples froze on their oars, terrified. "It's a ghost!" they cried out.

At once Jesus spoke to them. "It's Me! Don't be afraid!"

The disciples peered, straining to see. And Peter said, "Master – if it's *really* You, tell me to walk on the water towards You!"

"Come!" said Jesus.

The disciples watched in silent awe

204

as Peter climbed over the side of the boat – and began to walk towards Jesus! He took a few steps in perfect safety. Then he suddenly realized what he was doing. He noticed the wind and the waves – and he was afraid. Immediately, he began to sink.

"Help! Help me, Master!" he cried.

Instantly, Jesus reached out and caught him. "You have so little faith!" He said. "Why did you doubt?"

Together they got into the boat. And at that same moment the wind ceased to blow, and the sea became calm.

In the moonlight, the disciples looked at Jesus. Reverently, they spoke. "Truly – You are the Son of God."

They crossed the Sea of Galilee, and came safely to the other side. And the next day, the people who had seen the disciples set off, said, "Jesus is over on the other shore. But He wasn't in the boat when it left here – and there was only one boat..."

205

# The Man Who Couldn't Hear

There was a man living in the territory of the Ten Towns who was deaf.

Life was hard for him. He could never hear the voices of people joking and laughing. He couldn't hear music, or bird-song, or stories.

And because he couldn't *hear* words, he couldn't learn to speak correctly; also, he may have had something wrong with his tongue.

So he had great difficulty in making himself understood. He couldn't easily ask for what he needed; or tell what had happened to him. He couldn't share good news, or be comforted when life was sad. He felt lonely; isolated; as if no one cared.

But some people *did* care. And they heard that Jesus – who healed the sick – was nearby.

Eagerly, they rushed to tell the deaf man. Panting, they found him. Then they stopped. *How* to tell him?

They stood in front of him, excitedly waving their arms about, crying, "Jesus is nearby. Jesus!"

Puzzled, the man tried to make out what they meant. Impatiently, they shouted, "Jesus! Quickly! Before He's gone!"

Still the man didn't understand. Then one of them seized his arm. "Come with us!" he signed.

Still puzzled, but aware of their excitement, the deaf man went with them.

As usual, there was a crowd around Jesus. But they stood back to let the little group get through. Jesus looked at them – at the eager faces of the little group; at the puzzled face of the deaf man.

"Please!" begged the people who had brought him. "This man is deaf. And he can't speak properly. If You will just touch him – he will be healed!"

Jesus looked at them again; at the crowd thronging around. Then, gently, He took the bewildered deaf man by the arm, and led him to one side, a little way apart from all the noise and confusion. The deaf man gazed at Jesus' face, trying desperately to understand. Jesus didn't try to speak to him. Instead, He put His fingers into the man's ears. The man nodded. His ears *were* the trouble...

Jesus touched the man's tongue. Again, the man nodded. He *couldn't* speak... Jesus had understood his problem, *and* had let him know. Here was someone he could *trust*...

Jesus looked up to Heaven. He groaned. Then He said, "Ephphatha!" which means, "Open up!"

At once the man's ears were clear. He could hear! He could hear perfectly! He could hear the voices of the crowd a little way off; the sound of the wind in the trees; the song of the birds! Joy surged through him. He tried to speak – and found he could! His tongue was working correctly!

The people who had brought him saw his glowing face; heard him using his voice! And they too were overjoyed.

Jesus smiled at them. "Don't tell anyone!" He said.

But they couldn't help it. They were so glad, they couldn't keep quiet about it. And people who had known the deaf man before were utterly amazed.

"Jesus does everything!" they said. "He can even make deaf people hear, and dumb people speak!"

The news about Jesus spread. And a group of ten sick men heard of Him...

207

# The Ten Lepers

Jesus was now making His way along the roads which bordered Samaria and Galilee. And ten men who had the dreaded disease of leprosy learnt He was going to pass quite close to the place where they were living.

Leprosy was dreaded because – once caught – no one knew how to cure it. The disease would eat away at whichever part of the body was affected. Fingers and toes could be lost; faces disfigured. The ugliness alone was enough to dread, without the added problems of trying to manage with only stumps of fingers or toes. And because leprosy showed up as white patches on the skin, it was impossible to hide it for very long. Every healthy person feared catching it; so lepers were forced to leave their homes and go and live outside the village.

They could never again kiss the people they loved, or hug their children; never mix with their former friends. Indeed, they soon began to dread meeting anyone, because of the fear on other people's faces when they saw a leper; and the way they would be shouted at to go away.

There was no hope. Lepers were utterly isolated and miserable. They were forced by law to wear torn clothes; to let their hair grow long and untidy; to cover the lower part of their faces; and to call out, "Unclean! Unclean!" if they saw anyone.

But *these* ten had heard that Jesus healed sick people... Only would He heal *them*? Would the crowds who always followed Him even let them get near enough to ask? One of the men – a Samaritan – was even more worried, for Jesus was a Jew; and for many years the Jews and the Samaritans had disliked and mistrusted each other.

But the lepers resolved to try...

They watched and waited near the road to a village. And sure enough, at last, they saw Jesus coming. Other people were with Him, as they'd expected. Not daring to attempt to get close, the lepers called out. "Jesus! Master! Help us!"

Jesus heard their voices, turned to look for them, and saw their troubled, desperate faces. He called back to them. "Go and let the priests examine you!"

The lepers were silent for a moment, looking at each other. Go and show themselves to a *priest*! They'd had to show themselves to a priest when they first caught the disease. It was the priests who decided which people *did* have leprosy, and must go and live outside the village. People only went *back* to the priests if they wanted to prove they were well, and didn't have leprosy after all. Yet Jesus *must* have seen the patches of leprosy still upon them...

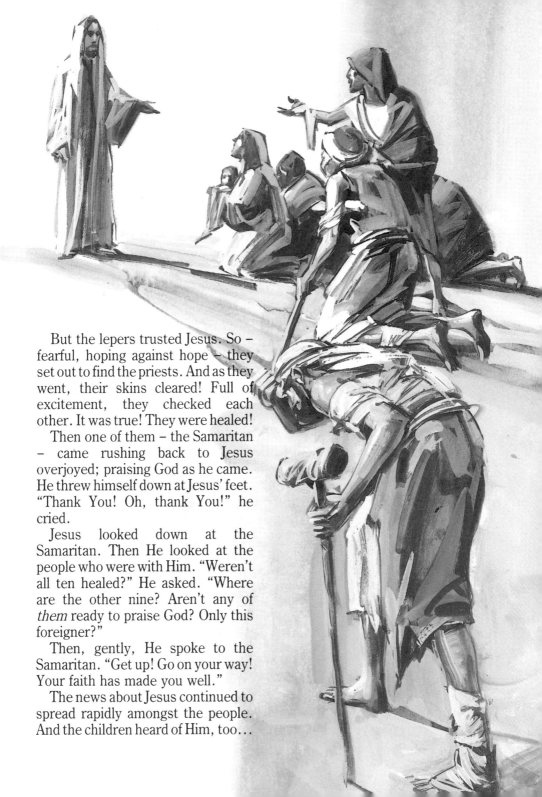

But the lepers trusted Jesus. So – fearful, hoping against hope – they set out to find the priests. And as they went, their skins cleared! Full of excitement, they checked each other. It was true! They were healed!

Then one of them – the Samaritan – came rushing back to Jesus overjoyed; praising God as he came. He threw himself down at Jesus' feet. "Thank You! Oh, thank You!" he cried.

Jesus looked down at the Samaritan. Then He looked at the people who were with Him. "Weren't all ten healed?" He asked. "Where are the other nine? Aren't any of *them* ready to praise God? Only this foreigner?"

Then, gently, He spoke to the Samaritan. "Get up! Go on your way! Your faith has made you well."

The news about Jesus continued to spread rapidly amongst the people. And the children heard of Him, too...

*Matthew 19 : 13–15; Mark 10 : 13–16, 32, 33; 20 : 17–19;*
*Luke 18 : 15–17, 31–34; Isaiah 53 : 7-12*

# The Children and Jesus

The children who were old enough to understand longed to see Jesus for themselves. And the mothers and fathers wanted to ask Jesus to bless their sons and daughters. But it wasn't easy to get small children safely through the crowds which usually surrounded Jesus.

One day, a group of parents and children came eagerly towards Jesus as He sat and rested for a while. This could be their chance! They could reach Him, talk to Him, listen to Him! Excitedly, the children tried to run on ahead.

But the disciples turned, and saw the little group. "Why are you trying to bother Jesus with all these children?" the disciples asked the parents, harshly. "He can't talk to you now!"

The disappointment was so great, the mothers and fathers stood for a moment in silence. After all their efforts to get here – to get their *children* here – they would have to go away...

But Jesus had heard the disciples' words; and He spoke angrily. "What are you doing? Let the children come to Me! Don't try to stop them! The Kingdom of Heaven belongs to such as these!"

He opened His arms wide; and the children ran to Him. He said to the people who were watching, "I tell you all – if you don't receive the Kingdom

in the same spirit as a child does, you'll *never* enter it!"

The parents were happy and smiling now. Jesus took each of the children into His arms, and blessed

them. The listening people tried to understand what He had said. They were to accept God's Kingdom in a spirit of trust, the way a young child trusts his or her parents.

Presently the mothers, fathers and children, happy now, went back to their homes. Jesus and His disciples continued on their way towards Jerusalem. He intended to be there for the Feast of the Passover. But the people who followed Him were afraid.

Jesus had been walking a little way in front of His disciples. But when He noticed their anxious faces, He called them to one side. He knew exactly what was troubling them. The chief priests and the Pharisees had often been angry at the things He had said and done. They'd made up their minds He wasn't the Son of God, the Messiah; but just an ordinary man. They were afraid that the people would try to make Him their king; that there would be trouble with the Romans; that they themselves would suffer. So they were just waiting for a chance to kill Jesus. And the disciples thought that if He went to Jerusalem, He would be walking into a trap.

"Listen." Jesus tried to explain. "We *are* going to Jerusalem. The Son of Man *will* be handed over to the chief priests and the teachers of the law. He will be condemned to death by them. They will hand Him over to the Roman soldiers, who will mock Him, torture Him, crucify Him. This *must* happen, just as the prophets foretold. But three days after He has been killed, the Son of Man will rise to life again."

The disciples listened; but they couldn't understand. They didn't know what He was talking about. They only knew He was quite set in His purpose; and that they loved Him. If *He* went to Jerusalem – so would they.

First, they had to pass through the city of Jericho, and, as usual, someone was waiting eagerly for Jesus to come.

# Bartimaeus

Bartimaeus lived in Jericho. He was blind.

There was no work he could do, so unless he was to starve, he had to sit all day by the roadside, begging for money.

As he sat there, he could tell by the sounds many things about the people passing by on the road. He could tell if they were hurrying or strolling; whether they were alone or in groups; if they were excited or sad. He caught many snatches of conversation. Some of the people knew him, and stopped to talk to him.

So Bartimaeus heard about Jesus: that He loved people; had done many wonderful things; that He *healed* people...

If only Bartimaeus could get to Jesus! It seemed impossible. It took

213

him all his time to feel his way along the streets of Jericho to his place here, just outside the gates; to the position he had chosen because so many people passed by on their way to and from Jerusalem...

That was it! Jesus was on His way to Jerusalem! He would be coming this way!

For a moment Bartimaeus was full of excitement. Then he began to think. Wherever Jesus went, there were crowds. How could a blind man possibly push his way through a crowd, to find a person he couldn't see?

Disappointment flooded through him. But – maybe – if he just sat here, and called out to Jesus... Only would he be able to make himself heard?

All through the long, hot, dusty days Bartimaeus sat by the roadside and worried. Then, at last, he heard the sounds of an excited crowd – distant at first, but getting closer.

"What's happening?" he called out.

"Jesus of Nazareth is coming!" a passer-by answered.

Bartimaeus' heart began to thump. He took a deep breath...listened for the crowd to reach him...be going by... Waited until he guessed Jesus was passing him...then – "Jesus!" he shouted. "Help me!"

"Sssh!" Sharply, people at the edge of the crowd hushed him. "Be quiet!"

Bartimaeus took no notice. "JESUS!" he shouted, even louder.

"JESUS, SON OF DAVID! HELP ME!"

Amidst all the noise and bustle, Jesus heard Bartimaeus. He looked round, and saw him. Saw that Bartimaeus was blind, unable to make his way through the crush.

"Bring that man to Me!" Jesus said.

Now hands were urging Bartimaeus to get up. Voices said, "Come on! Jesus wants you!"

Heart pounding, Bartimaeus threw off his cloak in case it should get in his way. He scrambled to his feet, and let himself be led into the midst of the crowd. The guiding hands let go of him; he knew he must be standing in front of Jesus.

He heard Jesus' voice. "What do you want Me to do for you?"

"Oh!" Bartimaeus replied. "If only I could see!"

Jesus answered, "Then see. Your faith has healed you."

And at once, light began to dazzle Bartimaeus. He put up a hand to shade his eyes. He could see the sunshine! He could see the trees! The sky! The faces of the crowd! He could see *Jesus.*

No longer would he have to sit begging by the roadside! He'd never sit there again! His sight was perfect!

Joyfully, Bartimaeus gave thanks to God. Then he joined the crowd following Jesus, rejoicing at every fresh thing he saw.

And when the crowd saw Bartimaeus, they all praised God, and were glad.

Meanwhile, in Jericho, someone else was longing to see Jesus...

# Zacchaeus

In Jericho lived a tax-collector called Zacchaeus. Zacchaeus was rich, but much of his money had come from cheating people; collecting more money than was rightfully due in taxes. Almost all Jews hated tax-collectors. Zacchaeus had almost stopped inviting anyone to his house for a meal. He had few friends. He was very lonely.

One day, as he sat by himself, he heard the sounds of many people passing by his house. What could be going on? Zacchaeus went outside to find out. The road was thronged with people. Zacchaeus listened to their excited voices. "Jesus is coming this way!" they were saying.

Zacchaeus had heard of Jesus. He had heard that Jesus was friendly, even towards tax-collectors...

Zacchaeus wondered what He looked like. He longed to see Him...

But Zacchaeus was a very short man. He was right at the back of the crowds now lining the road; and they wouldn't let him through. When he tried to squeeze to the front, they glanced down, saw who it was, and moved even tighter together.

Zacchaeus felt desperate. He could tell by the sounds of excitement that Jesus was getting closer – was almost here! He would pass by without Zacchaeus getting even a glimpse of Him! Unless –

Zacchaeus had an idea. Further along the road was a sycamore tree...

Zacchaeus ran; hot; perspiring in his anxiety. Breathless, he reached the tree. He was in time. Panting, he began to climb. He'd not climbed a tree for years, but he hadn't forgotten how to do it... In fact, it was easier now that he could reach further...

Soon, the wealthy tax-collector was perched in the branches of the tree. Now he had a perfect view! He could see right down the road. He could see the crowd coming towards him. And – in their midst – he could see Jesus. Somehow, he knew at once which one was Jesus...

Hardly breathing, Zacchaeus watched the crowd getting closer and closer. Now they were passing by the sycamore tree... Some of them were right underneath him... *Jesus* was almost there...

And suddenly, Jesus stopped. He looked up – straight at Zacchaeus. And He spoke. "Zacchaeus! Come down! Today I must stay at your house!"

Zacchaeus took a moment or two to realize what Jesus had said. Then, filled with excitement and joy, he came scrambling down. Jesus wanted to stay with *him*!

"You're very welcome!" he cried breathlessly. "It's just along here!"

*Now* Zacchaeus was not squeezing along the back of the crowd. He was leading the way, with Jesus beside him. The people had watched everything. They began to mutter angrily. "Look at that! Jesus is actually going to visit the house of that cheat!"

Zacchaeus heard the words. He stopped. "Master," he said, "I'll give half of my belongings to the poor. And if I've cheated anyone – I'll give him back four times as much!"

There was a gasp of surprise from the people. Jesus said to them, "Salvation has come to this house today. This man, too, is a son of Abraham! And remember – the Son of Man has come especially to seek out people who have done wrong, so that they can believe in Him, and be sorry for their wrong doing. And God will forgive them."

Zacchaeus heard the words; and felt happier than he had ever done. Gladly, he led the way into his house.

When Jesus had visited Zacchaeus, He continued on His way towards Jerusalem.

And people began to think of other things He had taught them.

Some of the things Jesus taught  *Excerpts from Matthew : 5; 6; 7*

# The Sermon on the Mount

One day, when Jesus saw the crowds following Him, He went on to the mountain side, and sat down. People gathered all around Him; and He taught them. Here are some of His sayings:

Happy and blessed are those who know they must trust in God; for the Kingdom of Heaven shall be theirs.

Blessed are those who mourn, and are sad; for they shall be comforted.

Blessed are those who are not proud, but humble; for they shall inherit the whole earth.

Blessed are those who greatly desire to do right; for they shall be satisfied.

Blessed are those who are merciful towards their enemies; for mercy shall be shown to them.

Blessed are those whose thoughts are pure; for they shall see God.

Blessed are those who make peace; for they shall be called the children of God.

Blessed are those who suffer for what they know to be right; for theirs is the Kingdom of Heaven.

If men persecute you, and call you names, and tell lies about you because you love Me – rejoice, and be glad; for your reward in Heaven will be great.

If you are My followers, you are like salt, which gives flavour to food. Or you are like a light for the whole world. So don't hide your light where it can't be seen! When you do good, people will see it; and they will give praise to God, your Father.

You have been told, 'You shall not kill'. But *I* say to you, thoughts which make you *feel* like murdering someone are also wrong.

You have been told, 'An eye for an eye, a tooth for a tooth'; to obtain vengeance equal to the wrong done to you. But *I* say to you, do not take revenge on anyone who acts wrongly against you.

You have been told, 'Love your friends, hate your enemies'. But *I* say to you, love your enemies. Pray for those who do you wrong. This way you will become sons and daughters of your Heavenly Father. For He makes His sun to shine and rain to fall on the good and bad alike. Why should God give you a reward for loving the people who love you? Even tax-collectors do that! And if you talk only to your friends, you've done nothing special...

If you help those who are in need, don't tell everyone about it. Your Father in Heaven will see; and He will reward you.

When you pray, talk quietly to God. He is your Father, and knows what you need even before you ask Him.

Pray like this: Our Father, which art in Heaven, hallowed be Thy name. Thy Kingdom come, Thy will be done, on earth as it is in Heaven. Give us this day our daily bread. And forgive us our debts as we forgive our debtors. And lead us not into temptation, but deliver us from evil. For Thine is the Kingdom, the power and the glory, for ever. Amen.

And don't worry! Your Heavenly Father knows what you need. Put His Kingdom first – try to do as He wants – and everything you need will be given to you. Don't worry about tomorrow. Tomorrow has enough worries of its own.

Don't judge other people, saying they are right or wrong, or you will be judged yourselves. It's as if you saw a speck of sawdust in someone else's eye, and never noticed a huge plank of wood in your own!

If your son asked for bread, would you give him a stone? Or if he asked you for fish, would you give him a snake? If *you* know how to give good gifts to *your* children, how much more will your Heavenly Father give good gifts to those who ask Him!

Always treat other people the way you would like *them* to treat *you*. This is what the law is about.

As they listened, the people were amazed; because Jesus taught them with certainty, not in the usual way of the teachers of the law.

He finished His teaching that day by telling – as He often did – a parable, a story with a secret meaning...

# The House on the Rock

This is the parable Jesus told at the end of His sermon on the mount.

There were two men. Each one wanted to build a house. The first man understood how important it was for his house to have good, firm foundations; so he dug deep into the ground until he came to solid rock. There he laid the foundations, and built his house on them.

Presently a storm began to blow. The wind howled around the house. The rain poured down. The rivers overflowed their banks. Water swished roughly around the walls of the house, and the wind battered against them.

But the house was built on strong foundations, and it did not fall.

Jesus said, "Anyone who hears My words, and acts on them, is like the wise man who built his house on the rock. When troubles come, that person will not give in, but will stand firm."

The second man cared nothing about having strong foundations for *his* house. He built it on sand.

When the storm came, the flood waters rose. The wind hurled itself against the house. Without good foundations the house had no chance. It fell down with a mighty crash.

Jesus said, "Anyone who hears My words and does *not* act on them is like the foolish man who built his house upon the sand. When troubles come, that person will not be able to manage, and will give in under them."

Jesus told other parables...

221

# The Sower

Wherever Jesus went, crowds of people gathered round, wanting to listen to Him. He often told them parables – stories with secret meanings which they could work out. This is another of the parables of Jesus.

A farmer went out to sow some seed. As he walked up and down his field, he scattered the grain in handfuls from the basket slung over his shoulder.

Some seed fell on the path, where it was either trampled into the ground or swooped on by the birds, who pecked it up hungrily.

Some seed fell on a rock, where the earth was shallow. The seeds sprouted, but the young corn could not put down roots, and the plants soon withered and died in the sun.

Some seed fell amongst thorn bushes. The corn grew – but so did the thorns. They choked the corn, and soon those plants died too.

But some seed fell on the good rich earth. The plants put down deep, strong roots. The corn grew tall, and ripened in the sun. By the time of the harvest it was a splendid crop – a hundred times more than the farmer had sown.

Jesus' disciples couldn't work out the meaning of this parable, so they asked Him to explain it.

The seed stands for God's word. Some people listen to God's word carelessly. The Devil can easily make them forget what they've heard. That is the seed which fell on the path.

Some people listen gladly, and believe for a short time. But as soon as any trouble comes, they stop believing. That is the seed which fell on the rock, and had no roots.

Some people hear the message, but their minds are so full of other thoughts, there's no room for God's word. That is the seed which fell among thorns.

But some people listen to God's word, believe it, and try to live as God wants. That is the seed which fell on good ground, and gave a fine harvest.

# The Good Samaritan

A lawyer wanted to test Jesus with a difficult question.

"Master," he said, "what must I do if I am to inherit eternal life? To live forever in God's Kingdom?"

Jesus knew why the lawyer asked the question. He turned it back to the questioner. "What does the *law* tell you about this?"

The lawyer answered, "I must love the Lord my God with all my heart and with all my soul and with all my strength; and I must love my neighbour as much as I love myself."

"That's right," said Jesus. "If you do that, you will live."

But the lawyer wanted to prove to the people listening that he hadn't asked a *simple* question. How could he make it more tricky? He thought quickly. "But – who *is* my neighbour?" he asked.

Jesus answered with a parable.

Once, a man was going down from Jerusalem to Jericho. The road was lonely, and dangerous for travellers. Alongside it were rocks behind which robbers often lurked, waiting to pounce on unwary travellers.

The man hurried along, glancing fearfully around as he went. But it was no use. Suddenly a band of robbers sprang out. They knocked him to the ground, stripped him of his clothes, stole all that he had been carrying, then disappeared back amongst the rocks, leaving him lying by the roadside, half dead.

For a long time the man lay in the hot sun, too weak and injured to move, hoping desperately that someone would come and help him.

At last, he heard footsteps approaching. Feebly, he raised his head to see who was coming...

It was a priest! Surely a priest would help! Step – step – step – step. The poor injured man could hardly *believe* it. The priest had walked by on the other side!

The man's head throbbed more painfully than ever. The sun beat down. He longed for a drink of water...for someone to come and help him. His eyes closed.

Dimly, he heard more footsteps. As they neared, he opened his eyes. A Levite was coming! A servant of the Temple. Surely someone who served God in the Temple would help! Yes...the Levite was coming over...bending down...looking at him...

And then the Levite straightened himself up and walked on.

The injured man groaned in despair. He would *die* here, by the roadside...

More footsteps. The clip, clop, clip, clop of a donkey's hooves. Once more the man made the effort to open his eyes; to see who was coming... He sank back with another groan. It

was a foreigner. A Samaritan. Everyone knew that Samaritans were *useless*... certainly no friends of the Jews. No use expecting help from *him*. The man closed his eyes, all hope gone.

But the footsteps slowed. The donkey clip clopped to a halt. The injured man felt gentle hands touching him. He looked up. The Samaritan was helping him! Bathing his wounds with oil to soothe them and wine as an antiseptic. Bandaging the hurt places as best he could. Offering the injured man a drink of cool, clear water...holding it to his lips...supporting his head as he drank...

The Samaritan refused to leave the man lying by the roadside. The injured man tried to stand; but he was too weak and ill. His head spun; if the Samaritan had not supported him he would have fallen.

"It's no use," he groaned. But the Samaritan led him to the patiently waiting donkey; helped him on to its back. Then, slowly, carefully, the donkey picked its way along the stony road until they came to an inn.

"We'll rest here for the night," said the Samaritan.

He led the man inside, and took care of him, attending to his wounds once more, and bringing him food and drink.

But by the morning, the injured man was still not well enough to continue with his journey.

"No matter," said the Samaritan. "You must stay here until you are fit to go on."

And, knowing the robbers had stolen all the man's money, the Samaritan spoke to the innkeeper.

"Here are two pieces of silver. Take care of him. If it costs more than this, I'll pay you the rest when I come back this way."

The lawyer had been listening intently to the story.

"Now," said Jesus, "which one of those was a neighbour to the man who was robbed and beaten?"

The lawyer answered, "The one who was kind to him, and helped him."

And Jesus said, "Go, and follow his example."

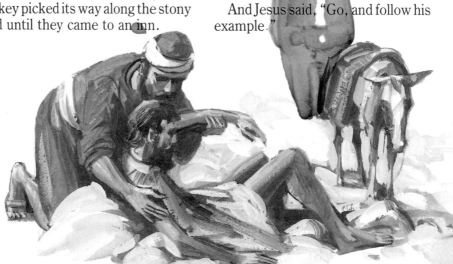

# The Lost Sheep, and the Lost Coin

The Pharisees and the teachers of the law were muttering amongst themselves. "Just look at that! Jesus is talking to tax-collectors, and people who have done wrong! *Again*! He's even *eating* with them!"

Jesus heard what they said. And He told them a parable.

"Imagine a shepherd who has a hundred sheep. When he counts them one evening, he finds only ninety-nine. One of his sheep is lost! What does he do? He leaves the ninety-nine where they are safe, and goes in search of the one. And he will *keep* searching. Searching – searching – weary – footsore; but never giving up. And at last he finds his sheep that was lost. He is full of joy! The sheep is tired, near exhaustion. So, tenderly, the shepherd picks it up, puts it over his shoulders, and carries it home. And he calls out to his neighbours, 'Look! Be glad with me! I've found my sheep that was lost!'"

Jesus looked at the Pharisees and the teachers of the law.

"I say to you – God is like this shepherd. And there will be more joy in Heaven over one person who realizes he has been doing wrong, is sorry, and changes his ways, than there will ever be over ninety-nine good people who were doing right all the time."

The Pharisees and teachers of the law were listening; frowning, displeased. Jesus told another parable, trying to make His meaning clearer.

"Imagine a woman who has ten pieces of silver. Suddenly she realizes she has lost one of the coins. What will she do? She is very distressed. With shaking hands, she lights the lamp, placing it so that its light shines into every corner of her house. She fetches her broom and sweeps carefully, searching everywhere, until at last she sees her coin, glinting in the light of the lamp!

She snatches up her coin, holding it safe, calling to her friends and neighbours, 'Come in! Let's celebrate! I lost my coin, but now I've found it! Be glad with me!'"

And Jesus said to the listening people, "I tell you, there is joy amongst the angels of God over one person who is sorry for his wrong-doing."

And He told another parable about this...

# The Prodigal Son

This is another of the parables of Jesus.

Once a man had two sons. The older son was hard working and obedient. But the younger son never wanted to work; never wanted to do as he was told; and was never content.

"It's so *boring* at home!" he complained.

He knew his father was rich, and owned a lot of property. He also knew that when his father died, everything would be shared out between himself and his brother. But who knew how long it would be before *that* happened? Why should he have to wait for his father to *die* before he could enjoy himself?

So – not caring about his father's feelings at all – he demanded, "Give me my share of everything *now*!"

The father loved his son very much. He guessed the lad might leave home as soon as he had enough money, and he knew how much he would miss him. But the youth was old enough to go. The father didn't want to *force* him to stay by keeping him short of money.

So the father divided everything fairly between his two sons.

"Great!" thought the younger one. And soon after, he collected up everything he owned, and went off to a distant land.

People soon found out he had a lot of money. They came to his parties, accepted his presents, and pretended to be his friends.

For a while the young man enjoyed himself. He bought whatever he wanted, and did just as he liked. But soon the money was gone. His new 'friends' went, too. Worse. There was a famine in the land.

Now the young man was quite alone, with no money, no food, no friends, no family. He tried to get a job; but he'd never learned how to do anything properly. No one would employ him, until at last a man offered him work looking after pigs.

The lad took the job. No one spoke to him. No one cared about him. His clothes were in rags; and he was so hungry he wished he could share the pigs' food.

One day, as he sat watching the pigs snuffling and rooting around, he began to think about home. He remembered how kind his father was. He remembered that even the servants had enough to eat.

"I don't deserve to be called a son any more," he said to himself, "but perhaps my father would give me a job... I'll go back and ask him."

So the youth set out on the long walk home. Weary, half-starving, footsore, he trudged along. Maybe his father wouldn't let him into the house at all. Maybe his father had

forgotten all about him by now...

But far from forgetting, his father had never stopped watching for him, peering down the road every day, hoping...hoping...Missing his son. *Wanting* him back.

And now, in the distance, a thin, shabby figure appeared, limping along. Could it be...? The father strained his eyes, shading them against the sun.

Yes! Yes! It wasn't the finely dressed young man who'd gone marching off many months ago; but it was his son, all the same!

The father opened his arms and ran down the road.

The youth could hardly believe it. His father was hugging him, welcoming him, overjoyed to see him!

The son tried to say how sorry he was he'd done wrong; and to explain he only expected to be treated as a servant now.

His father was already calling to the servants. "Hurry! Bring my son fresh clothes! The best we have! And get a feast ready! I'm so happy! It was as if my son was dead; but now he's alive again!"

So they began to have a party. The elder son, coming back to the house, heard music and laughter. He called to a servant, "What's happening?"

The servant explained, ending, "Now your brother is back, there's a great celebration!"

"Celebration!" cried the older brother. He was so furiously jealous, he refused to even go inside the house.

The father came hurrying out to him, because he loved both his sons equally. "Come to the party!" he cried.

The older son answered angrily. "I've stayed here and worked hard for you all these years, and you've never given *me* a party! *He* takes half your money, goes off, wastes it, and then when he's got nothing left he comes home. And you have a *party*!"

"Son," said his father, "everything I have is yours! The party isn't for your brother, it's for all of us! It's right to be glad and celebrate; because he was lost to us, and now he's found."

Jesus said God is like the father in the story. He never stops loving us. He's ready to forgive everyone who is sorry they have done wrong. And He is *overjoyed* when everything is well again.

# The Midnight Visitor

Jesus was trying to explain more about prayer to His disciples. He told them a parable.

"It's midnight. You're at home. Suddenly, there's a knock on the door. You open it – and standing there is a friend of yours. He's on a journey, and he's stopped at your house for a rest and a meal. You welcome him gladly, invite him in – and then you realize. You don't have a *thing* to give him to eat! It's the middle of the night! Where can you get food at this hour?

"You think desperately – and you remember your friend along the road.

"Quickly, you run to his house. It's in total darkness. But you bang on the door. You call out to him. 'Please! Will you lend me three loaves of bread? A friend of mine has turned up unexpectedly, and I haven't got any food for him!'

"You wait. After a moment, you hear a sleepy voice from inside the house.

"'Go away! Stop bothering me! The door's locked for the night. I'm in bed, and so are all my family. I can't get up *now* and give you bread!'

"What will you do?

"You don't go away. You keep on knocking, and calling to him. At last you hear him stumbling about in the pitch darkness inside his home. He lights the lamp. He comes to the door. And he gives you the bread, because you wouldn't stop asking."

Jesus' disciples listened to the story, wondering about its meaning. Jesus said to them, "In your prayers, ask, and keep on asking. If you – being ordinary human beings – know how to give good things to him that asks, how much more will *God* give good gifts to *you*! So ask. And if it is for something God knows will be good for you, you will receive it."

# The Talents

Jesus told another parable.

A rich man was going on a journey. It wasn't practicable to take his money with him; so he called his three servants to him, to leave the money in their charge.

To the first servant he handed five talents of money; to the second he handed two talents; and to the third he handed one talent. Each talent was worth several hundred pounds. The rich man had divided up his money according to how he thought each servant would be able to manage it.

Then he went off on his journey.

The first servant took the five talents, and went to trade with them.

He did so well he had soon doubled the amount of money trusted to him.

The second servant also traded with his money. He, too, doubled the amount.

But the third servant thought, "Suppose I try to trade with this money? I might lose it all! Then my master will be furiously angry with me! Anyway – it's such a small amount. It can't matter much *what* I do, as long as I don't lose it. I'll just keep it safe. I'll hide it!"

And he went and dug a hole in the ground secretly; and there he buried his talent.

After a long time, the rich man came back from his travels. His three servants came to him. The first said, "Master, I traded with the five talents you trusted to me; and I made five more. Here are ten talents."

The rich man said, "Well done, good and faithful servant! You've been trustworthy over a few things. Now I will put you in charge of many! Come and share my happiness!"

Then the second servant said, "Master, I took the two talents you trusted to me, and I made two more. Here are the four talents."

And the rich man said, "Well done, good and faithful servant! You've been trustworthy over a few things. Now I will put you in charge of many! Come and share my happiness!"

The third servant had been watching. Now, reluctantly, he came forward. He could see he had to make some excuse...

"Master," he said, "I knew you were a hard man. You gather harvests which you haven't sown. I was afraid to do anything with the

money, in case I lost it. So I kept it in a hole in the ground. Here it is."

The rich man was furious. "You bad, lazy servant! In all this time you have done no work for me at all! You knew I reaped where I hadn't sown, did you! Then why didn't you at least put my money in the bank, where it would have earned interest for me? You should have been braver, and used your chance to serve me!"

And he ordered, "Take that talent away from him, and give it to the servant who has ten! For to every person who has something, more will be given, until he has plenty. A person who uses his opportunities will find his life growing richer and richer. But a person who wastes his chances will have nothing. His life will grow even poorer than it was before. Now take this useless servant, and send him away!"

Jesus is like the master in the story. His going on a journey is like Jesus ascending into Heaven, and leaving His followers to continue the work of increasing God's Kingdom on earth. They can do this by using their special gifts or abilities in the way God wants – no matter how small or unimportant their particular gift may seem to be.

235

# Jesus as the Good Shepherd

Jesus moved steadily on towards Jerusalem, although He knew what would happen to Him there. On the way, He tried to explain more about Himself to His disciples.

They were used to seeing shepherds caring for sheep. They knew that if danger from a lion or a bear threatened the flock, a good shepherd would try to protect his animals. He would be ready to die in the attempt, rather than leave them to their fate.

Also, the disciples had seen shepherds searching for fresh pastures for their flocks; finding cool streams where they could drink in safety; searching for lost lambs; watching tenderly over the ewes; knowing each animal individually.

So the disciples understood something of Jesus' love and care for *them* when He said, "I am the Good Shepherd. The Good Shepherd gives his life for his sheep... I am the Good Shepherd, and I know My sheep. And they know Me. As God the Father knows Me, so I know the Father... And I lay down My life for the sheep.

"No man takes it from Me. I lay it down Myself. I have power to lay it down; and I have power to take it up. This I have been told to do by My Father."

Many people heard the words Jesus said; but they argued amongst themselves over what He meant. Even the twelve did not understand at that time. And some of the people grew angry.

"He is speaking blasphemy!" they said. "He is making Himself out to be God!"

And they wanted to stone Him.

But Jesus slipped away from them. He left Judea and went back across the River Jordan. And many of the people there believed in Him.

But He did not stay there long...

# Mary, Martha and Lazarus

In the village of Bethany, about three kilometres from Jerusalem, on the side of the Mount of Olives, lived three friends of Jesus – Mary, Martha, and their brother Lazarus.

Martha had often invited Jesus to stay at their house. Once when He came she had bustled about, getting a meal ready, trying to make everything specially nice for their visitor; making herself hot, flustered and cross.

And she was even more cross because her sister Mary wasn't helping at all – just sitting there, listening to Jesus! It wasn't fair!

For a while Martha toiled alone. Then words burst from her. "Master – my sister is leaving me to do all the work! Don't You care? She should be helping me! *You* tell her!"

Jesus had answered gently, "Martha – you're worrying about many things. But they're not really as important as the thing which Mary has chosen to do. I won't take it from her."

Then Martha had realized that listening to Jesus, talking to Him, was more important than getting special meals ready, or being over fussy about the housework.

Jesus thought of them as His good friends. Now, as He walked with His disciples, a man hurried up to Him.

"There's a message for You from Mary and Martha!" the man said urgently. "Your friend Lazarus is very ill!"

Jesus said quietly, "Lazarus must die from this sickness… God's glory will be shown because of it."

237

And though He loved all three of them very much, Jesus did not set off at once for Bethany. Instead, He remained where He was for two more days. Then He said to His disciples, "Let's go back to Judea."

They answered in alarm, "The people there want to stone You!"

But He answered, "Our friend Lazarus is asleep. I am going to wake him."

The disciples were puzzled. Surely, if you were ill, sleep was a good thing?

"Master – if he sleeps, he'll get better," they said.

Jesus saw they didn't understand; so He spoke plainly. "Lazarus is dead. And because of what you will now see, I'm glad I wasn't there. Because now, you will believe."

The disciples looked at one another. Thomas was absolutely certain Jesus would be stoned to death if they went. Even so, he said, "Come on! Let's all go, so that we can die there with Him!"

By the time they neared Bethany, Lazarus had been buried for four days. Many of the Jews had come to comfort Mary and Martha. Now, some of them saw Jesus and His disciples coming along the road towards the village, and rushed to tell the sisters.

Mary remained sitting, quiet and still. But Martha couldn't bear to wait for Jesus to arrive. She hurried out of the house, and ran to meet Him while He was still outside the village. As soon as she reached Him, she cried out, "Lord – if You'd been here, my brother wouldn't have died!"

Then, a little more calmly, hoping against hope, she added, "But I know that God can do whatever You ask Him...even now..."

Jesus' eyes were full of sympathy and understanding. "Your brother will rise to life again," He said.

Martha answered falteringly. "I know he will rise to life in the resurrection, on the last day," she said.

Quietly but clearly, Jesus said, "*I am the resurrection and the life. He that believes in Me, though he were dead, yet shall he live. And whoever lives and believes in Me shall never die. Do you believe this?*"

Martha met his eyes steadily. Quietly, calmly, she replied, "Yes, Lord. I believe You are the Christ, the Son of God, come into the world."

When she had said this, she slipped away, back to the house.

"Mary," she whispered, "Jesus is almost here. He wants to see you."

There was something different about Martha, a kind of excitement... Mary roused herself from her grief, and hurried out to meet Jesus. The Jews who had been in the house with her, trying to comfort her, said, "See how quickly she moved! She must have gone to mourn at Lazarus' grave. We'd better go after her."

So they followed.

Mary almost ran along the road towards Jesus. Sobbing, she reached Him, threw herself down at His feet, and used exactly the same words as Martha.

"Lord – if You'd been here, my brother wouldn't have died!"

When Jesus saw how she wept, and that her friends wept also, He was distressed. "Where have you buried him?" He asked.

"Come and see," they answered. And as they led Him to the place, Jesus wept. Some of the watching Jews said, "Jesus must have loved

Lazarus very much!" But others said, "He could make blind men see! Couldn't He have stopped Lazarus dying?"

Now Jesus had reached the tomb. It was a cave, with a large stone rolled across the entrance to close it.

Jesus said, "Take away the stone."

There was a pause. Then Martha said, "Lord – by now the body will smell. He's been dead for four days..."

Jesus answered her. "Didn't I say that if you believed, you would see God's glory?"

So – hesitantly at first – not quite knowing what to expect – the people moved the stone away.

Jesus spoke to God. "Father, I thank You because You have heard Me. I know You hear Me always; but I am speaking these words aloud so that all the people standing here may *know* that You sent Me."

Jesus finished His prayer. Then He called loudly, "Lazarus! Come out here!"

And the man that had been dead came out! His hands and feet were still wrapped in grave clothes; and his face was still covered by a cloth.

The people stood silent, awestruck.

"Help him off with those grave clothes!" Jesus said. "And let him go!"

And they did.

Then very many of the Jews who had seen all this believed that Jesus was indeed the Messiah, the Son of God.

But some of them went to the chief priests and the Pharisees, and told them what had happened.

The chief priests and the Pharisees called an urgent meeting of their special court, the Sanhedrin.

"He's got to be stopped!" they cried. "If we let Him go on like this, *everyone* will believe in Him! The Romans will come and destroy us – our Temple – our whole nation!"

"Better *one* man should die!" said Caiaphas, the High Priest, meaningfully.

From that day on, the chief priests and the Pharisees plotted to kill Jesus.

Jesus, knowing this, went secretly to a village called Ephraim. And there He stayed until the time was right for what He knew must happen...

# Palm Sunday

Now it was nearly time for the Festival of the Passover. Many people were going to Jerusalem to prepare themselves for it, as was the custom. They kept looking for Jesus amongst the crowds in the Temple.

"Will He come, do you think?" they asked each other. "Probably not. He *must* know about the command from the Pharisees and the chief priests that if anyone knows where He is, they are to report it. Those chief priests and Pharisees are just *waiting* for a chance to arrest Him…"

Jesus did indeed know of the command. But it did not change His

mind. He set out from Ephraim with His disciples.

As they came near to a village called Bethphage, on the Mount of Olives, He said to two of them, "Go into the village. You'll see a donkey tied up there. You'll know which donkey I mean because she'll have a young colt beside her – a colt which no one has ridden yet. I want you to untie the colt, and bring it here to Me."

The disciples nodded. It was better, they thought, for Jesus to stay out of sight.

Jesus went on, "If anyone asks you

241

what you're doing, just say, 'The Master needs the colt, and will send it back again soon.'"

The disciples nodded again. But they were puzzled. Why did Jesus need the donkey?

Later, they remembered some words which the prophets of long ago had spoken. They had foretold that the King of the Jews would come to His people humbly, riding on the colt of a donkey...

But now they went into Bethphage, as Jesus had asked them. Sure enough, there was the colt, tied up exactly as Jesus had said. They untied it.

Some people who had been watching them suspiciously called out, "Hey! What are you doing?"

The disciples answered, "The Master needs it, and will send it back soon."

It sounded like a code message. The people were silent, and the disciples led the colt away.

Jesus was waiting for them. When the disciples realized He was going to ride on it, they spread their cloaks on the colt's back, to make a saddle.

A crowd had begun to gather. Word spread as quickly as ever.

"Jesus is coming!"

People threw their cloaks down in the road so that Jesus might ride over them. Some people cut branches from the palm trees, and spread *them* in the road, or waved them like banners.

Now, as Jesus and His disciples moved forward, with Jesus riding on the donkey, there was a crowd in front and behind. People were shouting, "Hosanna! Blessed is He that comes in the name of the Lord! Hosanna to the Son of David! Hosanna in the highest!"

Many people in the crowd still didn't understand that Jesus' real purpose was to tell them about God's Kingdom. By riding on a donkey and not a war horse, Jesus tried to tell the people that He was not a conquering king.

So Jesus returned to Jerusalem; not sneaking in quietly, afraid of the plots of the chief priests and the Pharisees – but openly, courageously, in the middle of a cheering crowd.

As they entered the city streets, people already there were asking, "Who *is* this?"

And Jesus' followers replied proudly, "This is Jesus! Jesus of Nazareth!"

And Jesus went, as the custom was, to the Temple...

# Cleansing the Temple

When Jesus reached the Temple Courts, He stood still, anger rising within Him as He saw what was happening.

Young goats and lambs stood trembling in pens. They were waiting to be bought and used as sacrifices. Caged doves and pigeons were there also.

And there were the money-changers – men who sat at tables with piles of coins in front of them, ready to change money for the people who wanted to pay the Temple tax.

As Jesus watched, He saw the money-changers were cheating. Giving less change than was due, to people who weren't able to work out the proper amount for themselves – or who were afraid to argue even if they realized what was happening.

Jesus had to show that this was wrong. Besides, the Temple must be kept for the worship of God and not for buying and selling. He scattered the coins, so that they rolled *everywhere*. He overturned the tables. The money-changers sprang to their feet. Jesus overturned their stools also.

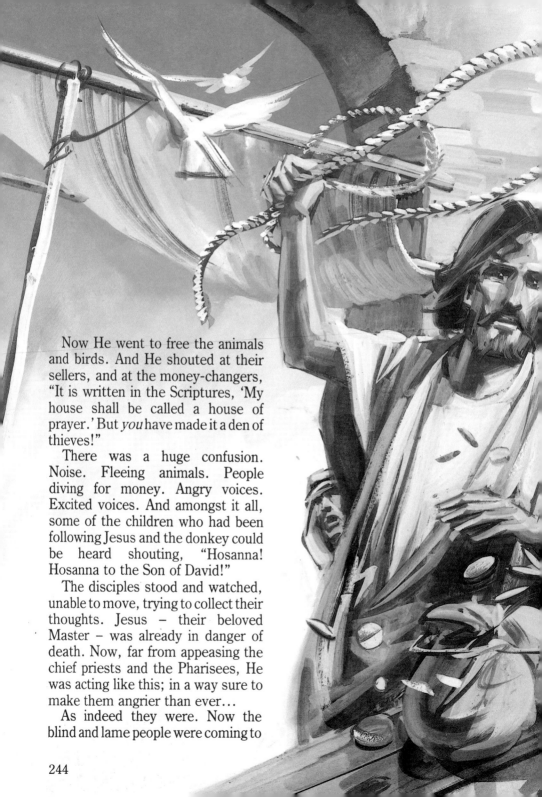

Now He went to free the animals and birds. And He shouted at their sellers, and at the money-changers, "It is written in the Scriptures, 'My house shall be called a house of prayer.' But *you* have made it a den of thieves!"

There was a huge confusion. Noise. Fleeing animals. People diving for money. Angry voices. Excited voices. And amongst it all, some of the children who had been following Jesus and the donkey could be heard shouting, "Hosanna! Hosanna to the Son of David!"

The disciples stood and watched, unable to move, trying to collect their thoughts. Jesus – their beloved Master – was already in danger of death. Now, far from appeasing the chief priests and the Pharisees, He was acting like this; in a way sure to make them angrier than ever...

As indeed they were. Now the blind and lame people were coming to

244

Jesus, begging for healing. And He healed them, there, in the Temple. The chief priests and Pharisees dared not touch Jesus for the moment. They were afraid of the crowd turning against them...

The children were still shouting, "Hosanna to the Son of David!" At last the Pharisees could let out some of their anger. On the *children*!

"Don't You hear what they're saying?" they demanded. "Tell them to stop shouting in the Temple!"

"Certainly I hear them," Jesus replied. "Haven't you read the Scriptures where this was foretold? 'Out of the mouths of babies and children you shall hear perfect praise.'"

Again, Jesus was making them look as if *they* – who were supposed to be the experts – hadn't studied the Scriptures properly. He went on, "If the people hadn't called out, even the stones would have taken up the cry."

And the Pharisees and chief priests said amongst themselves, "It's no use. It's as we said before. We're not succeeding in stopping Him at all. Next, He'll be leading the people to revolt. He *must* be killed. We'll have to capture Him secretly."

It was getting late in the day now. Jesus took his twelve disciples, and they left the noise and bustle of Jerusalem to go to the village of Bethany for the night.

And it was in a house at Bethany that a beautiful thing happened...

# Supper at Bethany

It was evening when Jesus and His disciples reached Bethany. Simon, who had been a leper, invited them to supper at his house. Some of Jesus' other friends were there too.

As the guests reclined at the table, a woman came into the room. In her hands she held an alabaster jar of precious perfume. Everyone stopped talking to watch her. There was something about the way she looked – the sorrow on her face...

Quietly, the woman went over to Jesus. Gently, reverently, she poured the perfume over His head and His feet. Then she dried His feet with her hair.

The lovely scent of the perfume filled the room. The guests looked at her, silently, puzzled.

But Judas Iscariot, who was in charge of the disciples' money, spoke angrily. "What a waste! That perfume could have been sold! It's worth more than a year's wages! The money could have been given to the poor!"

And some of the other disciples agreed. The woman shrank back. Her action of love – the action with which she'd tried to tell Jesus she knew sorrow and suffering was to come to Him, and that she cared *desperately* – her action had been misunderstood. She'd been stupid. Wasteful.

But *Jesus* had not misunderstood.

"Leave her alone!" He said. "What she has done is beautiful. There will always be poor people amongst you, whom you can help. But you will not always have Me. She poured this perfume over Me to prepare My body for the burial which is to come. And I tell you – wherever the news which I came to give you is told, throughout the whole world, what she did here will also be told. Her action will *never* be forgotten!"

Then the woman felt protected from the disciples' harsh words; and she loved Jesus more than ever.

But Judas was furious. And seeing this, Satan seized the opportunity to put wicked thoughts into Judas' mind – thoughts which led to action.

For in his anger, Judas went secretly to the chief priests and officers of the Temple Guard.

"I know where Jesus is," he told them. "I will tell you where He goes. You will be able to capture Him in a quiet place – away from the sight of the crowds who follow Him."

The chief priests rubbed their hands together. They thought they were to be rid of Jesus at last.

They promised Judas Iscariot thirty pieces of silver as a reward. And Judas started to watch for a chance to hand Jesus over to them.

# The Withered Fig Tree

Early in the morning Jesus and His disciples set out from Bethany to walk to Jerusalem.

On the way, Jesus felt hungry. He noticed a fig tree growing by the roadside. It seemed to be a good, strong tree, with plenty of leaves. It looked as if it would be full of fruit, just as Jerusalem appeared to be full of people who were ready to follow Him.

But when Jesus went over to the tree, and searched amongst its branches, He couldn't find one single fig. What it had promised wasn't there at all – just as the people in Jerusalem would soon show how little they *really* cared about Him.

Jesus said to the tree, "You will never bear fruit again." And the fig tree withered up in the sunshine.

The disciples were amazed. "Why did it wither so quickly?" they asked.

Jesus said to them, "If you have enough faith and trust in God, you will be able to do much more than wither a fig tree! You will be able to move mountains! When you pray *as God wills*, believe that you have whatever you ask for. But make sure you have forgiven anyone you are holding a grudge against. And your Heavenly Father will forgive you the things *you* have done wrong."

Still talking, they went on towards Jerusalem.

# The Widow in the Temple

When Jesus and His disciples reached Jerusalem, they went straight to the Temple. A large crowd gathered, as usual; eager to hear Jesus' teaching.

"Beware the teachers of the law!" He warned them. "They walk around full of their own importance. They have places reserved for them in the Synagogues; and they sit in the best seats whenever there is a feast. But in secret they cheat the poor and take away their homes. Then they stand where everyone can see them and recite long prayers, so that people will think how good they are. God is not deceived! They will be punished as they deserve!"

The disciples stood listening, afraid for Him; for this kind of teaching was going to anger the authorities still more... Yet they could understand that Jesus couldn't *bear* to see people betrayed by the very men who should have been showing them the love of God, and His true will for them...

Now, as Jesus sat there, He could see people putting money into the offering box. Many rich men came; swaggering their way through the crowds; dropping their silver and gold coins into the box with a loud clatter; hoping everyone would be impressed by the amount they had given.

But presently, a woman whose husband had died came into the Temple. It was clear that she was very poor. She was pale, and shabbily dressed. Humbly, she crept to the offering box. Quietly, as if hoping no one would notice, she dropped in two small copper coins.

Then she would have crept away, ashamed that her offering was so small. But Jesus spoke to the listening crowd. "I tell you – this poor widow has given more than any of those rich people gave!"

The crowd gaped at Him. How could He say that? Hadn't He *seen* the two tiny coins?

Jesus explained. "The rich men gave out of their plenty. It was such a small proportion of their wealth, they won't even notice it has gone. But this woman has given God all the money she had, because she loves Him. She gave her all. No one can ever give more than that."

Now the crowd understood. The widow hurried away; but there was a warm glow in her heart.

Judas had been standing watching all this. He was still waiting for a chance to betray Jesus...

# Preparing for the Last Supper

It was the first day of the Festival of the Passover. Jesus' disciples asked Him, "Where shall we eat the Passover meal?" for they were wondering if *anywhere* in Jerusalem was safe.

Judas was listening.

Jesus took Peter and John to one side. "Go into Jerusalem," He said. "As you enter the city, you will meet a man carrying a pitcher of water. Follow him. He will lead you into a house. Say to the owner of the house, 'The Master asks, which is the room where He may eat the Passover meal with His disciples?'

"He will show you to a large, upper room. That is where you must get everything ready."

Judas was baffled. He couldn't follow Peter and John without arousing suspicion...

Peter and John set out. Sure enough, they met the man carrying the pitcher of water. It was a secret sign. Carrying water was normally women's work.

There was no need to speak. Keeping well back, hearts beating fast, Peter and John followed him.

He led the disciples safely to the house. The owner showed them to the upstairs room, just as Jesus had promised. Peter and John began the preparations.

When they had finished, the two disciples returned to Jesus and the others. And in the evening, the twelve went with Him to the upper room.

In that hot, dusty country it was the custom for a servant to wash the feet of anyone coming into a house. But now, the disciples went straight to the table. None of *them* intended to act as a servant.

So – as the meal was being served – *Jesus* stood up, took off his outer robe, and wrapped a towel around His waist.

The disciples watched; first in amazement, then with shame, as Jesus poured water into a basin and started to wash their feet, drying them with the towel around His waist.

He reached Peter. Peter cried, "Master – do You mean to wash *my* feet?"

"You don't understand now what I'm doing," Jesus replied, "but you'll understand later."

"You'll never wash *my* feet!" Peter said, feeling he couldn't bear to have Jesus acting as servant for him.

"If I don't wash you, you'll no longer be My disciple," Jesus answered.

Then Peter cried, "Oh, Master – wash my hands, and my head, as well!"

Jesus answered, "Anyone who has had a bath only needs to wash his feet. His body is clean."

Then He said, "All my disciples are clean, except one…"

He knew that Judas meant to betray Him that night…

When He had washed all their feet, He took off the towel, and put His robe on again. Then He sat once more at the table.

"Do you understand?" He asked, "You call Me 'Master', and 'Lord'; and so I am… I, your Master, have washed your feet. And you should be ready to wash one another's feet – to work for one another. I did this so that you could copy Me. Don't be ashamed to carry out such tasks. No servant is greater than his master; nor is any messenger more important than the one who sent him. If you serve one another, you will be happy and blessed. And whoever is kind to any messenger of *Mine*, is being kind to Me; and to the One who sent Me."

Now they were ready to start their meal.

*Matthew 26 : 21–35; Mark 14 : 17–31; Luke 22 : 14–23, 31–34;*
*John 13 : 21–38; 14 : 1–31; 18 : 1, 2*

# The Last Supper

It was their last supper together. Jesus began to be very troubled. "I tell you truly," He said, "one of you who sits at the table with Me will betray Me."

Only Judas knew exactly what He meant. The other disciples all began to be upset, fearing that they might indeed betray Him in a moment of carelessness or fear.

"Is it I, Lord?" they asked. "Is it I?"

John was sitting next to Jesus. Peter whispered to John, "Ask Him which one of us He means!"

John moved very close to Jesus. "Master," he pleaded, in a low voice, "who is it?"

Jesus answered, "It is he to whom I give the bread."

He dipped some bread into the sauce – and handed it to Judas.

"The Son of Man will die as it has been foretold," He said. "But it will be terrible for the man who betrays Him. It would be better for that man if he had never been born."

Judas met Jesus' eyes; and tried to bluff it out. "Surely, Master, You don't mean me!" he said.

But Jesus *knew*. "Go, and do what you have to do," He replied.

And Judas got up, and went out into the night.

None of the other disciples realized what was happening. They knew Judas was in charge of the money. They thought Jesus had told him to go and buy something they needed; or even give some money to the poor.

During the meal, Jesus took the bread, and gave thanks to God for it. Then He broke it, and shared it out amongst the eleven, saying, "Take this, and eat it. It is My body, broken for you. Do this in memory of Me."

The disciples looked at Him, puzzled, distressed. Jesus took the wine; and when He had given thanks to God, He poured it out for the disciples, saying, "Drink all of it. This is My blood of the New Testament – God's new covenant with man, sealed with My blood. It is shed for you, and for many, so that your sins may be forgiven... Truly I say to you – I will drink no more of the fruit of the vine until the day I drink it new in the Kingdom of God."

Still they looked distressed.

"God's glory will be revealed," Jesus said. "My beloved friends, I shall not be with you much longer. So I give you a new commandment. Love one another, as I have loved you."

"Master, where are You going?" they cried. "We will come with You!"

"You cannot come with Me now," Jesus answered gently. "Later, you will follow Me."

"Why can't we come with You now?" Peter demanded. "I would *die* for You!"

"Peter," said Jesus, "all of you will desert Me, and run away. And before the cock crows three times, you will say three times that you never knew Me."

"I'll never deny knowing You!" Peter cried, deeply distressed.

Jesus went on, trying to comfort His special little group of friends. "Don't let your hearts be troubled! You believe in God – believe in Me, also. In My Father's house there are many rooms. If it wasn't so I would have told you. I go to prepare a place for you. And if I go to prepare a place for you, I will come again, and take you to Myself; so that where I am, there you may be, also. And where I am going you know, and the way you know."

Thomas said, "Lord – we *don't* know where You are going. So how *can* we know the way?"

Jesus answered, "*I* am the way, the truth and the life. No one comes to the Father, except by Me. If you have known Me, you have known the Father."

Then Philip cried, "Master – let us *see* God! *Then* we will know!"

Jesus said, "Philip – have I been so long with you, and still you haven't known Me? If you have seen Me, you have seen the Father."

He looked around at their troubled faces. "If you love Me, obey My words. And I will ask the Father to send you another comforter, who will be able to stay with you for ever. I will not leave you comfortless. I will come to you. A little while, and the world shall see Me no more. But *you* see Me. And because I live, you shall live also... Peace I leave with you, My peace I give unto you. Let not your heart be troubled, neither let it be afraid."

And when they had spoken some more, they sang a hymn, and went out.

Everywhere was in darkness. They came to the Garden of Gethsemane.

And Judas knew where they had gone...

# In the Garden of Gethsemane

The Garden of Gethsemane was dark, shadowy in the moonlight. Jesus said to His disciples, "Sit here, while I go over there and pray... Peter, James, John – come a little further with Me..."

Peter, James and John went with Him. They could see He was very distressed.

"Keep watch," He said. "My sorrow is so great, it almost crushes Me."

He went a little way apart from them, and knelt on the ground. He prayed, "Father – all things are possible with You. Take this cup of suffering from Me... But let Your will be done; not Mine."

He came back to Peter, James and John. Instead of keeping watch as He had asked, they had fallen asleep; utterly weary after the long, hard day.

Jesus said, "Simon Peter – are even *you* asleep? Couldn't you keep watch for just one hour?"

The three disciples woke, ashamed; feeling terrible that they had let Him down when He was in such distress.

"Keep watch," He said again. "And pray that you may not do wrong..." Then He looked at them with gentleness and compassion. "You *want* to stay awake; but your bodies are very tired," He said.

He went away again to pray. In agony, He said, "Father, if this cup of suffering is the only way – Your will be done..."

He came back to the three. Once more they had fallen asleep. Once more He woke them. They could find no words to say to Him.

A third time Jesus prayed. A third time He returned and found them sleeping. This time, He said, "Are you *still* asleep?" And then, urgently, "Look! The hour has come! Let's go! Here comes the one who will betray Me!"

The disciples awoke, suddenly aware of the lights of torches and lanterns in the garden – of a crowd carrying sticks and swords – of soldiers – of the Temple Guard, sent by the chief priests...

They struggled to their feet. But now Jesus was not *trying* to get away.

He stepped forward, calm, quiet; facing the rabble. "Who are you looking for?" He asked.

"Jesus of Nazareth," they answered.

"I am He," Jesus replied.

Judas came pushing his way to the front. He went to Jesus.

"Do what you have to do," said Jesus.

And Judas kissed Him, saying, "Master." For this was the secret sign he had arranged with the chief priests.

"Is it with a kiss you betray the Son of Man?" Jesus asked him.

Then the soldiers moved forward to arrest Jesus. Peter, furious, seized a sword and cut off the ear of the servant of Caiaphas, the high priest.

But Jesus touched the man's ear, and healed him.

"Put down your swords," He said to His followers. "For he who lives by the sword shall die by the sword!

Don't you think I could ask My Father for help? He could send legions of angels to defend Me. But if I do, the Scriptures will not be fulfilled. Do you think I will not obey My Father's will?"

And He spoke to the crowd. "Am I leading a revolt? Is that why you come to capture Me with sticks and swords? Didn't you see Me every day, teaching in the Temple Courts? You didn't arrest Me then!"

Then he said to the soldiers, "*I* am Jesus of Nazareth whom you have come to arrest. Let these others go."

And His disciples, seeing what was going to happen next, all deserted Him, and fled.

# The Trials of Jesus

Now Jesus was in the hands of His enemies. They bound Him, and led Him away. The disciples, afraid for their own lives, deserted Him and fled. But Peter and John, tormented by love, fear and sorrow, couldn't bear not knowing what was happening. So they stopped, turned, and began to follow after Jesus, keeping well back, hidden in the darkness.

The chief priests, the elders and the temple guards took Jesus to the house of Caiaphas, the high priest. First Jesus was questioned by Annas, father-in-law of Caiaphas. Then He was taken before Caiaphas himself to be put on trial by the Sanhedrin, the Jewish high court.

Peter and John waited outside, in the courtyard. It was a cold night, and the servants had made a fire. Shivering, Peter moved towards it, trying to warm himself. He saw people being taken into the house – people who were prepared to tell lies about Jesus; for the chief priests were determined to have Jesus killed, even though He had done nothing which deserved death.

Jesus listened to the many lies which were told; but He remained silent until at last Caiaphas said, "Tell us. Are You the Son of God?"

There was a hushed pause as everyone waited for the answer. Jesus said, "Yes, as you have said.

And you will see the Son of Man sitting at the right hand of God, and coming in the clouds of Heaven."

"He speaks blasphemy!" cried Caiaphas. "We need hear no more!" And he tore his cloak, as was the custom with the Jews when they heard blasphemy. "What do you think should happen to Him?"

"He must be put to death!" shouted the chief priests and the elders. And they began to strike Him.

Outside, Peter heard the cries. As he shivered, one of the maids noticed him. "You!" she said. "You were with that man!"

"No!" cried Peter, in fear. Hastily he left the fire, and went out to the gateway.

Another girl saw him, and said, "This man was with Jesus."

"I tell you I don't know Him!" shouted Peter.

But later, other people standing there said, "You *are* one of them. We can tell you come from Galilee by the

way you talk."

Peter was desperate. "I tell you *I DON'T KNOW HIM*!" he cried. And then, as the people looked at him with hard, unfriendly eyes, Peter heard a cock crow twice.

He remembered what Jesus had said to him. "Before the cock crows twice, you will say three times that you don't know Me."

Then Peter rushed away to be by himself; and he cried, for his heart was breaking.

It was dawn. The chief priests and the elders took Jesus under guard to Pilate, the Roman governor of that district. Judas saw this. He realized Jesus had been condemned to death and he couldn't bear it. He took the thirty pieces of silver which had been his reward for betraying Jesus, and hurried to the chief priests and elders. "I was wrong!" he cried. "I've betrayed an innocent man!"

They answered cruelly. "Why should we care? What you did was up to you."

Judas flung the money at them. Then, unable to live with the thought of what he had done to Jesus, he went out and hanged himself.

Now Jesus stood silently in front of Pilate. Pilate questioned Jesus.

"They say You have been calling Yourself a king. Are You King of the Jews?"

"You say that I am," said Jesus.

The chief priests and elders told many more lies, but Jesus answered not one word.

Pilate was puzzled. "Don't You

hear what they're saying against You?" he asked. Still Jesus remained silent.

A crowd of people had collected, stirred up by the chief priests and the elders. Pilate said to them, "I can't find anything to charge this man with."

The chief priests and the elders thought quickly. They must say something which Pilate *would* think was a crime.

"He has been trying to start a riot in Galilee!" they cried.

"He's from *Galilee!*" said Pilate, in great relief. "Then it's nothing to do with me. You must take Him to Herod. Herod rules in Galilee."

Herod was in Jerusalem at that time, because of the Feast of the Passover.

So Jesus was taken to stand yet another trial.

At first, Herod was pleased to see Jesus. He'd heard about the miracles Jesus had done, and he wanted to see some now. He asked many questions, but Jesus would not say one word, although the chief priests and elders still continued their lies. At last Herod grew furiously angry. He and his soldiers dressed Jesus in a beautiful robe, cruelly making fun of Him. Then they sent Him back to Pilate.

The crowd followed. Some were jeering; but some were friends of Jesus, and they were silent, almost overwhelmed with sorrow.

Pilate was faced once more with trying to make a decision.

"No one has found this man

guilty!" he cried. "I'll have Him whipped, and then let Him go."

But by now, many people in the crowd had been worked up by the chief priests and the elders into a kind of madness.

"No, no! Free Barabbas instead!" they howled.

Barabbas was a murderer. Pilate knew that at this feast one prisoner was always released. By this he'd hoped to save Jesus. But the crowd howled for Barabbas; and Pilate was afraid. He didn't want a riot.

As he stood there, wondering what to do with Jesus, a message came to him from his wife. "I've had terrible dreams because of this man! Don't have anything to do with it!"

The crowds were still shouting. Pilate cried once more. "Which of the two do you want me to free? Jesus or Barabbas?"

"Barabbas!" they yelled.

"Then what shall I do with Jesus?" asked Pilate.

"Crucify Him!" they yelled.

"Why? What wrong has He done?" pleaded Pilate.

But they shouted even louder. "Crucify! Crucify!"

Pilate was too weak-willed to act against the mob. He sent for a basin of water. In front of them all he washed his hands, as a sign that *he* wasn't making the decision.

So Barabbas was freed, and Jesus was whipped, and handed over to be crucified.

# The Crucifixion

The Roman soldiers stripped Jesus of His clothes. They dressed Him in a purple robe, and put a crown of thorns on His head. They put a staff in His hand; cruelly making fun of Him, kneeling down in front of Him, and saying, "Hail, King of the Jews!"

Then they took the staff, and struck Him with it.

Once more, Pilate took Jesus out to show Him to the people. Surely now they would have pity on Him! But still the crowds shouted, "Crucify! He says He is the Son of God! By our law He must die!"

Pilate took Jesus to one side, and tried to question Him again: but Jesus would not answer.

Pilate had never met anyone like this before. "Don't You know I can either set You free, or have You crucified?" he asked.

Then Jesus replied, "You would have no power at all if it wasn't given to you by God."

The crowd was shouting again. "If you let this man go, you are no friend of Caesar's! Anyone who says He is king is in opposition to Caesar!"

That was it. Pilate was very much afraid of Caesar. So he finally handed Jesus over to be crucified.

The soldiers put Jesus' own clothes on Him again. Then they forced Him to carry a heavy cross to the place called Golgotha.

By now Jesus was so weak, He fainted on the way up the hill. A man

– Simon of Cyrene – was called out from the crowd to carry the cross for Jesus.

At the place of execution Jesus' friends watched, helpless, as the soldiers nailed Jesus to the cross with one nail through each hand and foot. The hammer blows fell, and Jesus was in great pain; but He prayed to God, "Father, forgive them; for they know not what they do."

The cross was lifted and set into place. The soldiers sat down, and began to share out Jesus' clothes between them. They threw a dice to see who would win His robe.

As He hung on the cross, many people jeered at Him; and the chief priests and elders said mockingly, "Let Him come down from the cross now, and we will believe Him!" But

Jesus was intent on carrying out God's plan; and He would not answer them.

Jesus' friends – especially the women – stood nearby, hoping it might comfort Jesus to see them there. Even when most of the crowd had gone, they remained.

Two thieves were crucified, one on either side of Jesus. One thief was sorry for the wrong he had done, and asked Jesus to think of him. To him, Jesus said, "Today you will be with Me in paradise."

As Jesus looked down from the cross, He saw His mother, Mary; and His disciple, John: and said, "Woman, behold your son. Son, behold your mother." They realized He wanted them to be as mother and son and comfort each other.

Now He was in very great pain. He spoke some words which He had learnt from the Psalms as a boy. "My God, My God, why hast Thou forsaken Me?"

After a while, He said, "I thirst." So they soaked a sponge in cheap wine, and held it up to His lips.

Soon after that, Jesus said, "It is finished... Father, into Your hands I commit My spirit." And He died.

For the last three hours Jesus was on the cross there was darkness over all the land. As He died, there was a great earthquake, and the curtain which hung in the Temple was ripped in two.

The people were very much afraid. The Roman soldiers who had helped to crucify Him were terrified; and when they saw these things, they said, "Surely, this was the Son of God."

# The Burial of Jesus

It was a Friday when Jesus and the two thieves were crucified. Next day was the Jewish Sabbath.

So, on the Friday evening, the Jewish rulers went to Pilate and asked that the bodies be taken down from the crosses. They did not wish them to be hanging there on a holy day.

First, the soldiers broke the legs of the two thieves, so that they died at once. But when they went to break Jesus' legs, they found He was already dead. So, as the Scriptures had foretold, none of His bones were broken. To be certain of His death, one of the soldiers pierced Jesus' side with a sword. Blood and water flowed out.

The sorrowing disciples wanted to be given Jesus' body, so that they could bury it with loving care. A rich man, Joseph, from Arimathea, came to them. He was a member of the Sanhedrin, and had secretly believed in Jesus.

Now, he went boldly to Pilate, and asked for the body.

Pilate turned to the Roman soldiers. "Is Jesus dead already?" he asked in surprise.

The soldier reported how it had been. So Pilate gave Joseph permission.

Joseph went to Golgotha, to the place where Jesus had been crucified. Nicodemus, another member of the Sanhedrin who had so far been a secret follower, went with him.

Reverently, they took the body, and wrapped it in a new linen sheet, with spices, as was the custom of the Jews.

Then they placed Jesus' body in the tomb which Joseph had intended for his own use, when the time came for him to die. It had been freshly cut out of solid rock, and had never before been used. The tomb was in a garden, close to the place where Jesus had been crucified.

The women who had been with Jesus at the cross also took spices, and went with Joseph. They saw where Jesus' body was buried.

Then Joseph rolled a large stone across the entrance to the tomb, to close it. The sad day was almost over. The men went away, leaving

Mary Magdalene and another Mary still sitting facing the tomb, grieving bitterly.

At last the women, too, left the garden.

It was now the Sabbath day. The chief priests and the Pharisees went to Pilate, because even *yet* they were anxious.

"Sir," they said, "we remember that while this liar was still alive, He said, 'In three days I will be raised from the dead.' Command that a guard be set over the tomb until the third day has passed! Otherwise, His disciples may steal the body, and then spread the rumour that He *is* alive! The last lie would be worse than the first!"

"Very well," said Pilate. "Go and make the tomb as secure as possible. You may take a guard."

So the chief priests and the Pharisees went to the garden, taking the Roman soldiers with them. They put a seal on the stone so that it would be impossible to move it without the seal being broken. And they left well-drilled, highly disciplined Roman soldiers on guard.

And yet...

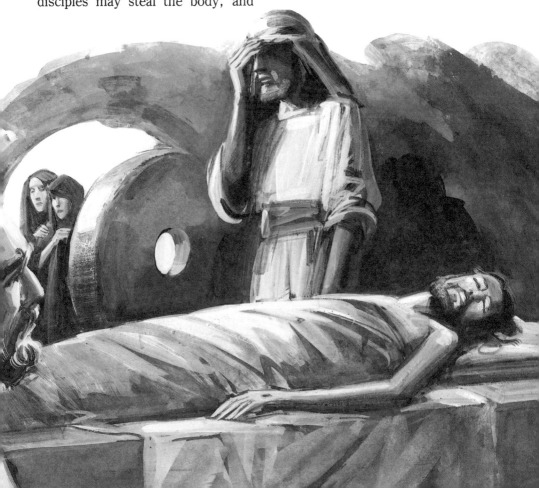

# The First Easter

At sunrise on the Sunday morning Mary Magdalene and some of the other women set out to go to the tomb, taking with them more spices with which to anoint the body of Jesus. They were still grieving deeply; looking for *something* which they could still do for Him.

It wasn't until they were on the way that they remembered the huge stone that had been rolled across the entrance. How would they move it? Even as they worried, there was a violent earthquake. In the garden, an angel of the Lord came down, rolled away the stone, and sat on it. His clothes were shining white; and when the Roman guards saw him, they fainted in terror.

Before the women reached the tomb, the angel had gone – and the soldiers had fled. Mary Magdalene, hastening along in front of the others, saw that the stone had been rolled away. In great distress, she ran back to find Peter and John.

Now the other women arrived at the tomb. Fearfully, they crept inside... They gazed around. Jesus' body was no longer there! And suddenly, two angels in shining white clothes stood beside them. The women were terrified.

"Don't be afraid!" said the angels. "You are looking for Jesus, who was crucified. But why are you looking for the living among the dead? He is not here! He is risen! See – that is the place where His body was laid! Remember what He told you! Go and give this message to His disciples, *and* Peter. Tell them He is going before you into Galilee, and you will see Him there."

Then the women remembered that Jesus had said He would rise on the third day.

They turned and ran as fast as they could, rushing to get back to the disciples with the news.

But Mary Magdalene had already reached Peter and John. "They have taken Him away!" she sobbed. "And I don't know what they've done with His body!"

Stricken with fear and grief, Peter and John ran to the tomb. John reached it first. Near the entrance, he saw the cloths in which Jesus' body had been wrapped. He stopped. Peter, panting, breathless, didn't pause. Straight into the tomb he rushed.

He saw the linen cloth; and he saw the wrappings which had bound Jesus' head. They were lying separately, neatly rolled up.

And he believed.

Then John, too, entered the tomb. He and Peter looked at each other.

Incredulous, exultant joy began to fill them. Puzzled, still not fully understanding, they returned to the house.

But Mary Magdalene had not gone all the way back to the tomb with them. Now she stood alone in the garden, weeping. Presently, she stumbled forward, and looked into the tomb. And there she saw two angels, sitting where the body of Jesus had been laid – one at the feet, one at the head. She thought they were ordinary men.

"Woman – why are you crying?" they asked.

"Because they have taken away my Lord, and I don't know where they have put Him," she sobbed.

She turned around, and saw someone standing there. But she did not recognize Him.

"Woman – why are you weeping?" He asked. "Who is it you are looking for?"

Half blinded by her tears, Mary thought He must be the gardener. "Oh, sir – if *you* took Him away, please tell me where you have put Him!" she begged. "I will go and get Him!"

Then Jesus said, "Mary!"

She turned fully towards Him, looked at Him. "Rabboni!" she gasped in Hebrew. "Master!"

"Don't touch Me," Jesus said. "I haven't yet gone back to My Father. But go to My friends, and tell them I am returning to My Father, and your Father. I am returning to God."

Mary, overjoyed, hastened back to the disciples. She found a group of them. "I have seen the Lord!" she cried. And she gave them His message.

But the disciples could not accept the good news. In spite of all the times Jesus had tried to explain it – to prepare them for what was to happen – they wouldn't believe He had risen.

It was late on the Sunday evening. The disciples had gathered in the room of a house. All the doors were locked, for the disciples were afraid; terrified of the Jewish authorities.

And suddenly, Jesus was standing amongst them.

"Peace be with you!" He greeted them, in the old way. The disciples gazed at Him in fear, thinking He was a ghost. He held out His hands, so that they could see the marks left by the nails. And He showed them His side, where it had been pierced by the Roman soldier's sword.

"Touch Me!" He smiled. "You can't touch a ghost!"

Then, seeing they were still unsure, He said, "Have you any food here?"

They gave Him some; and He ate it.

At *last* the disciples could accept the truth. This was no ghost! It was their Master! Risen! Alive! They were full of joy.

But Thomas was not there when Jesus appeared to them. As soon as he came in, they cried, "We have seen the Lord!"

Thomas shook his head. "Unless I can see the marks of the nails, and touch them, and put my hand into the wound in His side, I won't believe!" he said.

And he continued to grieve deeply.

Meanwhile, some of the Roman guards had gone to the chief priests...

268

# The Roman Guards Talk to the Chief Priests

Some of the guards who had been at the tomb when the stone was rolled away went to the chief priests, telling them everything they had seen.

The chief priests, pale-faced, trembling, went to the Jewish leaders. This story that the soldiers told must not be allowed to spread...

Together they worked out a plan.

"Look," they said to the guards, "you must say that the disciples came in the night and stole the body while you were asleep."

And they offered the soldiers a large sum of money as a bribe. The soldiers hesitated. They should *not* have been asleep...

The chief priests grew more agitated. "If Pilate hears about all this, we'll make him believe you were completely blameless," they urged. "You've no need to worry."

So the guards took the bribe, and spread the false story. And many of the Jews believed it.

But more of Jesus' disciples were beginning to learn the truth...

# The Walk to Emmaus; and Thomas

On that first Sunday evening two of Jesus' followers were walking sadly home to Emmaus from Jerusalem. And Jesus Himself drew near to them.

Buried in their grief, they didn't recognize Him. He began to walk with them, asking them what they were talking about so unhappily. One of them – Cleopas – said, "How can you not know what's been happening in Jerusalem these last few days? *Everyone* knows!"

"Tell Me," said Jesus.

Then Cleopas told Him how they had all felt that Jesus had been a very special prophet; the One who would set Israel free from the Romans. But He had been crucified. Some of the women were now talking of finding the tomb empty. They were claiming that they had seen angels, who told them that Jesus was alive again... But who could believe *that*?

Jesus answered, "You are so *slow* to believe! It was *necessary* that all those things should happen!"

And He began to explain everything to them, beginning with the books of Moses.

As they walked and talked, the two followers began to feel happier. Excited...

They reached Emmaus. Jesus was going to walk on. But Cleopas said, "It's getting very late. It will soon be dark. Spend the night here with us."

So Jesus went into the house with them. A meal was prepared, and they sat down to eat. Jesus took the bread, and blessed it. Then He broke it, and handed it to them. There was something familiar in the way He did it...

271

Suddenly they recognized Him! And in that moment, He disappeared from their sight. Then they looked at each other, their faces ablaze with joy.

"It was Jesus! The stories the women told were true!" they cried. And they rushed all the way back to Jerusalem, to tell the other disciples.

But it was seven more days before Thomas was convinced.

Again the disciples were in the room, with the doors shut and locked as before. Suddenly, Jesus was there with them.

"Peace be with you," He greeted them. Then, as they gazed at Him, He held out His hands. Gently, He spoke to Thomas. "Put your finger in the marks of the nails; and put your hand into the wound in My side. And do not doubt, but believe."

Thomas did not need to touch the nail prints, nor put his hand into the wound. Filled with a mixture of awe, love, and almost overwhelming joy, he whispered reverently, "My Lord and my God!"

Jesus said, "Do you believe because you see Me? Happy are those who have not seen Me, and yet have believed."

# Breakfast on the Shore

Jesus had said He would go before His disciples into Galilee. Now, seven of the twelve waited there for Him, near the shores of Lake Tiberias. Peter was one of the seven. He was longing to see Jesus again – yet still desperately upset about having three times denied knowing Him...

Suddenly, he felt he could no longer bear to sit about doing nothing. He sprang to his feet. "I'm going fishing," he said. It would be like the old days; before he'd even met Jesus.

"We'll come with you," said the others. Anything was better than this waiting...

So they got into a boat, and cast off. All night they fished; but they caught nothing. Dejectedly, they began to sail towards the shore.

It was very early in the morning – barely light. As the boat came closer to land, the disciples could see the figure of a man on the beach; but they didn't realize who it was.

273

He called to them. "Have you caught any fish, My friends?"

"No," they answered.

He said, "Throw your net on the right side of the boat. You'll find some fish there."

James, John and Peter looked at one another. Once before, someone had told them to do that...

They let the net down – and immediately it was full of fish – so many, they couldn't haul in the net! And John said, "It *is* the Lord!"

Peter waited no longer. He tucked up his robe and waded ashore, splashing and stumbling in his eagerness to get to Jesus. They were about a hundred metres out. The others stayed in the boat, rowing it to shore, hauling the net behind it.

When they landed on the beach a fire was already alight, with fish cooking on it. There was bread also.

Jesus said, "Bring over some of the fish you've just caught."

And while the others stood gazing at Him, Peter jumped into the boat and pulled the net ashore by himself. There were one hundred and fifty-three fish altogether; yet the net was not torn!

"Come and have breakfast," Jesus invited them.

Still none of the disciples ventured to ask, "Who are You?" They were sure it *was* Him. He was the same – yet He was different...

Jesus took the bread and gave it to them, as He had done so often before. Then He shared out the fish.

When the meal was over, Jesus said, "Simon Peter, do you love Me?"

"Yes, Lord," Peter answered. "You know I love You."

"Care for My little ones," said Jesus. "Simon – do you *truly* love Me?"

Peter answered again, "Lord, You *know* I love You."

Jesus said, "Care for those who follow Me."

And a third time He said, "Simon Peter – do you love Me?"

Now Peter was upset. "Lord," he answered, "You know everything. You *know* I love You."

Jesus said, "Care for My followers." And He added, "Peter, truly I say to you – when you were young, you dressed yourself, and went wherever you wanted to. But when you are old, you will stretch out your hands; and another will dress you, and carry you where you do not want to go."

It wasn't until much later that Peter realized those words had been foretelling his own death on a cross. All he knew *now* was that he had been given the chance to say three times that he loved Jesus; and that Jesus had forgiven him for those three times he'd declared he didn't even know Him. And besides that, he had been given special commands to carry out for his Master.

Some days later, the other disciples were also entrusted with the task of continuing Jesus' work on earth. They had gone to a mountain in Galilee, as Jesus had told them to. When He appeared to them there they worshipped Him, although some of them doubted it was really Him. Then He came closer, and spoke to them.

"All power is given to Me, in Heaven and on earth," He said. "Go, therefore, and teach all people everywhere; baptizing them in the name of the Father, and of the Son, and of the Holy Ghost; teaching them to obey all the commands I have given you. And lo, I am with you always, even unto the end of the world."

Soon, the disciples were to start this task. But first, they were to see something marvellous...

# The Ascension

For forty days after His crucifixion, Jesus appeared at different times to His disciples. Some of His followers had doubted; but by now the eleven were absolutely convinced of the truth of His resurrection.

As they ate their last meal together, He said to them, "You must wait here in Jerusalem for the gift which My Father will send to you. The gift of the Holy Spirit."

They still didn't fully understand. There were still many questions they wanted to ask. But He knew He could no longer remain on earth with them. He led them out of the city, to the Mount of Olives.

"When the Holy Spirit comes to you, you will receive power," He promised them. "And you will speak for Me in Jerusalem, in Judea and Samaria, and in the uttermost parts of the earth."

He lifted up His hands to bless them; and even as He did so, He was parted from them; taken up into the skies. And a cloud hid Him, so that they could see Him no longer.

As they gazed upwards, two men dressed in shining white appeared beside them, and spoke to them.

"Men of Galilee, why do you stand gazing upwards into the sky? This Jesus, whom you have seen taken up into Heaven, will one day return in the same way."

Filled with joy, the disciples went back to Jerusalem. There, in the upper room, they prayed.

And while they were waiting for the gift which Jesus had promised them, they spent much of their time in the Temple, praising God.

# The First Whitsun

Fifty days after the Feast of the Passover came the Feast of Pentecost. Ten days earlier, Jesus had ascended into Heaven. The disciples were still waiting for the gift of the Holy Spirit which He had promised them. They had chosen Matthias to be one of the twelve in place of Judas Iscariot; and they began to be known as the apostles. Now, on this Feast of Pentecost, they were all gathered together in the room of a house.

Suddenly, there came a sound from Heaven like a rushing, mighty wind. It filled the whole house. And as they looked at each other in awe, they saw tongues of fire appear, divided so that a flame rested above each one of them.

And they were all filled with the Holy Spirit of God, as Jesus had promised them.

They began to speak – and found they were talking in different languages, guided by the Holy Spirit.

At that time, Jews from many nations were living in Jerusalem. They believed in God, and worshipped Him. When the news about the apostles spread, a crowd of these people came to listen. And they were utterly amazed: because each one of them heard the apostles speaking in *their* language. Languages which the apostles had never *learned*.

"Aren't those men all from Galilee?" they asked one another. "How is it we can hear them talking about God in our own languages? What does it mean?"

Some of the listening crowd jeered, "They're drunk! That's what it is!"

But Peter stood up boldly in front of them all; and the other apostles stood with him. No longer were they hiding in a locked room! They were about to tackle the whole might of the Roman Empire, *and* their own Jewish authorities. And they were going to do it in the name of Jesus.

"Listen to me!" said Peter. "These men aren't drunk! For one thing, it's only nine o'clock in the morning!"

Then he told them how the Scriptures had said God's Holy Spirit would be poured out on men. That their sons and daughters would prophesy, and their young men would dream dreams. And he told them about Jesus.

Around three thousand people heard, and believed; and they were baptized.

And many signs and wonders were performed at that time.

Now all the believers shared everything they had. They gave each person what he needed. They met every day in the Temple Courts, and in each other's homes. They ate together, prayed together, learned together.

They were happy, and they praised God. More and more people believed each day.

But the authorities were watching...

278

# The Lame Man at the Beautiful Gate

In Jerusalem there lived a man who couldn't walk. There was no work he could do, so he was forced to beg for money. Every day he was carried to the gate which was called Beautiful, and left there. It was a good position to have, because many people passed by on their way to and from the Temple.

One afternoon soon after the first Whitsun, he had just been left in his usual place when he saw Peter and John coming. They were on their way to the Temple to pray.

"Please!" he called out. "Give me whatever you can spare!"

Peter and John stopped. "Look at us!" said Peter.

They're going to give me some money! thought the lame man, looking up expectantly.

Then Peter spoke. "I don't have any silver or gold," he said, "but what I *do* have I give you! In the name of Jesus Christ of Nazareth – get up and walk!"

The lame man gazed at Peter, astounded. Peter stretched out a hand to him. Bravely, the man clasped Peter's hand and struggled up. Immediately, he felt strength flow, first into his ankles, and then into his feet. Cautiously, he let go of Peter.

He could stand!

279

Overjoyed, he took a few steps, testing his new ability. He could walk!

He could run!

He could jump!

His face shone. Peter and John, smiling, went on into the Temple. And the man went with them – jumping, and walking, and praising God.

People already in the Temple Courts saw him; and they were amazed. "Isn't that the lame man who sat at the Beautiful Gate asking for money?" they asked one another. "What's happened to him?"

They began to crowd around, all trying to get a better look. The man

was afraid, and clutched hold of Peter and John.

Peter spoke to the people. "Men of Israel, why are you so surprised? Why are you staring at us as if we'd made this man walk by our own power?"

And he went on to tell them about Jesus.

The people listened – and so did the Sadducees, the priests, and the captain of the Temple Guard...

"Jesus *was* the Messiah!" Peter declared. "He was sent from God, as the Scriptures foretold! And after He had died on the cross, He rose to life again! He came to bring everlasting life to us all!"

The priests, the Sadducees, and the captain of the Temple Guard were furious! *Again* someone was preaching this message of resurrection!

Pushing their way through the listening crowd, the Temple Guard arrested Peter and John.

By now it was late in the evening; so the two apostles were thrown into prison for the night.

"You can wait there till morning!" the captain of the Guard told them menacingly. "Then the court will decide what should be done with you!"

But in spite of the arrest, very many of the people who had been in the Temple Courts that day believed the message preached by Peter and John. Now the number of believers in Jerusalem had reached five thousand or more. And the Jewish authorities were very worried indeed...

# Peter and John on Trial

Next morning, Peter and John were brought from prison, and put on trial before the Sanhedrin – the Jewish court. Caiaphas, the high priest, was in charge of the proceedings – the same Caiaphas who had tried Jesus. Now, he ordered that the lame man also be brought to the court.

"Stand in front of us!" Caiaphas ordered Peter and John, sternly. They obeyed, standing straight; bravely meeting the eyes of their accusers, even after the night in prison. Annas – Caiaphas' father-in-law, formerly high priest himself – spoke.

"Tell us – How did you do this thing? This healing?" he asked.

Then Peter was filled with the power of the Holy Spirit. Unhesitatingly, he replied, "If you

have called us here to answer for our good deed of yesterday – when this lame man was healed – then you, and all the people of Israel should know. It was by the power of Jesus Christ. The One whom you rejected. He is the only One with the power to save."

The Sanhedrin were amazed. Peter and John were just ordinary men. Yet they had this surprising courage, and the ability to speak fluently... Truly these men had been with Jesus...

"Wait outside!" ordered Caiaphas.

Peter and John obeyed, still under guard.

Then the members of the Sanhedrin discussed anxiously what could be done.

"Everyone in Jerusalem knows they have performed this miracle," they said. "It's no use trying to deny it. But we must tell them not to *dare* to speak any more in the name of Jesus! Otherwise this belief is going to spread!"

So Peter and John were recalled. Once more they stood in front of the Sanhedrin.

"In future, you are not to speak or teach in the name of Jesus!" ordered Caiaphas.

Courageously, Peter and John replied, "Decide for yourselves – is it right that we obey God, or that we obey you? We *must* tell everyone the miraculous things we have seen and heard!"

The Sanhedrin were even more furious. They made many threats of what would happen to Peter and John if the two apostles continued to preach. But in the end, they had to let them go. As before, the Jewish leaders were afraid to act because of the people. They knew that at that very minute crowds were praising God for the miracle of the healing of the lame man – made even more remarkable now that people had learned he was over forty years old.

Freed, Peter and John went back to the house where they were staying. Soberly, they told the rest what had happened.

Then they all joined together in a prayer. "God who made the Heavens, and the earth, and the sea, and all living creatures – You know how Herod and Pontius Pilate plotted together. But they did to Jesus only what Your will had decided beforehand. Please hear the threats now being made to us. Give us the power of Your Holy Spirit, so that we can continue to preach Your message unafraid. And please continue to work miracles through the name of Jesus. Amen."

After they had prayed, their courage was restored. They knew themselves to be filled with the power of the Holy Spirit; and they *were* unafraid to speak God's message.

The believers continued to share everything they had. If they sold their land or their homes, they brought the money from the sale and gave it to the apostles to share out as it was needed.

But one man and his wife didn't want to give all the money from *their* sale...

# Ananias and Sapphira

Ananias, one of the believers, sold some of his land, and received a fair price for it. He had watched other believers handing their money over to the apostles; but he wanted to keep back some of his. Who knew when he might need it himself? He discussed it with his wife Sapphira; and together they agreed not to tell anyone the exact amount.

So Ananias hid a part of the money. The rest he took to Peter. Solemnly, he laid it down at the apostle's feet.

But Peter said sternly, "Ananias, why have you done this? You've let Satan make you lie to the Holy Spirit! You've kept some of the money from the sale of your land for yourself! You haven't lied to *me* – you've lied to *God*!"

When Ananias heard these words, he fell to the ground and died.

Some of the young men in the group carried him out, and buried him.

Presently, Sapphira came into the house where the believers were. She was quite unaware of what had happened. Peter showed her the money Ananias had brought.

"Sapphira," he said, "is this truly the price your husband was given for the land?"

Sapphira nodded. "Yes," she lied. "That's the full amount."

Then Peter said, "How *could* you both agree to test the Holy Spirit? Your husband is dead. Here come the young men who carried him out and buried him. And they will carry *you* out, as well!"

Sapphira was so overcome, she also fell down and died; and she was buried beside her husband. And everyone who heard this story was full of fear.

But the twelve apostles were performing many miracles of healing, and doing other wonderful things.

The believers met regularly together in Solomon's Porch. Those who didn't belong were afraid to join them there, although they were held in high regard. But all the time, more believers were being added to the group. Sick people were carried out into the streets and laid there on beds, so that as Peter walked by at least his shadow might fall on them. People came from all the towns around Jerusalem, bringing with them those in need of healing. And every sick person was made well.

And the high priests and the Sadducees watched...

# The Apostles Imprisoned

As the number of believers increased, and people crowded to listen to the apostles, the high priests and the Sadducees grew very jealous.

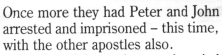

Once more they had Peter and John arrested and imprisoned – this time, with the other apostles also.

But that night, as the apostles tried to sleep, an angel appeared to them. And the angel *unlocked the prison doors*, and let them out!

"Go!" he said. "Return to the Temple. Tell people more about this new life you have found."

The apostles, hardly believing what was happening, hastened silently away from the prison, and made their way through the dark streets.

At daybreak they were once more in the Temple, teaching the people.

The high priest had called a full meeting of the Sanhedrin for the morning. When the Jewish leaders had arrived, they sent officers to the

prison, ordering that the prisoners be brought before them.

Presently the officers came back, looking shaken. "Sir," they said, "the jail was locked securely. The guards stood outside the doors. All seemed to be in order. But when we went inside – the jail was empty! The prisoners had gone!"

"What?" cried the chief priests and the captain of the Temple Guard. And as they looked at one another, wondering exactly what could have happened – and what they were going to *do* about it – a messenger panted up.

"Those men you arrested yesterday! They're in the Temple Courts! Teaching the people!" he said.

"Leave this to me!" cried the captain of the Guard.

Furiously, he went to the Temple, taking some of his men with him. But when they reached the Temple Courts, the crowd was so large they dared not seize the apostles by force. The people might have turned against them...stoned them...

So, forcing himself to be polite, the captain *asked* the apostles to accompany him to the Sanhedrin.

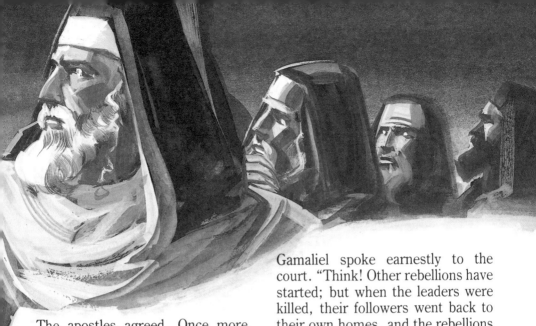

The apostles agreed. Once more, they stood before the high priest and the Sadducees.

Caiaphas shouted, "We *forbade* you to speak in the name of Jesus of Nazareth, or to continue preaching about Him! Yet you are still doing so! What is more, you're trying to make us guilty of having killed Him!"

Peter and the others replied steadfastly. "We must obey God rather than men. It was God who raised Jesus from the dead. We *must* tell people this; and that the Holy Spirit has been given by God to all who obey Him."

When they saw that Peter would not be silenced, the Sanhedrin called for the apostles to be put to death immediately. There was uproar.

But a Pharisee called Gamaliel shouted, "Wait!"

As the hubbub died down, he ordered the guard, "Take the twelve of them outside for the moment."

When this had been done,

Gamaliel spoke earnestly to the court. "Think! Other rebellions have started; but when the leaders were killed, their followers went back to their own homes, and the rebellions were over. So *I* say, in this case, leave the apostles alone! If their actions are only from men, the whole thing will fizzle out, as usual. But if it should be from *God* – nothing *we* do will stop it. And you will be fighting against God Himself."

There was silence. Gamaliel's words rang true. The Sanhedrin hestitated now about insisting on a death sentence...

So instead they had the apostles cruelly whipped; ordered them never to preach about Jesus again; and let them go.

The apostles left the court, not cowed, overcome by the beating; but rejoicing, because God had thought them important enough to be allowed to suffer in the cause of their beloved Master.

And wherever they went, they continued to tell people about Jesus.

But more trouble from the authorities was bound to come...

# Stephen

The number of believers was growing every day. They were still trying to share everything; but some of them had begun to grumble.

"The widows of the Greek Jews aren't being given as much food as the widows of the Hebrews!" they complained.

The twelve apostles called a meeting. "Look," they said, "we can't stop preaching God's message just to wait on you at the table! My friends – choose seven men whom you know to be wise and fair. They can take over the task of distributing things between you. Then *we* can go on giving our time to prayer, and teaching the people – which is our special work."

So the believers chose seven men. They were presented to the apostles, who blessed them.

Amongst the seven was a man called Stephen. Besides being full of wisdom, he was a great preacher. He also performed many miracles.

The Jewish leaders were frightened. This new Gospel of Christ was spreading too fast, too far. Even a great number of *priests* had started to believe. And people were taking less and less notice of the law of Moses.

When Stephen started to preach, certain members of the Synagogue were amongst the crowd listening to him. They argued with him; but he was filled with the Holy Spirit, and his answers were too wise for them to trap him. So they bribed men to tell lies about him. Then they roused the elders and other leaders against him, and had him brought before the Sanhedrin, where they continued their false accusations.

The members of the Sanhedrin listened, watching Stephen intently. To their amazement, they saw that – far from showing fear or distress – his face shone.

"What do you say to these charges?" the high priest asked him angrily.

Stephen seized his chance. He replied fully, beginning with the lives of Abraham and Moses, and finishing with an accusation against the Jews themselves. "You are all the same!" he cried. "You've always killed or persecuted the prophets! Now you have murdered Jesus Christ, the Son of God!"

His listeners were so *furious* they gnashed their teeth at him. But Stephen looked upwards. "I see Heaven open, and the Son standing at God's right hand!" he said.

The people in the court put their hands over their ears, to hear no more. Then, screaming and shouting, they rushed towards Stephen, seized him, dragged him out of the city, and began to throw stones at him.

Some of the men who had falsely accused Stephen now slipped off their outer robes, the better to hurl the stones. And they gave their clothes to a young man called Saul to watch over.

As the stones rained down on him, Stephen remained steadfast, praying, "Lord Jesus, receive my spirit." When he could no longer stand, he collapsed on to his knees, crying out loudly, "Lord, do not remember their sin against them!"

And so he died.

The young man Saul watched approvingly...

That same day, all the believers in Jerusalem began to be persecuted; and many of them fled.

Stephen was buried by the believers, with deep mourning. But the young man Saul was so determined to destoy all the believers, he went from home to home in Jerusalem, searching for them, dragging them off to prison.

The believers who had fled were now scattered throughout Judea and Samaria; but wherever they went, they preached about Jesus. So the Gospel of the Kingdom of God began to spread.

One of Stephen's companions – Philip – had gone to a city in Samaria. And he began to preach there.

# Philip and the Ethiopian

Crowds came to listen to Philip as he preached; and he healed many sick people. There was much happiness in the city.

Then an angel appeared to him, with a message from God. "Philip – you must go south, to the desert road that goes from Jerusalem to Gaza."

Leave the city, where things were going so well, and travel to a road through the desert which practically no one used? Philip was puzzled.

But he obeyed. Reaching the road at last, he stood by the edge of it. Why had God sent him *here*?

Then, in the distance, he saw a chariot. It was coming towards him from Jerusalem. Soon it would pass the spot where he was standing.

The Holy Spirit spoke to Philip. "Go across to that chariot, and stay close to it."

So, as the chariot passed, Philip joined in with it, running along at its side. He saw that inside the chariot sat a man from the country of Ethiopia. To Philip's amazement, the Ethiopian was reading aloud from the book of Isaiah – part of the Scriptures. He had reached the words, "He was led as a sheep to the slaughter; and like a lamb dumb before His shearer, so He opened not His mouth."

Panting, Philip called out, "Do you understand what those words are about?"

Startled, the Ethiopian looked up, and saw Philip. "How can I understand, if no one explains them to me?" he said.

"*I* can explain," Philip panted.

"Really?" In delight, the Ethiopian ordered his driver to pull up. "Will you come and sit with me?" he asked Philip.

Thankfully, Philip accepted.

The chariot drove on. The Ethiopian explained that he was an official in charge of the treasury of the Queen of Ethiopia. He'd been to Jerusalem to worship God. Now he was on his way home.

Philip could see that the man was rich, and would have much influence amongst the people of Ethiopia. *Now* he realized why God had wanted him to be here at this particular time...

The Ethiopian turned back to the words of Isaiah. "Who is the writer talking about?" he asked. "Does he mean *he* is the sheep led to the slaughter? Or is he speaking of someone else?"

Then Philip told him the story of Jesus. The Ethiopian listened closely; and as he listened, he believed.

Now the chariot was travelling along the road, past some water. "Look!" cried the Ethiopian. "Can I be baptized here? At once?"

Philip nodded. "Yes. You can."

"Stop!" the Ethiopian ordered his driver. Amidst the cloud of dust kicked up by the horses' hooves, the chariot stopped. Philip and the Ethiopian climbed down. They both went into the water; and Philip baptized the Ethiopian.

As they came out, the Holy Spirit suddenly took Philip away. His work in that place was finished; and the Ethiopian could see him no longer. Unperturbed, he continued on his way home, full of happiness.

Philip found himself at Azotus. He journeyed on to Caesarea, preaching as he went.

But back in Jerusalem, Saul was still violently persecuting the believers...

# Saul on the Road to Damascus

The young man Saul wasn't satisfied with persecuting only the believers in Jerusalem. He went to the high priest.

"Give me letters of introduction to the rulers of the Synagogues in Damascus," he said. "I will go there. And if I find any followers of Jesus among the worshippers, I'll arrest them – men *or* women – and bring them back here to Jerusalem! This talk about Jesus of Nazareth must be stopped!"

The high priest gave the letters to Saul; and the young man set off grimly, taking with him others who would help him in his intended task.

But as he travelled along the road to Damascus, he was suddenly surrounded by a light of unearthly brilliance.

Saul fell to the ground. He heard a voice speaking to him. "Saul, Saul, why do you persecute Me?"

Trembling, Saul whispered, "Who are You, Lord?"

The answer came. "I am Jesus, whom you are persecuting."

Jesus? The One whom believers kept saying was alive? Could it be that Saul had been *wrong*...?

Still trembling, he asked, "Lord – what do You want me to do?"

"Get up," Jesus answered. "Go into Damascus. There you will receive your instructions."

The men who were travelling with Saul stood silent, fearful. They could hear the voice, but they could see no one...

Saul stumbled to his feet. He put a hand to his eyes. He couldn't see! He was blind!

One of the men with him took Saul's hand. "Come," he said. "We'll lead you the rest of the way to Damascus."

Terrified, Saul went with them. They took him to the house of a man called Judas. There Saul sheltered. For three days he could not see; and during that time he refused to eat or drink. But he *did* pray...

Living in Damascus there was a believer whose name was Ananias. The Lord Jesus came to him in a vision. "Ananias!" He said.

Ananias was startled for a moment. Then he answered steadfastly, "I am here, Lord."

"You must get up, and go to Straight Street, to the house of a man called Judas," said the Lord. "There you must ask for Saul, from Tarsus. He has been blinded; but now he is praying. And he has had a vision in which a man named Ananias comes to him and places his hands on him, so that his sight is restored."

Ananias was full of fear. "But Lord, I've heard about this man! He's done terrible things to the believers in Jerusalem! And he's only *come* here to arrest all the believers! He's brought letters of authority from the high priest himself!"

Jesus answered quietly, "Ananias – go to him. I have chosen him to be My messenger, both to the Jews and to the people of other nations. I will speak to him Myself, and show him how much he must suffer in My name."

Ananias swallowed hard; but he set out for the house in Straight Street. But there he hesitated. Suppose Saul was waiting to trap him?

He forced himself to knock on the door. At once he was admitted, and shown into the room where Saul was.

For a moment, Ananias stood and gazed at him. This man who had been so cruel, so harsh, now sat blind and helpless, praying to God in distress.

Ananias went forward, and placed his hands on Saul, as Jesus had told him to. "Saul, my brother," he said gently, "Jesus Himself has sent me to you. The same Jesus who met you on the road to Damascus. He sent me so that you might be able to see again, and be full of the Holy Spirit."

At once it seemed as if something like fish scales fell from Saul's eyes. His face began to shine with joy.

"I can see!" he cried. "I can see!"

He got to his feet, stumbling a little, weak from his three days' fasting. Quietly, he spoke. "I *believe*," he said. "And I want to be baptized."

So he was baptized immediately. And as soon as he had had something to eat, his strength returned to him.

But soon he was to be in danger…

# Saul's Escape from Damascus

Saul stayed with the believers in Damascus for a while. He began to use as much energy in helping them as he had *previously* used in having them killed. He preached in the Synagogues; and everyone who heard him was utterly amazed.

"Isn't this the same Saul who was persecuting the believers in Jerusalem?" they asked one another. "Listen to him now! He's claiming that Jesus *was* the Messiah – the Son of God!"

Saul's preaching grew so powerful, the rulers of the Synagogues in Damascus couldn't answer his arguments. Frightened and angry, they decided he must be killed.

"He'll be leaving the city soon," they said. "He'll have to go through *one* of the gates. If we set a watch on *all* of them, we'll be bound to catch him!"

But Saul's friends heard of the plot, and warned him.

"There *must* be a way to get you safely out of Damascus," they said anxiously. "If you can't go through the gates, you'll have to go over the wall!"

But the walls around Damascus were strong and high, as was the custom in those days...

"I know!" cried one of the believers. "We'll get a big basket and some strong ropes. Then, when it's dark, Saul can sit in the basket, and we can lower him down through an opening in the wall!"

It would be very risky; but no one could think of a better plan.

So that night, a group of believers moved stealthily to the place they had chosen. They fastened the ropes securely to the basket, and let it hang through an opening in the wall. Bravely, Saul climbed into it. "Right," he whispered.

They paused for a moment, listening. If anyone should discover them, it was possible they would *all* be killed...

But there was silence everywhere. As quickly as they could, Saul's friends let out the ropes. Down went the basket, bumping against the wall, swinging backwards and forwards. More believers were waiting at the bottom, peering upwards, holding their breath.

Saul landed safely. Rapidly, he was helped out of the basket. Losing no time, he thanked his friends, and set out on the road back to Jerusalem.

Arriving, he went to find the believers there. But they were terrified of him. They wouldn't accept that he too was a believer now.

Then Barnabas said, "Saul – *I* trust you. I'll take you to the apostles."

Barnabas told the apostles how Saul had met with Jesus on the

Damascus road, and that he had been preaching in the Synagogues of Damascus.

The apostles accepted Barnabas' words. So the believers in Jerusalem made Saul welcome, and invited him to stay with them.

Just as he had done in Damascus, Saul began to preach powerfully in the Synagogues. He also talked with the Greek-speaking Jews. But they became angry, and plotted against his life.

When the believers discovered this, they took Saul to Caesarea, then sent him on to Tarsus, where he would be safe.

And for a while the persecution of the church throughout Judea, Galilee and Samaria ceased; and with the help of the Holy Spirit, more and more people began to believe.

Meanwhile, Peter travelled around the countryside, preaching to the people about Jesus, and healing the sick.

One day he was sent for urgently...

295

# Dorcas of Joppa

In Joppa there lived a lady called Tabitha, or Dorcas. She was a believer; and all the people in the church in Joppa loved her. She was always thinking up a kindness she could do for someone. And she was always making new clothes for people – especially those who were poor.

One day Dorcas became ill and died. The people were very distressed. They felt they couldn't bear to part with her until they had had time to get used to the idea. So instead of burying her body at once, as was the custom, they washed it with loving care and placed it in an upstairs room.

As they grieved, one of them said, "If Peter were here, he might be able to help."

And another said, "But he *is*! He's in Lydda! And when he arrived there he healed Aeneas – who hadn't been able to get out of bed for the last eight years!"

The believers looked at each other with growing hope. Lydda was only a few miles from Joppa!

Hastily, two of them set out. They found Peter, and begged him to come back with them. Peter agreed.

As soon as they reached Joppa, the believers took him to the upstairs room. There the widows whom Dorcas had helped so much were standing weeping. They showed Peter the clothes she had made for them while she was alive.

Gently, Peter asked them all to leave the room. When they had gone, he knelt down and prayed. Then he turned towards the body. "Dorcas – stand up!" he said.

And she opened her eyes, and looked at him...

When she saw it was Peter, she sat up. He held out his hand, and helped her to her feet. Then he opened the door of the room, and showed her to all the people who had been waiting outside. They had been hardly daring to hope. Now they *saw*! She was alive again!

There was great rejoicing. The story spread all over Joppa, and many more people became believers.

A tanner (leather worker) called Simon invited Peter to stay at his house. And while he stayed there, Peter had a very strange dream...

# Peter Meets Cornelius

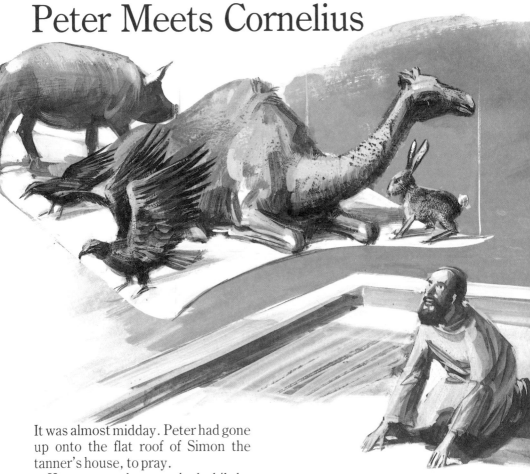

It was almost midday. Peter had gone up onto the flat roof of Simon the tanner's house, to pray.

He grew very hungry. And while he was waiting for a meal to be prepared, he began to dream about food.

He thought he saw something that looked like a large sheet. It was being lowered down to earth by its four corners. In the sheet were all kinds of creatures – animals, birds and reptiles. And a voice said, "Get up, Peter. Kill, and eat!"

Peter was very hungry. But according to the law of Moses, these animals were unclean; not to be eaten by the Jews. Peter answered, "Oh no, Lord! I've never broken the law by eating anything which is common or unclean!"

The voice spoke again. "You must not call unclean that which God has cleansed!"

Three times this happened. Then the sheet rose again into the sky.

Peter sat there, troubled. What did

the dream mean? Was it *really* about food? Or was there more to it than that…

As he puzzled, he heard a loud knocking on the door of the house. Someone shouted, "Is Simon Peter staying here?"

The Holy Spirit spoke to Peter. "Do you hear those three men? They're looking for you. I Myself have sent them to you. Go with them."

The men had come from Caesarea with a message from Cornelius, a Roman centurion. Peter invited them in for a meal and a night's rest. Then he and some of the other believers from Joppa accompanied them back to Caesarea. The journey took almost two days.

At last they arrived at Cornelius' house. It was full of people. Cornelius had asked his close friends and relations to come and listen to what Peter would say.

When Peter reached the doorway, Cornelius knelt to worship him.

"Get up!" said Peter. "I'm only a man – not a god!"

As they went into the house, Peter began to understand the meaning of his dream. Jews had always been forbidden to visit anyone of a different nation, because foreigners were thought to be ritually unclean – they didn't keep the Jewish religious laws. Now, Peter realized he must call *no one* God had made 'unclean'.

He explained this to Cornelius; and then said, "Now – why did you send for me?"

Cornelius said, "An angel told me

to! He knew exactly where you were to be found! So I obeyed him. Please – tell us about the Lord Jesus!"

Peter nodded. "I realize now that God's Kingdom is not just for Jews, as we thought. Anyone, of any nation, who believes in Him and obeys His words is equally acceptable to Him."

Then Peter told Cornelius and his friends and relations about Jesus. "And," he finished, "the sins of everyone who believes in Him will be forgiven, through His name."

As Peter spoke, the Holy Spirit came down on everyone who was listening; and they all began to praise God.

Some of the Jews from Joppa were amazed. How could God pour out His Holy Spirit on *Gentiles* – people of other nations? But Peter said, "These people have received the Holy Spirit just as we did! So who can refuse to let them be baptized, also?"

No one could refuse. They were baptized in the name of Jesus; and a Roman centurion became a follower of Jesus Christ.

When Peter went back to Jerusalem, the believers there said, "How could you stay in the house of *Gentiles*? And *eat* with them!"

So Peter told them the whole story, beginning with his dream, and ending, "God gave these people the Holy Spirit, exactly as He gave it to us. How could *I* stand against *Him*?"

Then they understood; and they praised God.

But the time of peace for the believers was ending…

# Peter in Prison

King Herod decided to start persecuting the believers again. He arrested John's brother James, and had him killed by the sword.

The Jews were pleased; and Herod, seeing this, had Peter thrown into prison, intending to have him put on trial and killed as soon as the Festival of the Passover was over. Remembering the last time Peter had been arrested, Herod said to himself, "I'll make certain he doesn't escape *this* time!" And he gave orders that Peter be guarded day and night, by four soldiers at a time.

The believers in Jerusalem were in great distress. James had been killed. Were they to lose Peter also?

They began to pray. From early morning until late at night – even all *through* the night – they pleaded with God that Peter might be spared. Day after day they prayed. Nothing happened. On the night before his trial – their last chance – they were still praying...

In prison, Peter was asleep. He was chained hand and foot. The door was locked. Two soldiers were in the cell with him, to guard him. Two more stood outside, guarding the iron gate. Surely escape was impossible...

But suddenly, Peter felt someone shaking him by the shoulder. He started up, half awake. Then he

299

rubbed his eyes in disbelief. An *angel* stood in the cell beside him, and a light shone in the darkness. "Quickly! Get up!" said the angel.

Get up! Couldn't the angel see the heavy chains? Even as the thought came into Peter's head, the chains fell off. Yet the clanking didn't disturb the guards... They seemed to be fast asleep...

Peter scrambled to his feet.

"Get dressed, and put on your sandals," the angel said. "Then pull your cloak around you, and follow me."

As hastily as he could, Peter obeyed. Was this really happening? Or was it a dream?

Silently, the angel opened the cell door. Peter went with him. They passed the sleeping guards, and came to the huge iron gate. To Peter's utter amazement, it swung open by itself. Through the gate they went.

They walked along one street; and suddenly, the angel left Peter.

Alone in the starlight, Peter looked around. It was *true*! He really *was* out of prison! God had sent the angel to rescue him! Peter began to hasten along the road to the house of Mary, John Mark's mother.

Inside the house, the believers were praying for Peter's release. And there came a loud knocking at the outer door...

Rhoda, a servant girl, went fearfully to answer the knock. Guessing that whoever came would be alarmed, Peter called out, "It's me! Peter!"

*Peter*! Rhoda was overjoyed. Not stopping to open the door, she ran straight back to the believers.

"Peter's here!" she cried. "He's at the door!"

Although they had been praying for this very thing, they didn't believe her. "You must be mad!" they said.

"No!" she insisted. "It's him! Really it is!"

"It can't be him!" they said. "It's his angel!"

Meanwhile Peter, desperately afraid that someone would come along the road and discover him, was still knocking. At last, the believers went together to open the door. And they saw him.

"Hush!" Peter held up his hand; in their excitement they were likely to cry out and betray his presence. They took him inside, and listened eagerly as he told them what had happened.

"Tell James and the other believers about this," he said. Then he left secretly.

In the morning there was a great commotion at the prison. None of the soldiers could explain how Peter came to be missing. No one had seen anything – heard anything – remembered anything.

Herod was furious. He ordered that Peter be found. A thorough search was made; but Peter seemed to have vanished. Herod sent for the guards, and questioned them himself. Discovering that they had no satisfactory explanation, he commanded that they should all be executed.

Then he left Judea, and went to Caesarea. There he made a speech to the people. They – hoping to gain favour with him – shouted, "Surely he speaks not as a man, but as a god!"

Herod listened proudly, doing nothing to stop them, or give honour to the true God. And an angel struck him down, and he died.

But the good news of the Gospel continued to spread...

# Saul's First Journey

When the believers scattered after the killing of Stephen, some of them went to Antioch. There they spread the good news of the Gospel; and many people believed, and joined the church.

Barnabas came from Jerusalem to Antioch, to learn more of what was happening there. He was delighted, and encouraged the new believers so much that many more were added to their number.

He began to wonder about Saul. So he went to Tarsus, found him, and invited him to come to Antioch and help with the new church. Saul came. And it was at Antioch that the believers were first known as Christians – followers of Jesus Christ.

One day, the Holy Spirit said to the members of the church there, "Set Saul and Barnabas apart. There is special work for them to do." Then the people realized that God wanted Saul and Barnabas to leave Antioch, and take the good news to other places.

So when they had prayed and fasted together the believers blessed the two men, and watched as they set off on their journey. Barnabas' young cousin John Mark went with them, as a helper.

After various adventures – including a meeting with a magician on the island of Cyprus – the three came to Pamphylia. There John deserted the group, and went home. But Saul – now known as Paul – travelled on, with Barnabas.

They reached another Antioch. This one was in Pisidia. The Jews there asked Paul to preach in their Synagogue; and his sermon was so powerful, he was invited to preach again the following week.

When Paul and Barnabas went to the Synagogue on the next Sabbath day, they found crowds waiting outside. Gentiles as well as Jews had come to listen. Practically the whole town was there.

But the Jews were jealous. They didn't want to share the good news about Jesus with *Gentiles*. They began to argue with Paul, and insult him.

Paul preached even more boldly. "It was necessary that God's word should first be spoken to you," he said. "But you have refused to accept it. So we take the message to the Gentiles!"

The Gentiles were pleased when

they heard this, and many of them became believers. But the Jews were furious. They made trouble in the town for Paul and Barnabas. So the two men left, and went to Iconium.

There, much the same thing happened. Soon the whole town was divided between those who were for Paul and those who were against him. Some of those *against* plotted to stone the apostles to death; but Paul and Barnabas were warned in time, and they got away. They visited the towns of Lystra and Derbe, and the countryside round about.

In Lystra, there was a man who had never been able to walk. As Paul preached, he noticed the intent look on the man's face. This man believed! He could be healed!

Looking straight at him, Paul commanded loudly, "Stand up on your feet!"

The man jumped up – and *walked*! Everyone who saw it happen was utterly amazed. The news spread rapidly. Hundreds of people came rushing to see the lame man walk, and to get a glimpse of Paul and Barnabas.

"They're gods!" they cried. They named Barnabas 'Zeus', and Paul 'Hermes'. The priest of the temple of Zeus hurried to bring bulls and garlands of flowers, so that a sacrifice could be made.

Paul and Barnabas were horrified. "No!" they shouted. "We're not gods! We're men like yourselves! We came to *tell* you about God – the one, true, living God!"

At last the people were dissuaded. The noise died down. The priests went back to their temple. And then some travellers from Antioch in Pisidia, and from Iconium, arrived. They immediately recognized Paul and Barnabas.

Kill! Kill!"

Barnabas escaped. But Paul was stoned.

Thinking him dead, the people dragged him outside the city and left him there.

Distressed, sorrowing, the believers gathered round him. And to their joy, he opened his eyes! He had only been stunned. Courageously, he returned to Lystra.

Next morning he found Barnabas;

and the two of them travelled on, encouraging new believers and establishing more churches.

At last they arrived back at Antioch – the town from which they had started out; and the believers there listened, thrilled, as Paul and Barnabas told of their adventures.

The two apostles stayed a long time in Antioch. Then something happened...

The crowd was already disappointed. Now the newcomers turned the people against the apostles. The crowd became a howling mob, yelling, "Kill them!

# A Letter to the Churches

Some men arrived in Antioch from Jerusalem, and started to teach that Gentiles must keep Jewish customs, if they were to become Christians. Paul and Barnabas disagreed very strongly with this, so they and some other believers set off for Jerusalem to argue the question with the apostles there.

On the journey, Paul and Barnabas stopped at various churches, telling people that Gentiles were now entering the Kingdom. Everyone heard the news with joy.

But in Jerusalem some of the church members insisted that before Gentiles could become Christians they *must* agree to keep all the laws given by Moses to the Israelites.

The apostles and elders called a special meeting. After they had argued for a while Peter stood up. He told them about his dream, and the way God had sent the Holy Spirit to the Gentiles in the house of Cornelius.

Then Paul and Barnabas spoke, telling especially about the wonderful things *they* had seen God do amongst the Gentiles.

Finally James stood up. Firmly, he said, "I think we should write to the Gentiles. We shouldn't make it hard for them to become Christians. We should simply tell them not to eat any food that has been offered to idols; that men and women must behave honourably towards one another; and that they must not eat anything which has been strangled, nor any blood."

This was agreed. A very important decision had been made. The Christian church was for *everybody* who loved and trusted God.

The letter was written. Judas, Silas, and some of the other believers in Jerusalem were chosen to return to Antioch with Paul and Barnabas to deliver it.

The people at Antioch listened gladly to its message. Judas and Silas gave them much encouragement, before returning to Jerusalem.

Paul and Barnabas remained in Antioch. But they were beginning to feel restless...

# Silas and Paul

Paul said to Barnabas, "Let's go back to the churches we founded, and see how they're getting on!"

"Great!" said Barnabas. "We'll take John Mark with us!"

"No we won't!" cried Paul. "He deserted us last time! I'm not taking him again!"

There was a fierce argument. Barnabas absolutely refused to leave his young cousin behind. So the apostles agreed to split up, and Barnabas and Mark sailed for Cyprus. Later, John Mark proved to be very trustworthy; and Paul himself said he was a valuable fellow worker, a comfort to him.

But for the moment, he asked Silas to be his new companion; and later, Timothy.

Paul and Silas travelled through Syria and Cilicia, visiting the young churches, and encouraging them. Paul wanted to go to other parts of Asia Minor, to tell the people there about Jesus. But something always happened to stop him from going. They had gone as far as Troas when Paul had a dream. A man from Macedonia stood before him, begging, "Come and help *us*!"

When Paul woke, he told his dream to Silas. They agreed that the dream had been a message from God. Troas was a sea port; so they all went down to the docks and booked a passage on a ship sailing for Neapolis.

Arriving at Neapolis they disembarked and travelled to Philippi, the chief city of the region.

On the Sabbath day they went down to the river bank, to the part which they knew was used as a place of worship by the religious women of the town. There they began to preach, telling the story of Jesus. One of the women who listened to them was Lydia, a seller of purple cloth. And as she listened, she believed.

She and all the members of her household were baptized; and she invited Paul and Silas to stay at her house. They accepted the invitation.

One day, as they were on their way to a prayer meeting, a slave girl met them. She could tell fortunes, and in this way made a great deal of money for her owners. Now she began to follow the two apostles, calling out, "These men are servants of the Most High God. They are telling you how you can be saved!"

She behaved in this way for many days. Paul became very troubled

about her. "She must be possessed by an evil spirit," he said. He stopped, and turned round to face the girl. Firmly he spoke. "Evil spirit, in the name of Jesus Christ, I command you to come out of her!" And the spirit obeyed.

Immediately, the girl was in her right mind. She was happy; but her owners were not. They realized that they would no longer be able to make money from her. Furiously, they grabbed Paul and Silas and dragged them before the magistrates in the local market-place. "These men are Jews!" they declared loudly. "They're upsetting the whole town teaching customs which it's against the law for Romans like us to practise!"

There was no proper trial. Soon the market-place was crowded with people shouting insults and accusations at Paul and Silas. Without giving them any chance to defend themselves, the magistrates declared them to be guilty. They were ordered to be stripped, beaten, and flung into prison.

The sentence was carried out immediately. And the prison jailer was told to take special care that the two men did not escape. So he had them put into the innermost cell, with their feet securely fastened in the stocks...

307

# The Earthquake

In prison that night, Paul and Silas couldn't sleep. So they began to pray and sing hymns.

The other prisoners listened in amazement.

Suddenly, at about midnight, there was an earthquake. The foundations of the prison were shaken. The doors of the cells swung open, and everyone's chains were loosened!

The jailer, startled into wakefulness, ran from his house to find out what had happened at the prison. All he could see was every door swinging wide open.

The prisoners must have escaped! He would be blamed! Knowing he could expect no mercy from the authorities, he pulled out his sword to kill himself.

But Paul called out, "It's all right! We're all here!"

The jailer shouted to his servants, "Quickly! Bring lights!"

And in the flickering light of the torches, he knelt in front of Paul and Silas.

Then he stood up, and led them out of the cell. "Sirs," he trembled, "what must I do to be saved?"

It was an extraordinary question for a jailer to ask. But Paul replied instantly. "Believe in the Lord Jesus Christ, and you will be saved. You and all your household."

The jailer and his household knew so little about Jesus that he asked if they could hear more.

Gladly Paul and Silas told the story. Then the jailer washed their wounds, and did what he could to make them more comfortable; and he and all his household were baptized.

He invited the two apostles into his house for a meal, full of joy because he and his whole family had come to believe in God.

At dawn, the magistrates sent police to the prison to say, "Those two men are now to be released."

The jailer hurried to Paul and Silas.

"You're free!" he cried. "You can go!"

"Oh no," said Paul. The jailer looked at him in amazement. Paul faced the police. "We were beaten in public, without a fair trial – although we are Roman citizens! Now the magistrates want us to leave quietly, without fuss. No! If they want us to leave, they can come here and tell us so themselves!"

The police were astounded. They reported back to the magistrates. And the magistrates were very worried. They hadn't realized Paul and Silas were Roman citizens. Beating a Roman citizen without first allowing him a proper trial was a serious offence...

Anxiously, the magistrates came to the prison. Humbly they led the two men out of the prison gates, and requested politely that they leave Philippi.

But Paul and Silas were not ready to go yet. First they returned to Lydia's house, to tell her what had been happening, and to encourage the other believers.

Then, when they were ready, they and Timothy set off again.

After many adventures – including having to split up for a while – they all reached Corinth. Here Paul grew discouraged. But God sent him a dream, saying, "Don't give up, Paul! And don't be afraid. I am with you. I have many followers in this city, and no one shall harm you."

No one in Corinth *did* harm Paul, and it was eighteen months before he travelled on.

# The Boy Who Fell Asleep

It was Sunday evening in a warm, upstairs room in Troas. Paul was speaking to the believers. He had much to say, for next day he was leaving. Midnight came; and Paul was still talking.

A boy called Eutychus had perched himself on a window-ledge to listen. Now, as Paul spoke on and on, Eutychus dozed off to sleep.

And he fell out of the window. He hit the ground with a thud – three storeys down!

There was an immense commotion. Everyone rushed downstairs and outside. They found Eutychus lying very still...

Somebody lifted the boy up. "He's dead!" they whispered.

Gently, they laid him down again.

Then Paul pressed his way to the front. He threw himself on top of the lad, hugging him. "It's all right," he said. "Don't be afraid. He's alive."

Everyone was amazed. But it was certainly true. Some of the people, much comforted, took Eutychus home. But Paul and most of the others went back upstairs. There they broke bread, and ate it. And Paul continued talking...

He spoke until daylight. Then he set off once more on his journeys.

# Paul in Trouble

Paul was in the Temple in Jerusalem. Suddenly, some of the Jews who had opposed him when he had visited their churches recognized him. They cried out, "Men of Israel, help! This is the man who teaches everyone against the people of Israel, and our law! *And* he's brought Gentiles into this Temple, defiling this holy place!"

The accusations were not true; but they started a riot. People came running from all sides, seized Paul, and dragged him out of the Temple.

Hastily, the doors were shut behind them. Then the mob tried to kill Paul.

A messenger rushed to tell the commander of the Roman soldiers, whose job it was to keep peace in the city. Hastily collecting up some of his men, the commander ran to where the crowd was. When they saw the soldiers coming, the mob stopped beating Paul up.

The commander arrested Paul, ordering that chains be put on him. Then he said, "Who is this man?

What has he done?" Immediately there was an uproar, with everyone shouting different accusations.

"Take him to the barracks!" the commander ordered his men. "We'll never find out the truth here."

The soldiers tried to obey. But when Paul reached the barracks steps the crowd became so violent they had to carry him.

Above the uproar Paul shouted to the commander. "May I say something?"

"Aren't you the leader of a band of terrorists?" asked the commander.

"No, I'm not!" said Paul. "I'm a Jew – since my parents were Jews. But I am also a Roman citizen, since I was born in Tarsus, a province of Rome. Please – let me speak to these people!"

The commander looked at Paul, then at the mob. "You can try," he said.

Upright, unafraid, Paul stood on the steps and motioned with his hands to the crowd to be quiet. Amazingly, the noise died down. Paul waited until there was absolute silence. Then he spoke in the language of Aramaic. And they listened.

He told them how he had persecuted the Christians; and that he had met with Jesus on the Damascus road. He reached the part where God had told him to take the message to the Gentiles...

That was it. So great was the outcry from the crowd, Paul could no longer be heard.

Fearing a riot, the commander ordered that Paul be taken inside the barracks. "Flog him, and question him!" he cried. "Find out the truth!"

As a centurion was about to start the flogging, Paul said, "Is it lawful for you to flog a Roman citizen when nothing has been proved against him?"

The centurion paused. Then he went to the commander. "Sir – this man says he is a Roman citizen. What will you do?"

They both knew the danger of flogging a Roman citizen without him having first been tried and found guilty.

The commander went across to Paul. "*Are* you a Roman?" he asked.

"I am," said Paul.

"I had to pay a large amount of money to get my citizenship," said the commander.

"I was born a citizen," Paul answered.

Hearing this, the men who had been going to question Paul backed away. The commander himself was worried to discover he had had a Roman citizen put into chains. But he still wanted to find out why the Jews had been accusing Paul so angrily.

So next day he released Paul from the custody of the Romans. But he also ordered an assembly of the chief priests and the Sanhedrin. And he brought Paul to stand before them.

# The Shipwreck and The Snake

The trial before the Sanhedrin ended in uproar, and Paul was taken back to the barracks.

Paul was downhearted. At his trial he'd angered the Jewish leaders so much, he felt he'd lost the chance of speaking to them at all. But God spoke to him in a dream. "Take heart, Paul! You have witnessed for Me in Jerusalem. Now you will witness for Me in Rome."

Paul was cheered. He had longed to see Rome. And he realized that God could fulfil one of His own purposes through what had just happened.

That night, to save Paul from yet another attempt on his life, the commander sent him under a huge guard to Caesarea. Felix, the governor there, could arrange the trial.

Felix had him imprisoned in Herod's palace until a fresh trial could be arranged. Then once more Paul stood before Ananias and the Sanhedrin. This time he was allowed to speak. But Felix made no judgement. "We'll wait until the commander arrives," he said. "Meanwhile, Paul is to be kept under guard. Allow his friends to take care of him."

So Paul was imprisoned again. Felix and his wife Drusilla often came to talk to him. Felix was hoping Paul would bribe him, and so obtain freedom. After two years, Felix was transferred; but he left Paul in prison because he wanted to please the Jews.

Festus, the new governor, wanted to know why Paul was in prison. He treated Paul with kindness, asking if he would like to go back to Jerusalem for a re-trial.

"No," said Paul. "I want to be tried by Caesar, in a Roman court."

Festus asked his counsellors for advice. Then he replied to Paul. "Very well. You have appealed to Caesar. To Caesar you shall go."

Before arrangements could be made, King Agrippa arrived in Caesarea. Paul was so famous a prisoner, the king wanted to speak to him. So Paul told again the story of Jesus. King Agrippa listened closely. "You almost persuade *me* to be a Christian," he said. And to Festus, he remarked, "If this man hadn't insisted on being tried by Caesar, he would have been set free." But Paul *had* insisted; and it was decided to send him to Italy.

Paul and some other prisoners were on board a ship bound for Italy. The ship's passage had been much delayed by bad weather. Now, as it lay at anchor in Crete, Paul warned the centurion in charge of the danger of sailing on.

But the centurion took the advice of the captain, who was unwilling to stay where they were for the winter. They set sail along the coast to reach a safer harbour.

At first there was a fair wind. But soon a hurricane sprang up. The ship was driven helpless before it. The situation was desperate. Shouting above the noise of the wind and the waves, the captain ordered that the cargo be thrown overboard to lighten the ship. Next day, the tackle was also thrown over the side. Still the storm raged, and the ship tossed up and down.

The crew and the prisoners gave up all hope of being saved. Then Paul stood in front of them. "Men!" he said. "If you'd taken my advice not to leave Crete, we wouldn't be in this

trouble now! Even so, take heart! For an angel of the God to whom I belong, and whom I worship, came to me this night! And he said, 'Don't be afraid, Paul! You *will* stand trial in front of Caesar. And God will save the lives of everyone who sails with you in this ship!' And I trust God that it will happen exactly as he says! But be warned – we will run aground on an island."

Sure enough, on the fourteenth night of the voyage the sailors could tell that the ship was nearing land.

They dropped four anchors, hoping to hold the ship off the rocks. Terrified, some of the sailors lowered a lifeboat, pretending they were going to drop more anchors. Really they were attempting to save themselves.

But Paul cried to the centurion, "Unless those men stay with the ship, they will be drowned!"

So the soldiers cut the ropes that held the lifeboat, and it fell away, empty.

As they waited for dawn, Paul urged, "Eat! You'll need all the

strength you can get! I tell you, not *one* of you will be lost!" And to encourage them, he took some bread, gave thanks for it, and ate it in front of them. Then they all took heart; and they too ate some food.

When daylight came, they saw they were near a sandy bay. They decided to try to beach the ship there. But it ran aground. Huge waves began to break it to pieces. "Kill the prisoners before they escape!" cried the soldiers.

"No!" shouted the centurion. "Jump overboard, all of you! Swim! Or grab a plank! Get yourselves to land somehow!"

This they did. And every one of them reached the shore in safety.

They were cold and wet. The islanders lit a huge camp fire to warm them. Paul collected some wood. As he put it on the fire, a snake driven out by the heat fastened itself on his hand. The watching islanders thought he would fall down dead; but Paul simply shook the snake off. Everyone waited, and watched. After a long time, when Paul was still obviously unharmed, the islanders decided he must be a god.

Publius, the chief official of the island, gave hospitality to the shipwrecked men. Learning that Publius' father was sick, Paul healed him; and after that many sick people came for healing.

It was three months before they set sail again, in a different ship. And finally, Paul arrived in Rome.

# The Letters to Christians

In Rome, Paul was allowed to rent somewhere to live, with only one soldier to guard him. He was under house arrest, so people came to *him*. He continued to preach fearlessly.

But in AD64 there was a huge fire in Rome. The Emperor Nero blamed the Jews; and the relentless persecution of Jews and Christians began.

According to tradition, Paul was one of the many Christians killed at that time because they refused to give up their faith.

But his words continued to live. While he was imprisoned in Caesarea he had spent much of his time writing letters to new Christians. And many of his letters were saved, to be read over and over again.

The letters are in the Bible; and so are letters from James, Peter, John and Jude. They are full of encouragement and wisdom, and are still treasured by Christians today.

# John's Vision

God sent John a vision of the future.

John wrote, "And after the judgement, I saw a new Heaven and a new earth... And I heard a voice out of Heaven saying, 'Behold...God is with men, and He will dwell with them... And God shall wipe away all tears from their eyes; and there shall be no more death, neither sorrow nor crying, neither shall there be any more pain: for the former things are passed away.' And the Holy City shall be very beautiful; and the glory of God shall be its light... The grace of the Lord Jesus Christ be with you all."

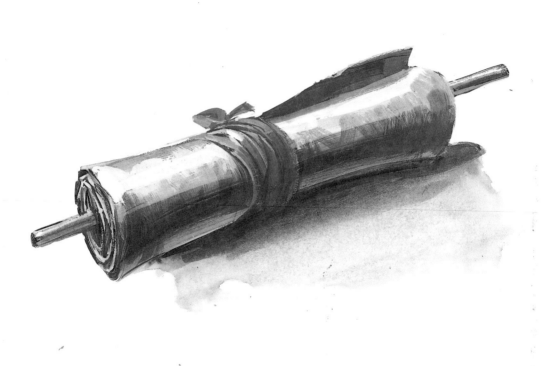